MY LIFE'S PLAYLIST

J.L. Taylor

Monkey Tales Publishing

ISBN-13:979-8-9942274-0-4

Cover design by: Art Painter
Library of Congress Control Number: 2018675309
Printed in the United States of America

This one goes out to the ones I love...

CONTENTS

PROLOGUE

You don't always know which songs will stay with you.

Most slip past unnoticed, dissolving into the noise of errands, car rides, and years you barely remember. They play once, maybe twice, and disappear without leaving a mark.

But a few arrive differently. They attach themselves before you realize what's happening—long before you understand why they matter, or what they're really about. They settle in quietly and refuse to leave.

Years later, when one of those songs comes on, it doesn't feel like nostalgia so much as recognition. Something opens. A door you forgot existed unlocks.

You don't just remember who you were; you remember how you felt.

This book is about those songs.

INTRODUCTION

I didn't set out to write a book, and I certainly didn't intend to write a memoir. This whole thing began as a simple playlist of my favorite Christmas songs. It was a harmless little project, something I could burn onto a CD and slip into my daughters' and wife's stockings. I pictured myself tucking a handwritten insert inside the jewel case—just a few lines about why each song mattered to me. Quick. Easy. Sentimental, but not too sentimental.

But the moment I started writing those notes, something unexpected happened. Every song dragged a memory up with it —some light, some heavy, some I hadn't revisited in decades. I thought I was making a playlist. Instead, I found myself sifting through the emotional archaeology of my life.

I wasn't writing about music anymore. I was writing about myself.

Which, let's be honest, sounds pretentious as hell. Who am I to warrant a memoir? This whole thing was supposed to be a simple gift for an audience of four. A homemade CD, a few notes tucked inside. Easy peasy. That was it.

A couple of Christmases ago, my oldest daughter, Maddy, gave me one of those *Conversations With My Father* books—the kind filled with questions about your childhood, your parents, your regrets, your dreams. As I flipped through the pages, I realized just how many stories I'd never told, how much history I carried around without ever setting any of it down in ink.

One of the questions asked, "Is there a song that reminds you of your childhood home?" I didn't have a single childhood home. I had several. But the more I sat with it, the more I kept landing on El Paso—not because it was *the* home, but because so many people, places, and memories spiderweb out from that West Texas town. It became the origin point for chapters I never expected to write.

A few days before Christmas, I was walking my dog, Colt, listening to the playlist I planned to burn onto that CD. "Little Drummer Boy" came on, and suddenly I was back at a welfare-funded daycare I hadn't thought about in years. I stopped walking, pulled out my phone, and started searching for Marty Robbins.

I rushed home and began writing what would later become the first chapter of this book, simply titled *El Paso*.

That's when this stopped being a CD project and became something else entirely. The more I wrote, the more I understood that these songs were stitched into both the good memories and the hard ones—the moments that built me and the ones I barely made it through.

This book isn't an exact chronology or a complete soundtrack. It's a mixtape—taped off the radio at just the right moment, imperfect and personal, arranged for reasons that only really make sense to me.

You won't know every song I write about. You don't have to. They aren't the point. They're markers of where I've been, the people I loved, the mistakes I made, and the moments that kept shaping me long after they were over.

Music outlasts almost everything. People leave, years disappear, and memory blurs around the edges—but a song can still drop you straight into a moment you thought you'd lost.

That's what these songs did for me. And maybe, if I've done this right, they'll remind you of the ones that shaped you, too.

MY LIFE'S PLAYLIST

EL PASO

I am in our small apartment somewhere in the Detroit suburbs. I am maybe four, maybe younger. My father is sitting on the couch, cigarette in hand. My mother is dressed in black, talking quietly to my aunt as she holds my baby brother. The room is dim, wood-paneled, heavy with cigarette smoke and the low hum of adult conversation.

And then "Funny Face" by Donna Fargo comes on the radio.

I don't remember the station. I don't remember the day. I don't remember why my mother was dressed nicely or what they were talking about.

But I remember the bright, sweet, unexpected chorus rising and something in me just...broke open.

My lower lip began to quiver and tears streamed down my face.

I wasn't scared or hurt, I was just overwhelmed by something I didn't know how to name. It was my first emotional reaction to a song, and it lodged itself so deeply inside me that I can still feel the shape of it fifty years later. Long before I knew anything about pop charts or genres, long before I understood the difference between sadness and beauty, I learned there was a place inside me only music could reach.

I don't remember my father being especially into music. I can't recall him ever talking about an album he loved or a song that moved him. There was no vinyl collection, no stereo system as the centerpiece of the living room. Maybe the radio was playing while he worked on his car, but I can't remember a single time he turned it up and said, "Now this is a good song."

But even without music, there was no mistaking who he was.

What I remember is that he was Robert Redford handsome and Steve McQueen cool. Muscle cars. Motorcycles. Marlboro Reds. He didn't drink, unless you count the gallons of black coffee he threw back every morning like it was water. He loved Denny's breakfast, his mom and dad, his sisters, and—for a time—me, my mom, and my little brother.

He was a charmer who could draw out giggles and blushes from waitresses, bank tellers, and cashiers with nothing more than a wink and a smile. Generosity and a willingness to help anyone, anywhere, anytime were traits he carried throughout his life.

Got a flat tire thirty-five miles from home with no money for a tow truck? He'd make that drive, fix the tire, and hand you gas money to get back. Dealing with a stubborn leak under the sink? He'd be over before you got off the phone, tools in hand, fixing things you didn't even know were broken.

What he lacked in formal education, he made up for tenfold in practical knowledge of the kind of things that will earn you lifelong friends and unforgettable stories. The kind people still bring up about you decades later.

"I remember that time your dad drove all the way to Sandusky, Ohio, just to help me get home after my transmission blew up."

His story, for me, begins in El Paso, Texas - that's where he met my mother.

He was a soldier stationed at Fort Bliss. She was a waitress at a diner downtown, not too far from the base gates. She barely spoke English and had immigrated to the U.S. from Chihuahua, Mexico, under circumstances that were... let's just say, less than legal. His parents had come up the Hillbilly Highway from Tennessee to Detroit, looking for a better life that didn't involve coal dust in their lungs.

The odds were stacked against them from the start. He was

twenty. She had just turned nineteen. Then she got pregnant with me.

At one point, my mother wasn't sure if my father was going to stick around after he had learned that she was pregnant. She moved across the border to Ciudad Juárez to stay with her sister while she figured things out and waited for me to be born.

She wasn't feeling well one day—understandably so, considering she was several months pregnant and uncertain about how she was going to raise a child on her own. She laid down on the couch to rest. The house was humble: adobe walls, a tin roof that rattled in the wind, and a screen door that creaked in and out with the breeze.

She was half-asleep when a taxi pulled up outside.

From the couch, she could only see the bottom half of the cab through the screen door. A pair of immaculately shined black dress shoes stepped out. Then olive green military-issue pants, creased so sharply you could slice paper on them. Then came the knock.

It was my father.

He'd come to bring her back to the States. Back to Fort Riley, Kansas, where he would be stationed next. Where they would get married. Where I would be born.

Soon after, my father was unceremoniously discharged from the Army for medical reasons. He had epilepsy. He'd sometimes suffer violent seizures that terrified my mother. These seizures would plague him for most of his life until medical science lessened their severity.

They moved to Michigan, where my father was from, hoping to carve out a life for themselves. But Michigan was hard on my mother. She didn't speak the language and was thousands of miles from her family. The culture shock was profound. She felt isolated. Trapped. And sometimes she'd leave for weeks at a time to go back to Mexico to visit her family. It put an enormous strain on a marriage that was already fragile.

It wasn't easy on my father, either. Although he had the support of family, his medical history made it hard to find steady work in a town where jobs meant long shifts on the line and working with heavy machinery to build cars. His epilepsy made him a liability. He eventually caught on with GM in facilities maintenance, but it wasn't the kind of job that paid well or promised security. He made just enough for them to scrape by.

And scraping by is exactly what they did.

This is what I remember from that time.

We were poor. Really poor. I remember eating bean burritos every day when I was little. Our apartment windows would fog in the kitchen from the steam rising out of the pot where pinto beans simmered for hours on the stovetop. I didn't know we were poor. That realization would come later. Back then, bean burritos were dinner. And lunch. And sometimes breakfast.

As time passed by, things between my parents grew harder. My mom's absences became longer, and my father, left alone with two young boys, did his best to hold things together.

During one of my mother's absences, my father met someone else. He was handsome and charming. It was inevitable, I guess, that someone would step into the space my mother had left. I have a hazy memory of being with him when he went to see her once. She sat on the hood of his car eating an ice cream cone as he leaned against it, Marlboro Red dangling from his lips. I remember feeling confused by what was happening.

What came next felt like a freefall. One day, I had a mom and dad. A house. Grandparents across the street, aunts, uncles, and cousins living within blocks of us. The next, we were living in a rundown low-income hotel in El Paso. My mother went back to waitressing at the same diner where she'd worked before I was born—where she'd met my father. My brother and I spent our days at a welfare-funded daycare.

That's how I remember it: sudden, jarring, like the floor dropped out from under us. But memory plays tricks. It wasn't quite that abrupt. There was a separation first. My mother left Michigan and took my brother and me back to El Paso, to a barely standing single-wide trailer. There, at least, she had family nearby. The rundown hotel happened a bit later.

My memories from that time are water-stained and faded, like old Polaroids that have been exposed to the sun too long. I can't tell you how long we lived in that trailer, but I remember a swing set—a small, rusted-out one in the middle of a patch of dirt we called a playground. I was pushing my brother on the swings when I saw him standing at the edge of the playground: my father. He kneeled down, took off his sunglasses, and hit me with that trademark raised-eyebrow smile of his. Movie-star handsome. Charming as ever.

I ran to him, leaving my brother to fend for himself on the swing. I hugged him tight, then took his hand. We gathered up my brother and I led him to the dilapidated single-wide trailer.

My mother opened the door and burst into tears. She and my father embraced. I'll never forget the sound of her sobs. I don't remember how long my father stayed with us in El Paso, but at some point, we all moved back to Michigan. That's when the cracks in the failing marriage deepened into fault lines.

When we returned, it was my father who started disappearing for days at a time. Each absence stretched longer than the one before, and the silence between them grew into a suffocating black cloud of anxiety and distrust. The tension continued to build until it finally broke one morning at breakfast.

That morning, it all cracked. My mother threw a tub of butter against the wall during breakfast. It hit with a loud thump, leaving a large grease stain that soaked into the cheap paint. The grease stain never really went away. Long after we scrubbed it, a faint shadow remained. It was a permanent watermark of the day everything came apart.

A few days later, my father's sisters arrived without warning. They came with black garbage bags and moved through the house like a cleaning crew on a mission. My mother was crying in the living room, held by one sister while the others moved through the apartment with grim efficiency, stripping closets, drawers, the hall rack. I hid in the bedroom closet, clutching a metal vacuum attachment like a weapon, ready to swing if anyone touched my father's things.

When they finally left, the apartment felt hollow. My mother retreated to her bedroom, sobbing quietly behind the door. I tried playing cars with my little brother, but then he began to cry. I helped him climb into bed beside her, and eventually, the three of us fell asleep like that, a small pile of grief in a too-quiet apartment.

When I woke, I half-expected to find it had all been a bad dream. But the stain was still there, just above the kitchen table, a reminder that some things, once broken, don't go back the way they were.

Years later, I learned the truth behind my father showing up in El Paso: my father didn't bring us back to Michigan to reconcile. He brought us back for leverage. Bringing us back to Michigan gave him the ultimate bargaining chip: sign the divorce papers, accept $68.00 a month in child support and airfare back to El Paso, or contest the divorce and remain in Michigan with no support, no job, no family, no friends, and two young boys to raise on her own.

My mother accepted the first option, and just like that we found ourselves back in El Paso, living in a welfare hotel.

Raising two young boys and living in a welfare hotel was not sustainable. We couldn't stay there forever, and my mother refused to let that be the end of our story.

Somehow, my mother scrounged up enough money to get us to California, where her sister was willing to take us in. I shared a bed with two cousins and immediately got lice. The backyard was all dirt and mud, engine blocks, broken appliances, and cars that hadn't moved in years. Everywhere I looked, there was tetanus just waiting to happen.

One of my cousins had a cheap record player—the kind that folded into a plastic suitcase. In a dusty stack of 45s, I found a copy of Marty Robbins' *El Paso*. I sat in the back room and played it over and over again.

And that was the beginning of music as escape for me, the first time a song felt like a doorway out of the life I was living.

The song made me think of my father. And my mother. The cantina in the song replaced the diner where they met. And for those four minutes and nineteen seconds, it all almost made sense.

I romanticized the memory of my father when I listened to that song. He was the jealous and hot-headed cowboy, my mother the wicked Feleena that danced and served drinks at Rosa's Cantina. A far cry from the lonely GI being served reheated pie by a Mexican waitress in a dingy El Paso diner. I would wonder if my father would have challenged another for my mother's hand. Was he the wild young cowboy, like in the song, wild as the west Texas wind? In my five-year-old mind my father was more than willing to shoot down any rivals that stood in his way.

I sat there, playing that song over and over, the needle crackling to life the images that filled my head—gunfights, twirling dresses, scenes I'd stitched together from imagination and longing. At some point, my aunt hid the record from me. She'd grown tired of hearing it.

I begged my mother to get it back. She did—but with rules. I could only play it twice. So, I made it count. I'd sit with my ear pressed close to the tinny, built-in speaker of the record player, listening, imagining, missing my father.

I wouldn't see my father again for over five years. By then, he was a stranger. The swashbuckling, muscle car days were long gone. Illness had taken its toll on him physically, though the charm remained.

As we both got older, we cultivated an uneven relationship

—familiar, but never quite comfortable. One of our last conversations came not long after I became a father myself. We talked about my mother, the divorce, the decisions he made, and any regrets he may have carried.

That conversation will stay private. It was filled with quiet admissions and vulnerable truths meant for no one else. I'll say this much: the divorce wasn't easy on him, either. Even if he did eventually marry the woman I remember sitting on the hood of his car all those years ago. She became his wife and remained so for the rest of his life. A steadfast, patient, and caring companion.

Still, anytime I hear Marty Robbins' *El Paso*, I can't help but picture my father as the jealous cowboy—the one who used a gun to shoot down a rival for my mother's affection. I see him clearly: tow-headed and blue-eyed, a handsome young man in a black cowboy hat, standing with a still-smoking six-shooter in hand. He's just gunned down the wild young cowboy who dared to share a drink with my mother. And there she is—young, maybe a little naïve—startled by the sound of the gunshot, wide-eyed as the handsome young stranger crumples to the floor. She did not know the spell she had cast. No idea how fiercely my father had loved her. Or how dangerous that love could become.

The song is cinematic—sweeping and evocative. It weaves a tale of unrequited love, Old West violence, heartbreak, and the desperate lengths a man will go to for the woman who owns his heart. It's a haunting ballad, sung with aching precision by Marty Robbins.

His voice doesn't just carry the melody—it carries the story. With that warm, rich tenor of his, Robbins doesn't sing El Paso so much as narrate it, like a gunslinger confessing from a porch at sundown. His vocals become the brushstrokes, each word painting scenes as vivid as any film: the dusty streets, the lamplit cantina, the clatter of horses in the dark, the thunder crack of pistols. You can smell the gunpowder, the leather of the holsters. You can feel the heartbreak.

It's more than just a country song—it's a masterpiece of musical storytelling. Gangster rap before the genre existed. Visceral. Violent. The final verses land like a gut punch, the consequences of jealousy paid in full.

You can see and hear it unfold as the posse chases him down, feel the burning pain in his side, the white puff of smoke from the rifle, the bullet traveling deep into his chest. That's how the song ends—bleeding, breathless, tragic. A Western in miniature, told through melody.

The guitar work is pure magic—country and western at its core but laced with flamenco-style flourishes that give it a haunting elegance. It's the sound of two worlds meeting: the dusty boots of a cowboy and the swirling skirts of a Mexican maiden. The melody weaves them together, binding romance and tragedy into a single thread. A tale of love, loss, and the price of passion—carried by a voice that sounds like it's lived every word.

Marty Robbins didn't stop with *El Paso*. He recorded two more songs—*Feleena (From El Paso)* and *El Paso City*—completing a musical trilogy.

Feleena serves as a kind of poetic origin story, diving deep into the life of the woman at the center of it all. It gives her a voice, a past, a longing of her own—transforming her from a symbol into a soul. It's slow, almost mournful, filled with backstory and heartache. You come away understanding why a man might kill or die for her. And why she would die for him.

Then there's *El Paso City*—the most haunting of the three. Robbins sings as himself, flying over El Paso years later, unsure why the land below feels so familiar. He wonders if the doomed cowboy from the original song is somehow a past version of himself. It's not just a sequel—it's a tale of reincarnation. A ghost story. A meditation on fate, memory, and the echo of lives once lived.

Together, the three songs form a sweeping, emotional arc—a Western opera in miniature. Love, jealousy, death, and the lingering mystery of what pulls us back to certain places, again and again.

I think deep down, my father and mother knew their love—like in the song—was in vain. Still, they took a chance. Gave in to the pull of something real, something fierce, even if it wasn't meant to last. In the end, my father rode off into the hazy factory-smoke sunsets of Detroit. My mother moved to California, two kids in tow, literally heading west to make a new life. Like characters from a song, they each followed their own verse—separate melodies spun from the same sorrowful chorus.

My father died when I was thirty-five. He met my daughter, his first granddaughter, before he passed. We made our peace. I don't fault him for how things ended between him and my mother. There are always two sides to every story—and I'm grateful I heard his before he was gone.

Maybe when I see him again, it'll be in El Paso. He'll be at the bar inside Rosa's Cantina—Robert Redford handsome, Steve McQueen cool, a Marlboro Red hanging from his lips. That's how I choose to remember him: a cowboy from Detroit, tossed into a story as wild as the west Texas wind that still echoes through El Paso today.

BAND ON THE RUN

After the whirlwind of El Paso and the hard reset that came with moving to California, my life took another unexpected turn. Not immediately. First came the lice infestations, cramped living conditions, and backyard tetanus traps disguised as broken toys. But eventually, we found a sliver of stability in a low-rent apartment complex in the center of Santa Ana, CA. That's where I met the man who would become my stepdad.

He lived upstairs from us. His domain was a quintessential 1970s bachelor pad with black light posters glowing on the walls, a high-end stereo system (complete with a reel-to-reel) he'd picked up overseas while in the Navy, and a refrigerator that held nothing but beer, hot sauce, and maybe some bologna.

The bathroom smelled like Aqua Velva and Barbasol, with a safety razor and toothbrush lined up along the sink. And of course, there was a fish tank—filled with exotic saltwater species. No self-respecting bachelor pad in the 1970s was complete without one.

He drove a beat-up 1967 Volkswagen Beetle, its 53-horsepower engine sputtering as he weaved through Southern California traffic. There wasn't a seatbelt in sight, and the dashboard was nothing but cold metal that may have been forged from melted-down Panzer tanks left over from the war. Had he slammed on the brakes, I would've gone flying into it with a loud clank, followed by the thud of me hitting the floorboard.

My stepdad wasn't classically handsome, not like my biological father. He looked more like a cross between Eddie Rabbitt and

Willie Nelson. He was wiry, with a scruffy beard and a quiet awkwardness that, even as a kid, I could tell set him apart from other adults. Today, I'd say he was likely on the spectrum —brilliant but socially awkward, tethered more to logic and numbers than to small talk or social niceties.

He'd grown up hard in Little Rock, Arkansas and Ponca City, Oklahoma—places where poverty was generational, and ambition often got ground up in the gears of the day-to-day grind of survival. He once told me he purposely tanked a calculus test in high school to avoid being invited to the end-of-year academic awards banquet. He did this because he didn't own a suit and couldn't afford to buy one. He was too proud, and maybe embarrassed, to show up in borrowed clothes.

What he lacked in polish, he more than made up for in intellect. The man was a mathematical genius, his mind a calculator disguised in bell-bottom denim and button-down shirts with collars roughly the size of the wings on a 737. He did two tours in Vietnam, first in the Army as a helicopter mechanic, and then again in the Navy aboard a carrier. His time in the military didn't make him hard; if anything, it made him softer in strange and unexpected ways. It was like he saw the world as a mathematical puzzle and he'd dedicated his life to trying to solve it one calculation at a time.

He was also tough as nails, and seemingly impervious to pain. He once accidentally cut one of his thumbs off while working with a router. Rather than panic, he calmly picked the severed digit up off the garage floor, placed it on ice in a plastic bag, and drove himself to the hospital, his bloody hand wrapped in shop towels. Another time, he fell from scaffolding while at work and severely broke his left wrist. He actually argued with co-workers to let him complete the job he was doing before going to the emergency room.

Where my father had been all swagger and cool, my stepdad was a mix of sci-fi nerd and eccentricity. They couldn't have been more different. And in that difference, I understood something important—about men, about love, and about how music enters your life from unlikely places, carrying truths we don't always recognize right away.

He met my mom in that apartment complex, a chance meeting forged by proximity, pain, and perhaps some shared need to start over. One was a single parent, trying to figure out how to survive and provide for her two sons; the other, a lonely man looking for some kind of meaning in his life. They carried their own kind of wreckage into the relationship. It wasn't always easy on them, or me and my brother.

And this is where the music comes back in.

That Volkswagen Bug had an 8-track player, and it played the soundtrack of my early California years. Not just Zeppelin and Sabbath—though yes, they were there, rumbling like distant thunder from cheap swap meet speakers—but also George Jones, Tom T. Hall, Dolly Parton, Merle Haggard, and Loretta Lynn. It was a strange musical mix. The rock made sense, but the country was where he was born and raised, he had lived the lyrics of those songs.

As great as the 8-track was, even better was that the VW also had an AM/FM tuner.

AM radio was where you tuned in to hear David and Shaun Cassidy, Bay City Rollers, the Osmonds, and Captain & Tennille. It was all bubble gum pop, easily digestible, meant for mass appeal and boosting the sales of 45 RPM singles. It was where the pages of Tiger Beat magazine came to audible life, meant to be heard on transistor radios strapped to the handlebars of banana seated Schwinn bicycles.

FM radio was AOR, short for album-oriented rock. This was music to be heard, listened to, not just consumed as product.

It was once said that during the 1970s, Led Zeppelin's "Stairway to Heaven" was playing somewhere on an American FM station at any given time. This feels true. FM stations are where you went to hear long cuts: Ted Nugent's "Stranglehold" in all its snarling, reverb-drenched glory; The Eagles' *Hotel California*, allowed to stretch out and build to the dueling guitar solos at the end of the song. These songs were not edited down to the fit the mold of the three-minute pop single. They were given space to breathe and not just exist as ambient background noise or the stuff of teen girl crushes. FM radio was serious, less static, in stereo, deep. It was where interstellar overdrives roared to life.

More importantly, FM radio was home to Paul McCartney and Wings' "Band on the Run". And I loved that song. A lot.

A multi-structured track, expertly constructed by McCartney, it always felt to me like the closest thing to a lost Beatles song he'd ever recorded. You can't tell me he didn't have John Lennon in mind when he arranged the phrasing of "If we ever get outta here..."—the defiance, the weary hopefulness. It's all there.

Though it peaked on the charts in 1974, it received massive airplay well into 1975 and beyond. With its three distinct parts —the subdued intro, the driving middle, and the bright, sing-along finish—it had something for everyone. DJs loved playing it. Listeners loved hearing it.

I have a vivid memory of that song playing in my stepdad's beat-up VW Bug. We were on our way to Pep Boys, the chain auto parts store that catered to gear heads like him. The opening chords spilled from the speakers, and he turned up the volume knowing how much I loved it.

We didn't speak through the first two sections. We just listened. I stared out the window, absorbing lyrics I didn't yet understand. Why was a pint needed? I had no clue.

And then the song lifted—*the rain exploded with a mighty crash*. We both fell into the sun. It was amazing.

Then chorus hit, and I sang along with everything I had: "Man on the run! Man on the run!"

My stepdad smiled and gently corrected me. "Not man," he said. "*Band* on the run." I looked at him, confused. Maybe even a little dubious. Why would a band be on the run?

That's when he explained McCartney's love of big ideas. That *Band on the Run* was rumored to have started as a concept album—maybe even a film—something like The Beatles' *Magical Mystery Tour*. He told me how McCartney often wove themes and characters into his music, how his work went beyond love songs and catchy choruses.

My five-year-old mind was blown. Tell me more about these concept albums. About magical mystery tours. About girls with kaleidoscope eyes.

We waited in the car, parked outside Pep Boys, so I could listen to "Band on the Run" in its entirety. When the song finally ended, we went inside and he picked up whatever it was he needed to keep the VW running—brake pads, spark plugs...I honestly don't remember.

That afternoon, he worked on the car, and later that evening, we had dinner at his apartment. Afterward, he let my younger brother feed the fish while my mom cleaned up. Then he fired up the reel-to-reel, and the room came alive. The speakers—outfitted with lights that pulsed in time with the music—flared as the dreamlike opening of "Band on the Run" filled the apartment.

My stepdad did a lot for me over the years. He took on a role that, by his own admission, he wasn't fully prepared for. It wasn't always smooth sailing and trips to Pep Boys. There were dark times, too. That's life. That's what happens when a 27-year-old man suddenly finds himself responsible for someone else's kids and chooses to raise them as his own.

There were growing pains—for him, for me, for my brother, my mom, and a couple of years later, my sister. But in the end, it worked out.

He taught me so much. Practical skills. Life skills. Lessons about what to do—and sometimes what *not* to do. We grew into our roles together, father and son.

More than anything, he was the one who kicked open the door

to a deeper understanding of music for me. He taught me how to listen—not just to the melody, but to the meaning. To think about what the lyrics were saying. To ask where a song came from. What it was really about.

It started with his simple explanation of how "Band on the Run" might have been part of a bigger concept. But from that moment forward, I wasn't just hearing songs anymore—I was immersing myself in them.

We bounced from one Santa Ana apartment to another, then into a small house, until eventually we landed in Montclair, California. These moves marked the beginning of what would become a long string of new homes and new schools.

I had just turned seven when we settled into the Montclair house. It was there my stepdad taught me how to use the reel-to-reel player. That opened up an entire world of music, giving me access to the albums he had recorded and carefully archived on tape.

Through those spools of magnetic ribbon, I found Creedence Clearwater Revival, their Bay Area swamp rock transporting me to a Louisiana bayou I'd never seen. I discovered the Rolling Stones, Mick Jagger's swagger and Keith Richards' open-tuned brilliance. Elton John sang about tiny dancers and yellow brick roads.

Then came the country artists—Willie, Waylon, and the boys. Kenny Rogers, lamenting about Lucille and four hungry children —which I misheard as four hundred children. In my version, Kenny and Lucille were remarkably prolific.

Fleetwood Mac was inescapable. They dominated the airwaves and my stepdad's turntable, their songs bleeding through every room of that little house.

If I were to make a mixtape of that time—songs that instantly take me back to those low-rent apartments in Santa Ana, "Band on the Run" would stand above them all.

That song represents a moment when, as a small boy, I had

something I hadn't felt in a long time: hope. Hope for a better life. A better place to live. The hope of having a dad again.

It still feels strange calling him my *step*dad. He's been in my life for half a century. He's just my dad—the man who stepped into a role he didn't have to fill but did.

As I write this, that same man is battling dementia and rapid-onset Alzheimer's. The math genius who once did calculus in his head now struggles to remember what day it is, or which stories he's already told. Some days he's still there behind his eyes, sharp and funny in flashes; other days he's adrift, his memories fraying at the edges. It's brutal and unfair, watching his hard drive fail after all the years he spent filling mine. I don't know how much time he has left, but I do know this: whatever the disease takes from him, it doesn't touch what he already gave me.

The day we spent driving to Pep Boys, "Band on the Run" playing on the radio—that's the memory I'll hold on to forever. That's *him*, right there in that moment. And that's me, finally feeling like I was no longer running alone.

SUSPICIOUS MINDS

In the early hours of August 16th, 1977, Elvis Presley died. His fiance, Ginger Alden, found him later that day, unresponsive on the bathroom floor at his Graceland mansion in Memphis, Tennessee. Emergency services were called around 2:30 in the afternoon, and he was transported to Baptist Memorial Hospital. Resuscitation efforts were futile, and Elvis was pronounced dead at 3:00pm. He was 42 years old.

The news of Elvis's death spread like wildfire. Major news outlets interrupted regular programming to announce the passing of the 'King of Rock & Roll'. My mother was watching *General Hospital* when the 'We interrupt this program to bring you this special report' cut in. She was glued to the TV the rest of the day, as was I. We sat and watched as talking head after talking head came on air to discuss Elvis's life and death. While I was aware of who Elvis was when he died, I got a crash course on his history and legacy via the retrospectives that aired posthumously. And I was hooked.

We were living in Montclair at the time and our living room was a full-blown testament to the era. My mother had my dad cover the walls of the living room with wallpaper that can best be described as a garish nightmare - a cream-colored backdrop with maroon velvet fleur-de-lis. To get from the living room to the hallway that led to the bedrooms, you had to pass through a set of swinging saloon doors. Then in the middle of the hallway, for no apparent reason, she had my dad hang a curtain of plastic beads.

Our furnishings were mostly rattan, even the couch. No matter where you sat, the sound of the rattan groaning in protest greeted you. One wall of the kitchen was covered in mirrored tiles. In a way, the Montclair house was my mother's version of Graceland via a carnival fun house.

Something about Elvis struck a chord in me that's still ringing decades later, but back then, at seven, it was simple: he was cool. Cooler than anyone I'd ever seen. The voice, the black leather suit, the way he moved—it all felt larger-than-life to a kid who mostly knew Saturday morning cartoons. I understood nothing about his struggles, that would come spilling out of books and documentaries later. At seven, you don't have a framework for tragedy. You just know when you like something, and I liked Elvis in the same way I liked Batman.

I tried to imitate the Elvis sneer in my second-grade school photo, a look that came out more goofy than dangerous. I spent part of my $2 allowance on gaudy gumball-machine rings because Elvis wore rings, and that was enough reason for me.

Networks worked feverishly to pump out made-for-TV Elvis movies, and I watched them all, including 1981's *Elvis and the Beauty Queen* (which was terrible). My favorite of those early Elvis TV films was 1979's *Elvis*, starring Kurt Russell. Directed by John Carpenter, 1979's *Elvis* focused on his rise to fame and personal struggles. It was my first glimpse into Elvis Presley the human being.

It wasn't until my teen years that the other Elvis—the real one, the complicated one—took shape. I devoured books about him, even the sensational, borderline character-assassination of a biography by Albert Goldman. That's when the rest of the story came into focus: the pressure, the sadness, the strange mythology of his life and death. But none of that was present for me in 1977. Back then, Elvis wasn't a cautionary tale. He was a superhero with sideburns.

About a month after his death, TV ads started airing for a two-album career retrospective. "The definitive collection of Elvis's greatest hits," the announcer promised. The album was available by phone or mail order only. Originally released in 1973, RCA had reissued this double-album to feed off of the public's grief. In reality, it was just a compilation of singles from 1956 to 1962, a snapshot of his early years. That didn't matter to me. I had no idea how deep his catalog went. I just knew I wanted that record!

My dad wasn't an Elvis fan, so we didn't have any of his albums. That made my acquisition of the double album more of a mission of cultural significance than just the simple want of a kid. The problem was, every time the commercial came on, I wasn't ready to write down the ordering information. So I devised a plan. I moved my little brother's chalkboard easel from our room into the living room and stationed it beside the TV. I effectively turned our living room into an Elvis record ordering command center.

I remember the moment when my plan came together. I was watching *Kimba the White Lion* after school. During the first commercial break, the screen suddenly faded to a shade of blue that perfectly matched the background of the album cover. Then a deep, authoritative voice boomed—at least as much as it could through the tinny speakers of our nineteen-inch Zenith:

"ELVIS LIVES — in this two-record limited edition release..."

Snippets of *"Hound Dog"*, *"Jailhouse Rock"*, and *"Don't Be Cruel"* played as images of Elvis flashed across the TV screen in quick succession. The narrator made it clear that this special collector's double-album would only be available for a limited time.

I bolted to the chalkboard, chalk in hand, and waited for the order screen to appear. When it did, I scribbled furiously: the phone number, the address, the price—everything. I don't remember the exact cost, maybe $7.98 or $8.99, but at that age it might as well have been a million dollars. There was no way I could ask my dad for it. This was clearly a "mom" situation.

She was preparing to cook dinner in the hall of mirrors we called the kitchen. I grabbed her by the sleeve and led her to the chalkboard like I was presenting crucial end of quarter sales data. I explained the household was suffering from a critical shortage of Elvis Presley records and that this *definitive, career-spanning* double album would solve that problem. Time, however, was of the essence, as this double album would be available for a limited time only. There was no time to deliberate, a decision needed to be made posthaste!

My sales pitch worked, because she didn't ask a single follow-up or clarifying question. She picked up the phone, dialed the number, and said we'd pay C.O.D. And that was that. Then came the hardest part of all: the waiting.

An eternity seemed to pass before the record finally arrived. Until then, my Elvis fixes came courtesy of the local TV stations that ran his movies in constant rotation—*G.I. Blues, Fun in Acapulco, Viva Las Vegas.* I couldn't tell you a single plot point from any of them, except that Elvis might've played a cliff diver in *Fun in Acapulco.* What I remember were the musical numbers. Most of the songs weren't great—the exception being "Viva Las Vegas". That tune cooks.

Four to six weeks later, the album showed up. My mom had it waiting for me when I got home from school, unwrapped and propped beside the record player. I rushed over, slid the first LP from its sleeve, and placed it on the turntable. Then, with surgical precision, I lowered the needle onto track one — "Hound Dog". Elvis's voice erupted through the living room speakers: *"You ain't nothin' but a hound dog..."*

Finally.

Listening to that album became my after-school ritual. I'd put on that double record and pretend our living room was the stage from *Aloha from Hawaii*, tossing plastic leis to my captive audience of one—my baby sister strapped into her swing.

Over time, side four became my favorite. Those five tracks

captured everything that made him extraordinary. His voice wasn't just sound—it was a presence. He had the uncanny ability to make any song completely his own.

From the playfulness of "Let Me Be Your Teddy Bear" to the lullaby-like "Love Me Tender" and the straight-up rock and roll of "Hard Headed Woman", I learned early that Elvis could sing anything. But it was the closing two tracks - "It's Now or Never" and "Surrender"—that stopped me cold.

Those songs revealed Elvis at his most ambitious—though I wouldn't understand that until much later. At seven, I didn't have the vocabulary to describe what I was hearing. I just knew it sounded different from anything on the radio or the records in our house. As an adult, I can hear the richness, the control, the way he seemed to sculpt sound rather than just sing it. But back then, all I knew was that Elvis's voice wrapped itself around me like a spell.

My second-grade teacher was Mrs. Cox, an older sprite of a woman who played the autoharp with gusto. Fridays were music day in her classroom, and she'd lead us through rousing versions of "This Old Man," "Bingo," "Farmer in the Dell," and other assorted public-domain toe-tappers. She seriously rocked out on that autoharp—an instrument I had never seen before or since.

Better yet, on Music Fridays students could bring in records from home for listening time. Unfortunately, my classmates mostly brought in novelty records: Rick Dees' "Disco Duck," Sha-Na-Na's parody-nostalgia albums, and even a 45 of "Convoy," because trucker culture was big enough in the 1970s to produce a hit single about CB radio slang. It was awful.

A second plan emerged.

I would bring my Elvis double album to the next Music Friday. Mrs. Cox would drop the needle on "A Big Hunk o' Love," the class would rock out, and they would hail me as a hero.

My mom carefully packed the record for me, and I carried it to school like it was an undetonated land mind, terrified of scratching the vinyl treasure inside. I walked so slowly that I was late to class.

After lunch, Mrs. Cox asked if anyone had brought a record for Music Friday. Up shot my hand—but so did the hand of a girl named Holly. What in the actual…? Competition was not part of the plan.

Mrs. Cox asked us to bring our records up front. I slowly lifted Elvis from the bag while Holly skipped forward, her braided ponytail bouncing like she was starring in her own musical. In her hands: the *Mary Poppins* soundtrack.

Mrs. Cox studied both covers. In one hand, *Mary Poppins*—safe, wholesome, Disney nonsense. In the other, Elvis Presley—regal, resplendent, the King himself in a white, tasseled jumpsuit. To me, it was a no-brainer.

But she didn't choose Elvis.

She sighed, handed the album back to me, and asked, "Your parents let you listen to Elvis?"

"Yes," I said. "I listen to Elvis every day."

Her eyes locked on mine, cool and judgmental.

"Not today. Not in my classroom."

And that was that. We were going to listen to *Mary Poppins*.

I sat frozen at my desk, numb, while Holly cheerfully explained how much she loved the movie and all the musical numbers in it—especially "Supercalifragilisticexpialidocious." Then she played it, and every girl in the room knew every word to every goddamn song, and sang along at full volume.

It was torture.

At the time, I had not seen *Mary Poppins*. Forty-eight years later, I still haven't. And I never will.

My constant spinning of the Elvis double album threatened to wear out the grooves in the vinyl. Then one day, out of thin air, a 45 rpm single of "Suspicious Minds" appeared in the house. I have no memory of my parent's buying it—it just showed up.

Maybe my mother bought it for me, or my dad, during a routine trip to K-Mart. How it arrived didn't matter. From the moment I heard those opening notes, "Suspicious Minds" became my favorite Elvis song. Ever. The double album finally got a much-deserved break.

Released in 1969, "Suspicious Minds" was Elvis's last number-one—a song that bridged rock, soul, and country. Its arrangement was complex, its theme mature: a plea against mistrust in a relationship corroded by doubt. The narrator begged for understanding, desperate to save love from emotional decay.

It was a sharp contrast to the Elvis I'd known up to that point. Songs like "Jailhouse Rock" were pure early rock & roll escapism. "Suspicious Minds" felt heavier. There was a pleading weariness in Elvis's voice, a sadness that sounded familiar in a way I couldn't yet understand. As an adult, I can hear echoes of my parents' divorce in that song—the fights, the accusations, the suspicion, the dull thud of a tub of butter hitting the wall. Back then, I didn't have the language for any of that. I just recognized the feeling.

That's a lot for a kid to hear and feel in a song, but I was a strange kid: emotional, introspective, quiet. The song didn't make me sad so much as it made me aware—however faintly—of how much calmer life had become since. I had friends in the cul-de-sac, was doing well in school, and felt—for the first time in a long while—secure.

My Elvis phase never really ended—it just kept shifting as I got older. When CBS aired *Elvis and Me* in 1988, right before I left for the Air Force, I watched it with the earnestness of someone trying to understand a hero from every angle. Dale Midkiff looked about as much as Elvis as I did—second-grade sneer notwithstanding—but the performance worked. It hinted at a more complex Elvis than the one on my childhood album covers.

By then, I was starting to realize that you could love an artist without pretending they were perfect. You could hold on to the magic while acknowledging the mess.

Peter Guralnick's *Last Train to Memphis* arrived in 1994, and that book was a revelation. It captured everything electrifying about Elvis's rise—his ambition, his innocence, the strange alchemy that occurs when talent meets timing. I must have read it three times, tracing his story the way some people trace family trees. When the follow-up, *Careless Love*, came out in 1999, I devoured that too. That second book was heavier, sadder, a chronicle of the unraveling. Together, those two volumes finally helped me separate the man from the myth and the myth from the music.

Even now, I'll pull them off the shelf and flip through certain passages. Not for the trivia or the timeline, but for the reminder of what first drew me in: the spark, the sorrow, the voice that could bend an entire song to his will.

Elvis was the first artist I ever loved, the first one who made me want to understand *why* music could make a person feel something. And even after everything I've learned about his life—the brilliance, the flaws, the loneliness so deep it swallowed him whole—my connection to him still comes back to that kid in Montclair, sitting cross-legged on a rattan couch, needle dropping onto "Hound Dog," hearing something that made the world feel bigger.

The myth came later.
The tragedy came later.
But the music—that was first.

STAR WARS MAIN THEME

On May 25th, 1977, a low-budget space opera that was set a long time ago, in a galaxy far, far away was released in theaters. That movie, Star Wars, would go one to become a runaway pop culture phenomenon.

The impact this movie had on me - and kid's all over the world - cannot be overstated. There simply wasn't anything like it before or since. I didn't get to see the movie until it had been in theaters a couple of weeks. My neighbors, Sean and Jason, had been boasting to anyone who would listen that they had already seen Star Wars four times by that point. They would breathlessly describe the special effects, how bad ass Darth Vader was, the coolness of Han Solo, Luke Skywalker's heroics, the brashness of Princess Leia, and of course, how a mystical energy known only as 'the Force' could guide our actions. I pestered and pleaded with my parents to take me to see it, but something always came up. One of those things was a trip to Disneyland, and I remember sulking a bit on the car ride there because I wanted to see Star Wars instead.

This desire was further fueled when another neighbor's house caught fire. Luckily, no one was hurt, but they had to move out for a while. One of the older kids that lived there approached me as they were packing up and handed me a stack of slightly burned comic books. This pile of comics included the first two issues of Marvel's adaptation of Star Wars. The cover of issue number one was amazing, depicting Luke Skywalker with lightsaber in hand, ready to take on the Galactic Empire. Behind him, Han Solo with his blaster taking aim at something out of frame. X-Wing, Y-Wing, and Tie Fighters were in the background, engaged in an epic dogfight around the Death Star. And looming over all of this, the head of Darth Vader, ominous and evil.

I must have read those first two Star Wars comic books a hundred times. I'd sit in my room and flip through the singed pages, studying each frame. The comic books smelled like smoke, and the corners of each page were charred, but I didn't care about that at all. What I did care about was the story, mainly how it ended as I only had half of it in comic form. Issues three and four were hard to come by as they sold out as soon as the local 7-11 received them. I had no concept of specialty comic book stores, and honestly, my parents probably wouldn't have taken me to one to pay a premium above the thirty cent cover price. Word on the streets of Montclair, CA was that new and back issues of Star Wars comic books were going for an astronomical FIVE DOLLARS at these places. My parents wouldn't understand.

My dad finally took me and my brother to see Star Wars at the Brea Mall in early July of 1977. My mother, being a Mexican mother, had me and my brother dress up as if we were going to a wedding. She made us wear button up shirts with sweater vests to go to the movie theater. In summer. In the Inland Empire of California. Still, that's how she did things. We had to wear our best clothes when leaving the house.

We sat in the packed theater that day, quite possibly the only three people on the face of the earth who had not seen Star Wars yet. The lights dimmed, my anticipation rose, and then the drumroll and brass of the iconic 20th Century Fox fanfare burst from the theater sound system. A brief pause and then the Star Wars logo filled the screen as the movie's main theme blasted out of the speakers. I sat forward in my seat to read the opening crawl, the words giving crucial context to what we were about to watch. Then the Rebel Blockade runner dashes across the screen, its laser cannons, in a futile effort, attempting to hold off the massive Imperial Star Destroyer in merciless pursuit.

It was unlike anything I have ever seen, before or since.

The next two hours went by in a heartbeat. I walked out of the theater in a daze, trying to process the epic story I had bore witness to. Over the next few days, I replayed the movie over and over in my head, reliving the duel between Darth Vader and Obi-Wan Kenobi, the cantina scene, the Milennium Falcon's escape from the Death Star, and of course, Luke turning off his targeting computer before taking that fateful final shot. The Force was strong with him.

Unlike today, there were no opportunities to re-watch movies on streaming or BluRay. Hell, VHS tapes didn't even exist in 1977, so we couldn't even watch the movie that way. If you wanted to see a movie a second time, you had to either go back to the theater or wait for it to show up, heavily edited, as the network movie of the week. Even though Star Wars had a remarkably long initial theatrical run (it remained in theaters for over a year, with some theaters playing it for up to 44 weeks), I didn't get to see it again until spring of 1979.

In the meantime, I got my Star Wars fix via comic books, the novelization (much more violent and descriptive of said violence than the comics or even the movie), toys, trading cards, and the soundtrack album.

The Star Wars Main Theme is one of the most instantly recognizable pieces of music in cinematic history. It is blazing and bombastic, a brass tour de force. The horns and strings soar, conveying grandeur, adventure, and heroism. The rhythm is bold and militaristic, yet also sweeping and uplifting. The regal melody builds tension and drama, and muscially conveys the hero's journey depicted in the film.

It was so popular that a professional trombonist and music

producer named Domenico Monardo recorded a disco infused version. Released in August of 1977 under the name Meco, the Star Wars Theme/Cantina Band single took John Williams' Star Wars score and reimagined it with funky basslines, heavy hi-hat drum loops, and Moog synthesizers.

Which was fine. I preferred the John Williams' version, although I will admit to owning the 45 of the Meco release, one of the many copies sold that helped that single reach number one on the pop charts.

My obsession with Elvis in late summer of 1977 collided head-on with Star Wars fever in the spring of 1978. Since discovering Elvis, I had become fixated on learning to play the guitar. I pestered my mom and dad to sign me up for guitar lessons. They always said no, with reasons that ranged from somewhat understandable to downright bizarre: I'd lose interest, guitars were expensive, lessons might interfere with school work, and, the strangest of all...my dad insisted I was too skinny and frail to handle the size and weight of a guitar.

Apparently, he thought I'd try plucking out a rudimentary version of the Eensy, Weensy, Spider only to be knocked out of my chair by the reverberation of the strings, subsequently being crushed under the weight of dreadnought bodied acoustic guitar.

Then one day, my mom told me she had signed me up for "music lessons", which I assumed meant guitar lessons. I lit up. Finally, guitar lessons! My own hero's journey of becoming the next Elvis was about to begin.

Only later that evening would the vague phrasing of "music lessons" reveal its full, shocking, and horrifying truth.

We arrived at the strip mall where the music store - and my long-awaited lessons - was located. My excitement was palatable and my mind buzzed with possibilities. What we would be learning on this first night? Chords? Picking technique? Maybe an Elvis song?

I bounced through the store's front doors and was immediately escorted to one of the classrooms in back. My mom followed close behind. I took an empty seat in the semi-circle of plastic chairs near the front of the room and gave a quick once over to the other kids in the class.

Something didn't feel right.

None of them appeared to fit the guitar player archetype I had in my mind. There were no young Elvises, Jimmy Pages, or even Guy Clarks sitting beside me. They kids were, to put it mildly, nerdy.

The only one that registered on my cool meter was a girl with flaming red hair, cat-rimmed glasses, and perfectly painted crimson nails. She was immacutaley dressed in a blue poodle skirt and black blouse. Her feet were adorned with what appeared to be bowling shoes. She was pretty and undeniably with it.

At this point, I still believed - despite all mounting evidence to the contrary - that I was attending a group guitar lesson. Then the instructor strolled in, and he made the nerdiest kid in the room look cooler than Marlon Brando in "The Wild Bunch".

He was sloppily dressed in shapeless, high water brown corduroy pants held up by rainbow colored suspenders a year or so before Robin Williams made them popular. He had paired this with an ill-fitting navy blue button up corduroy shirt, and a black vest adorned with yellow smiley face buttons. His gray wool socks sagged into awful looking brown shoes that looked like they were prescribed by a podiatrist. His hair was straight out of the Bozo the Clown style book. His bushy mustache was greasy. He looked like he smelled of soup and moth balls.

Strapped to all of this was an unholy monstrosity of a musical instrument. Something that looked like it had been cobbled together from the discarded remains of a piano, bagpipes, an autoharp, and maybe a car radiator. It was not a guitar. I didn't know what it was.

He introduced himself as Mr. Gurgich, and then welcomed us to our first accordion lesson.

Accordion? What the fuck is an accordion? That's exactly what I would have said... if I'd known how to swear at eight years old. Instead, I just sat there...gobsmacked and in shock. I glanced over to my mom, mouth open, eyes wide in bewilderment. She beamed at me from the back of the room, glowing with pride.

I slowly turned back towards Mr. Gurgich, still stunned. What the fuck is an accordion?

For the next several minutes, Mr. Gurgich squeezed the accordion, working both sets of keys and filling the room with what sounded like carnival music ripped out of a fever induced nightmare. It was music to go insane by.

After a few bars of a song he would stop and ask the classroom what style of music he had just played. I was clueless. The only person answering was the red haired girl. A whirlwind of notes would blurt out of the accordion and she'd raise her hand and answer without hesitation.

"Polka!"

"Dixie!"

"San Francisco!"

San Francisco, I wondered? What the hell was San Francisco music? Then a string of notes swirled around the room that I vaguely recognised. I yelled out.

"Egyptian!"

The red haired girl looked at me over her cat-rim glasses, which was infuriating. "No," she said smugly, "it's Morrocan."

"Yes!" said Mr. Gurgich, visibly impressed and glowing with approval of the red-haired girl's musical knowledge. By this point, I hated her almost as much as I hated the stupid accordion.

After the musical guessing game, we were all called up to the front of the room to pick out our own instrument. If my dad was concerned about a guitar being too heavy for me, well, he should have been out of his mind with worry over the dead weight of an accordion. I lugged the clunky and awkward case back to my seat and sat down. Taking a deep breath, I popped the latches and lifted the lid.

And there it was.

A laminated hardwood of a beast, its body wrapped in a white pearlescent veneer. The composite keys leered at me mockingly. I tried hoisting the thing out of the case, not knowing that the last unfortunate soul that tried playing the wretched thing did not properly secure the bellows. As I lifted, the bellows unfolded, sending one half of the accordion flopping back into the case with a dull thud. Mr. Gurgich immediately reprimanded me for mishandling the accordion. I gathered up all my strength and pulled both sides of the accordion onto my lap. And there it sat, like a semi-dead fish, trying to squirm away as I wrestled to keep the bellows from flopping open again.

Mr. Gurgich had assistants, consisting of older and even nerdier students, to help us strap in to our accordions. Yes, we had to strap and buckle into the things. They accordions were heavy and awkward. If I didn't have scoliosis before that class, I was well on my way. The accordion pulled on my spine and shoulders like a medieval torture device.

I looked around the room at the other pupils. They all seemed happy, especially the red-haired girl. Mr. Gurgich then described the parts of the accordion with soulless, clinical efficiency.

"These are the bellows," he said, patting the middle of the accordion. "They are the lungs of the instrument, pushing air through the reeds to create sound."

He tapped the right side. "This is the treble keyboard, where the melody is played."

Then the left. "Here you'll find the bass buttons. These control bass notes and pre-set chords."

Finally, he motioned toward the grille. "Now place your hand on the grille. This protects the internal reeds and mechanics. Think of the grille as the accordion's ribcage."

I just sat there in stunned, silent disbelief.

At some point, Mr. Gurgich demonstrated some rudimentary practice scales that used only the treble keyboard. He pointed to the keys and explained which notes each one produced, his chubby, Jimmy Dean breakfast sausage fingers gliding over them with surprising smoothness and dexterity. Then we were taught our first song. I believe it was Mary Had A Little Lamb...or Twinkle, Twinkle Little Star. The musical equivalent of finger painting.

And after what seemed to be an eternity, the first lesson was over. They gave us beginner sheet music with new songs for us to learn and practice before our next lesson. I numbly stuffed them into the accordion case.

I peppered my mom with questions on the car ride home. "What happened to guitar lessons? How did I get signed up for accordion lessons? Did you know about this?"

My mom was coy, dodging with a shrug, "I must have checked accordion instead of guitar on the sign-up sheet. It was a mistake."

I pleaded with my mom to correct it. "Can you fix it? Please? Can I switch to guitar?"

"You'll learn to like the accordion," she said cheerfully. "It looks like fun!"

"No, it's not fun, I hate it!" I snapped, fuming.

When we got home, I dragged the case, packed with the accordion and my shattered dreams of playing the guitar, into the house. My dad looked up from the kitchen table, "How was accordion class?"

This confirmed it. He knew. They both knew. I may have been young, but I wasn't dumb.

"I hated it," was my defeated response. "I want to play the

guitar."

This is when the awful truth was fully revealed.

My dad looked at me and said, matter-of-factly, "Your mom signed you up for accordion because she wants you to join a mariachi band."

There it was. This wasn't a mistake, this was betrayal, and the stench of it hung in the air. The accordion lesson was not because of an administrative or clerical error, it was by design. My mom took it upon herself to crush my musical guitar dreams because she wanted me to learn accordion. In her head, I would join or start a mariachi band and play Cielito Lindo while wearing a decorated traje de charro, a silk bow tie, and a giant wide-brimmed sombrero. At eight years old. Preposterous!

I pleaded in vain, "Please switch me to the guitar, please?" Tears streamed down my face, to no avail. My mom was steadfast. I would finish out the next three months of accordion lessons, and that was that. There would be no switching to the guitar.

I went to bed, resigned to my hellish accordion fate. I would have to endure three months of the accordion, Mr. Gurgich, and the smug red-haired girl.

So I went, and I learned how to play "Camptown Races", basic polka style songs, and whatever other nonsense Mr. Gurgich picked out for us. I did not enjoy one moment of it.

Then one day, a glimmer of hope...a new hope, if you will.

I was with my brother Chris over at our friends Larry and James's house. While Chris and James played in the backyard, Larry called me over to the family piano. He had something to show me. Larry sat at the piano bench, adjusted his distance from the keys, wriggled and stretched his fingers, and then played the Star Wars Main Theme. That glorious, powerful, anthem rang out from their upright piano and filled the house.

I stood frozen, in awe.

When he finished, I asked, "Can you teach me that?" I then told him the whole story, how my mom duped me into accordion instead of guitar lessons. Larry burst out laughing.

When his laughter finally subsided, he nodded. "Okay, I'll teach you."

His mom had an old accordion from when she was a kid. He promised to figure out how to play the Star Wars Main Theme on it and then teach it to me. I nodded enthusiastic and hopeful.

Something good might come out of this accordion mess after all.

Or not.

A few days later, I returned to Larry's house, dragging my accordion behind me.

I knocked on the front door.

Larry's father answered. He was a serious, disciplined Japanese man that did not suffer foolishness or fools. At all.

He eyed the accordion with a combination of disdain and bemusement. Then, "Lawrence is a piano player. He will not be teaching you how to play the Star Wars theme on the accordion. That would be a distraction."

My heart sank, the accordion case in my hand so heavy that it felt as if it could drag me down into the earth's molten core.

Larry'd father continued. "If you want to learn the theme, watch Lawrence play it on piano, then translate it to the accordion on your own."

Well, that was something.

I nodded, and he opened the door to let me in. Larry was waiting at the piano, posture perfect, serious and focused.

His father brought a chair in from the kitchen and set it beside the piano. I took a seat, unlatched the case, and carefully removed the white pearlescent beast. I strapped in, adjusted the buckles, and took a deep breath.

For the next hour, I watched as Larry played the Star Wars Main Theme repeatedly. First at half speed. Then again, half speed but only with his right hand, so I could focus on the melody. I mimicked and followed his movements on the treble keyboard.

The bass buttons were trickier. I couldn't figure out which button did what note wise.

That's when Larry's mom appeared.

She entered the living room with her own accordion. The one she had when she was a little girl. She took a seat next to me and began showing me the proper fingerings for the bass line.

Note by note, button by button, the music came together.

By the end of the session, I had working knowledge of how to play the Star Wars theme on the accordion. It wasn't pretty, not yet, but I had something to build on.

Over the next few weeks, I practiced relentlessly until I had it nailed down. Admittedly, it didn't sound as epic on the accordion as it did on Larry's piano. It honestly sounded like what you might hear while riding a carousel or at a Wisconsin polka festival, but it was still way better than "Old Joe Clark".

I kept showing up to my accordion lessons, day after day, week after week, mindlessly trudging through scales. Then, at the end of our second-to-last session, Mr. Gurgich made an announcement.

"For our final class," he said, hand clasped in front of him, "each of you will select a song you have learned to play as a solo piece. This will mark the end of your beginner's accordion journey."

Okay, then.

I had one week to perfect a song from the stack of sheet music we'd collected throughout the course of our lessons. I flipped through each piece, trying to summon an ounce of enthusiasm for one of them. Nothing. Every title filled me with indifference.

Eventually, I settled on "At The Village Inn", mostly because I was sure no one else would pick it.

The final lesson mercifully arrived. The red-haired girl showed up dressed to impress in what looked like an Oktoberfest starter kit. My disdain for her, already close to reaching critical mass, spiked to new heights. In today's parlance, she'd be called a try-hard.

The rest of the class looked like what they were, a group of eight- and nine-year-olds that were forced to suffer through accordion lessons. Had I been a bit more social during class, we probably would have all trauma bonded over the experience, brothers-in-bellows. One poor kid was forced to wear a cheap rental tuxedo. He looked like a lost ring bearer at a shotgun wedding who'd wandered into the wrong banquet room at the Ramada Inn. I felt nothing but pity for that poor, unfortunate soul.

The final class began. A special chair had been placed at the center of our semi-circle. Mr. Gurgich dramatically dubbed it "the hot seat", which earned a few polite chuckles from the family members who had shown to watch.

Mr. Gurgich began class with an overview of all we had learned over the past several weeks. I sat there silently, just wanting it all to be over.

Then, with a clap of Mr. Gurgich's hands, it began. One by one, we were each called up to the "hot seat". Each kid shuffled forward, accordion strapped to them like rucksacks, heads down, faces blank. To a casual observer, it might have looked less like an accordion recital and more like we were being called up to face summary execution. By that point, there really wasn't much of a difference.

I suffered through bleak performances of "Ode to Joy", "The Itsy Bitsy Spider", and, of course, "Mary Had a Little Lamb". Each played with rote and soulless efficiency and precision, yet utterly devoid of emotion.

Then the red-haired girl was called up. She approached the seat like she was taking the stage at Carnegie Hall, and curtsied, not once, not twice, but three times: first to Mr. Gurgich, then to the class, and finally to the assembled friends and family in attendance. It was all a bit much, but pulling off a triple-curtsy with a sixteen-pound accordion strapped to her sixty-pound frame was no easy feat. I'll give her that.

She then took her seat, gave a dramatic flip of her red hair, and launched into a medley of the polkas we had learned - "Beer Barrel Polka (Roll Out The Barrel)", "Little Diamond Polka", and "The Geese in the Bog Jig". I noticed she had unbuckled the bottom portion of her accordion, allowing her to manipulate the bellows with dramatic flair. The rest of the class had kept the bottom of their accordions buckled to maximize stability. Not her. No, she chose spectacle over practical control, wringing every last drop of stage presence from the grim proceedings.

Her performance wrapped to thunderous applause. She rose from the chair, repeated the triple curtsy, and then returned to her seat where she sat primly, entirely secure knowing that she had just brought down the house.

There was only one student left to perform. Me. And in that moment, I had a choice to make. I could continue down the road of accordion mediocrity, play it safe and be forgettable. Or, I could dare to be great. I could buck the sacred norms of accordion class etiquette, rage against the polkas, lullabies, and public domain folk songs we had all endured over the last fifty-five minutes and chart my own course.

I took a deep breath and approached the hot seat, the accordion feeling as heavy as a boat anchor. One assistant stepped forward to adjust the music stand. I calmly, coolly said, "I won't need that."

He froze, giving me a look—a flicker of surprise, maybe even respect—then stepped back, hand raised, understanding that whatever was about to happen would not be business as usual.

A flash of lightning through the windows and the rumble of thunder shaking the foundation of the building would not have felt out of place in that moment.

I sat, unbuckled the top strap of the accordion. A heartbeat later, I unbuckled the bottom. The bellows sprang open like a wild mustang, thrashing and threatening to break free of my grasp. I wrestled the unwieldy contraption into place, feeling its full heft settle against me. The accordion properly wrangled, I looked out at the class.

Then, I played.

The opening chord of the Star Wars Theme burst from the accordion like a thunderclap, jolting the room. Heads snapped up. This wasn't "Oh, Susannah". This was something else, something epic. From that moment on, the accordion and I moved as one. My right hand danced over the treble keys, deftly pulling the melody from the plastic and wood. My left hand worked the bass buttons, building a structural foundation that added resonance and weight. The bellows surged and contracted, an iron lung pumping life and cinematic drama into every note.

Then it was over. I emerged from my musical trance and looked out at the stunned audience. The red-haired girl sat frozen, mouth slightly agape. I had just taken her soul.

Bon Jovi may have seen a million faces and rocked them all, but I had just blown the minds of approximately thirty people - and it felt tremendous. Bon Jovi had nothing on me, not in that moment.

I rose slowly, deliberately. Then came the applause. From classmates. From parents. From the assistants who'd helped us strap in and fumble through scales. Everyone…except Mr. Gurgich.

He stood off to the side, arms crossed, face unreadable, but clearly unimpressed with my act of musical defiance.

In that moment, I turned the accordion into an instrument of civil disobedience, a pearlescent weapon of cool, a weapon of the Rebellion.

I never played the accordion again after that night. We all turned in our instruments and went our separate ways, never crossing paths again. Still, I have to wonder: when any of my former classmates hear the Star Wars Main Theme, do they think of the boy who dared to be great that night in 1978? Did that small act of insurrection inspire any of them to raise their own bar, to break from the path of average and blaze something new?

I know I still think about Larry when I hear the Star Wars Main Theme. In early 1980, Larry and his family moved to Japan. His father wanted him to study with the same piano teacher that had taught and mentored him. I don't remember all the details. It was obvious, even to an eight-year-old, that he was different, a musical prodigy. He was focused and driven and light years beyond the rest of us. I've often wondered if he became a concert pianist. When the internet became a thing, I tried finding him by typing combinations like "Lawrence," "Larry", "Japanese", "Piano", and "Montclair, CA" into early search engines. Nothing ever came up. Then again, I had little to go on…just a first name and memories that become fuzzier as the years pass by.

For me though, the Star Wars Main Theme will always take me back to the theater with my brother and dad, watching in awe as the adventures of Luke, Han, and Leia lit up the screen. But it also reminds me of those awkward nights spent strapped to an accordion, all because my mom had it in her head that I was destined to become some kind of mariachi wonder kid.

I never got signed up for guitar lessons.

Years later, my mom bought me a second-hand Applause round back guitar from a music store in Port Orchard, WA. The salesperson offered a new student discount on lessons, if we were interested. Before I could even answer, my mom cut in, 'No, thank you." Instead, she bought a used copy of Mel Bay's Beginning Guitar for $5.00.

And so, through that book, and years of aimless plucking, I became a truly terrible guitarist. But for a brief, shining moment in 1978, I was a brilliant eight-year-old accordion player. Eat your heart out, Weird Al!

A Toy Story

During the summer of 1978, Star Wars action figures finally started appearing on store shelves—more than a year after the movie's theatrical release. This was a huge deal. Up until then, the only kids we knew who owned any Star Wars figures were the lucky ones whose parents had sent away for the infamous Early Bird Certificate back at Christmas 1977.

Kenner, the toy company licensed to make Star Wars merchandise, along with 20th Century Fox and George Lucas himself, had completely underestimated the film's impact. They had no figures ready for the '77 holiday season, so they offered a placeholder: the Early Bird Certificate Package—a cardboard stand-up display and a promise that four figures would be mailed sometime in the spring of 1978. It was a bold, unprecedented move at the time.

My parents—especially my dad—didn't bite. He dismissed it outright, convinced it was a scam. "They'll take your money," he said, "then never mail the toys out." He was also certain the Star Wars craze would fizzle out like mood rings, pet rocks, and every other short-lived pop-culture obsession.

Then one afternoon, my friend Raymond rolled into the cul-de-sac with brand-new Han Solo and Darth Vader action figures. My buddy Sean and I stared at those 3¾-inch pieces of plastic like they were newly unearthed treasure.

"Where'd you get them?" we asked.

"Toys 'R' Us in Ontario," he said.

I ran inside. "Mom! Mom! They've got Star Wars figures at Toys

'R' Us! Can we get some?"

To my surprise, both my mom and dad were on board. My mom loaded me and my little brother Chris into the station wagon, and off we went to the Toys 'R' Us in Ontario, California.

The moment we parked, Chris and I bolted for the toy aisle. We scanned the shelves with frantic eyes—G.I. Joes, Stretch Armstrongs, Army men—but no Star Wars figures.

My mom found us standing there, shoulders slumped.

"They must have sold out," I said, trying not to cry.

Just then, a Toys 'R' Us employee walked into the aisle. My mom asked if the Star Wars figures were gone. The woman smiled. "No, we keep them up front behind the counter. Follow me."

We followed her to a glass case near the registers—and there they were. Dozens of Star Wars figures lined up beneath fluorescent lights like artifacts from another world. My mom told us we could each pick three.

I chose Luke Skywalker, Darth Vader, and a Stormtrooper, my hands literally shaking. Chris picked Han Solo, Chewbacca, and a Tusken Raider.

Looking back, our choices said more about us than we realized. I gravitated toward Luke—the farm boy who discovers he's meant for something bigger. Chris's love for Han Solo made sense too; he was already bold and fearless in ways I wasn't. As for Chewbacca and the Tusken Raider, he just loved anything that looked like a monster.

At home, we tore open the packages and spent the rest of the afternoon on the living room floor, reenacting scenes from the movie and inventing new ones. Those figures became more than toys—they became anchors, something solid we could return to whenever the world felt unsteady.

That day marked the beginning of a ritual that always brought my brother and me back together. No matter how different we were or how much we argued, we could always meet again in that galaxy far, far away. In those moments, there were no rivalries—just two kids fighting side by side against the Empire.

Our friends Sean and Jason joined in, and the adventure spilled into the cul-de-sac and backyard. Tatooine. The Death Star. Meanwhile, my Elvis and Bee Gees records spun in the background during quieter moments.

In a year that would soon be filled with moves and changes I couldn't control, those afternoons on the living room carpet and in that cul-de-sac were magic.

It wasn't just an adventure.
It was home.

YOU SHOULD BE DANCING

If the summer of 1977 belonged to Star Wars and Elvis, then 1978 was all about the Bee Gees. They were inescapable, every radio station, every roller rink speaker, every transistor radio in the park or strapped to the handlebars of a bicycle was playing a Bee Gees song. The *Saturday Night Fever* soundtrack, released in November of 1977, launched the Brother's Gibb to stratospheric fame they never could have imagined.

I was well aware of the soundtrack in early '78, but not the movie. *Saturday Night Fever* was rated R for language, violence, and sexual content — the three big taboos in my mother's book. That said, less than three years earlier, she'd dragged five-year-old me to the drive-in with my not-yet stepdad to see *The Exorcist.* It would not be hyperbolic to say the experience traumatized me at a cellular level. Sex, drugs, and naughty language were off-limits in the context of disco dancing, but a demon-possessed twelve-year-old girl spewing vulgarities while her head spun like a top was apparently just fine. I'll never figure that one out.

It was during a trip to Mexico in the summer of 1978 that I finally saw the movie. My mom and stepdad left me in the care of two older cousins in downtown Chihuahua while they went off to do whatever adults did in Chihuahua, Mexico.

Those cousins—Reuben, ten, and Chirrin, twelve—seemed like

full-grown men to eight-year-old me. They both had the wispy beginnings of facial hair, they both had jobs, and Chirrin was already driving my uncle's truck around town. I had a Huffy with a handlebar attachment that made fake motorcycle noises at the push of a button. We were not from the same planet.

Chirrin had already seen *Saturday Night Fever* at least fifteen times that summer. He was obsessed with the dance scenes, tolerating the rest of the movie just so he could watch John Travolta move. He'd sit in the back of the theater, studying every step, then practice the routines until he could perform them perfectly at the local dance halls. Chirrin was definitely a big deal to the Chihuahua girls.

He took me and Reuben to see it that day, even though none of us were eighteen. The rules were different in Mexico — mostly in that there didn't seem to be any rules at all. Three minors walked right into an R-rated movie without so much as a note from our folks.

There I sat, watching a poorly dubbed Spanish version of *Saturday Night Fever*, having no idea how completely my world was about to get rocked. The movie opens with John Travolta's character, Tony Manero, strutting through the streets of Brooklyn. He's wearing a tight red shirt, black pants, and carrying a bucket of paint for his job at the local hardware store.

It sounds ridiculous, but trust me: Travolta made it impossibly cool. He's stepping in time to the Bee Gees' "Stayin' Alive," each footfall hitting the pavement to that absolutely filthy beat — BOOM / WHAP / BOOM / WHAP — the bass drum landing like a ton of bricks, the snare a sharp slap to the face. At one point he checks out a girl, then checks himself out in a storefront window. A moment later, he stacks two slices of pizza and eats them on the go — still strutting, still in rhythm, still carrying that bucket of paint.

And somehow, every move *works*. There's not a single word of dialogue in that opening scene, yet you learn everything you need to know about Tony — he's young, cocky, stylish, and projects confidence in a world that offers him nothing. The music and the walk say it all.

In the span of six months, I was introduced to two of the coolest, baddest, most iconic men to ever walk the planet: Elvis Presley and John Travolta. It was a one-two punch to the solar plexus — discovering Elvis at the literal end of his life, and meeting Travolta just as his star was beginning its meteoric rise.

I already knew Travolta, sort of. He played Vinny Barbarino on *Welcome Back, Kotter*—a lovable goofball with great hair and zero ambition. But Vinny was a dim bulb compared to the supernova that was Tony Manero—a sweathog turned polyester-clad prince of the dance floor. Tony had presence. Swagger. He moved like the world belonged to him.

I got all of that just from the opening minutes of the movie, but *Saturday Night Fever* is more than well-choreographed dance sequences set to an amazing soundtrack. The story itself is dark — a gritty look at working-class life in Brooklyn that touches on racism, broken families, sexual assault, and suicide. It may have been marketed as a disco fairytale, but it's really a street-level drama pulsing with desperation and sadness. And dancing.

Of course, at eight years old, I didn't grasp any of that. I just thought Tony Manero was awesome. And I wanted to be just like him.

After the movie, we boarded an over-packed bus—bald tires, belching Exxon Valdez levels of black smoke—and headed back to my grandmother's house in La Mesa. Chirrin had a copy of the *Saturday Night Fever* soundtrack on cassette. He popped a cartridge into a tape player, fiddled with the rewind button, then queued up "You Should Be Dancing" and hit play.

And right there, in the middle of my grandmother's adobe house, deep in the heart of central Mexico, my cousin became Tony Manero. "You Should Be Dancing" opens with a thumping bass line, rapid-fire hi-hats, percussion that's pure propulsion, and Barry Gibb's falsetto slicing through the mix like a razor. The horns are adrenaline, the guitars jagged and funky. The rhythm section is tight, yet the whole thing feels so urgent it might spin out of control at any second. It's seductive, tribal, commanding —and it never lets up. This isn't just a song; it's an order. YOU should be dancing. Nothing else. Don't think. Move. Now. It's the heartbeat of the disco era—confident, sweaty, relentless. The kind of song that instantly turns any space into a nightclub, whether it's your kitchen, your car, or your grandmother's living room in La Mesa.

I watched my cousin recreate the dance sequence from the movie. His movements were precise—dead-on to what we'd just seen on screen. It was uncanny. When the song ended, I asked him to teach me.

A silence passed. Then, without saying a word, he picked up the cassette player, hit rewind, and for the next couple of hours he showed me everything he knew. Step by step, spin by spin, I followed him across the floor, both of us sweating and laughing as I learned.

Then the batteries died. Finding new ones in La Mesa wasn't easy, but we eventually tracked some down at a tiny corner store. I paid with a one-dollar bill my dad had given me and got several pesos back — exchange rates baffled me. Batteries in hand, we headed back to my grandmother's, popped them into the player, rewound the tape, and kept going.

When we returned to California, I begged my mom to buy me the *Saturday Night Fever* soundtrack. She relented, and off we went to K-Mart. Soundtrack in hand, we went home, where I immediately put on "You Should Be Dancing" and started practicing the moves my cousin had taught me. I even began choreographing routines to other tracks—Tavares' "More Than a Woman," Yvonne Elliman's "If I Can't Have You." My steps were clunky, uneven, and I always came back to "You Should Be Dancing." To the beat I knew. To the steps Chirrin had drilled into me. To that first rush of confidence and joy.

While I practiced the dance routine obsessively in the early weeks of the school year, my focus didn't last. Eventually, I drifted back to the usual things — playing with my Star Wars figures, riding bikes around the neighborhood, watching *Ultra-Man* and Sid & Marty Krofft shows like *Land of the Lost*, and, of course, listening to Elvis records. My dance moves went dormant.

School let out for winter break — or *Christmas Break*, as we called it back in the 1970s before political correctness ran amok.

Not long after we returned in January of 1979, a big announcement shook the classroom: the school was putting on a talent show. Each grade was only allowed four acts. That meant auditions.

My third-grade teacher, Mrs. Baumgaertner, stood at the front of the class and asked if anyone wanted to audition and, if so, what their talent was.

Tracy Thompson — pretty, blonde, popular — immediately raised her hand. She'd be performing a cheer routine with pom-poms. Of course she would. How could anyone compete with that?

A few heartbeats passed. Mrs. Baumgaertner looked around and asked again if anyone else wanted to audition. I swallowed hard, then slowly, almost meekly, raised my hand. She looked at me kindly.
"Jesse? What's your talent?"

I answered with one word, barely above a whisper.

"Dance."

We had one week until auditions, so I practiced with the intensity of an Olympic athlete. My moves were rusty — forgotten transitions, unbalanced spins — nothing felt natural anymore. Every free moment I was rehearsing. My family got sick of hearing "You Should Be Dancing," so sometimes I practiced without music, counting the beat in my head. At night, I lay in bed running the routine over and over — hundreds, maybe thousands of mental reps.

Audition day finally arrived. Each contestant had two minutes to show the judges what they had. I remember waiting in the wings as Tracy, pom-poms in hand, melted hearts with what I considered a rather middling routine. Whatever.

There were other acts too, some juggling, Larry playing classical piano, but I was locked in on what I had to do, pacing back and forth like a caged panther, awaiting my time to unleash the dancing beast within.

Finally, my turn.

I handed my copy of the *Saturday Night Fever* soundtrack to the teacher at the record player and gave her simple, specific instructions: "Track four — 'You Should Be Dancing.'" She nodded as if she understood.

But when the needle dropped, it landed on track three — "Jive Talkin".

Now, "Jive Talkin'" is a great song—funky, smooth—but it's no "You Should Be Dancing". The beat was different: slower, cooler. This was not the disco inferno I had been practicing to.

Panic set in. I waved frantically, trying to get her to move the needle to the right track. No luck. She just motioned for me to start. *Show us your talent, kid. Clock's ticking.*

I had to improvise. The moves I'd practiced for weeks didn't fit this rhythm. I spun, stepped, pivoted—making it up as I went —but nothing synced. The beat and my body were speaking different languages.

I gave it everything I had. When the music ended, I walked off stage convinced I'd blown it.

In my head, I was no match for Tracy with her pom-poms, or Larry with his piano solo, or whatever the hell Gabriel was doing with those tennis balls. Other kids auditioned too, but I don't remember them. I just kept replaying the disaster, cursing the nameless teacher who couldn't tell track three from four and had sabotaged my shot at glory.

The next day, the talent-show roster was posted—and lo-and-behold, I'd somehow made the cut. That meant two weeks to refine my routine and, more importantly, to find clothes worthy of an eight-year-old disco dancer.

The weekend before the show, my mom took me to JCPenney—which, in 1978, was kind of a big deal. We spent what felt like forever searching for disco clothes in a sea of corduroy pants and cotton-knit polos. Nothing. JCPenney was not built for the Bee Gees.

So my mom pivoted. We piled back into our yellow station wagon and drove from Montclair to a heavily Mexican section of Santa Ana. She knew a place—a small boutique tucked between a taqueria and a used-tire shop—where we found *the* outfit: a silky maroon polyester shirt, tan bell-bottoms, a belt wider than the Rio Grande, and platform shoes that added at least four inches to my height.

Perfect.

Over the next two weeks, I rehearsed my routine at every opportunity. I had it down cold. Or so I thought.

Two days before the show, the school held mandatory rehearsals — and that's when a new problem revealed itself. Travolta's iconic dance sequence in *Saturday Night Fever* clocked in at two minutes and twenty-five seconds, perfect for the audition time limit. But for the actual talent show, I was expected to perform the *entire* length of "You Should Be Dancing," which runs four minutes and seventeen seconds. That meant I needed an extra two minutes of choreography.

Panic.

The easy fix would've been to repeat a few steps, or even the whole routine. But the first half of the song didn't match the rhythm of the second half. Repeating moves would've made the routine janky and disjointed. Unacceptable. Plus, I don't do easy. Instead, I folded in some of Travolta's moves from the "Greased

Lightning" number in *Grease.* Bold move, but it would add a new layer to the performance.

Lucky for me, a lot of the *Greased Lightning* choreography was basically recycled *Saturday Night Fever* material. I poached what I needed and stitched it seamlessly into my routine. Perfect!

Or so I thought.

Here's the thing: four minutes and seventeen seconds is *a long time* for a just-turned-nine-year-old to dance. It already felt like an eternity rehearsing in the living room — what would it feel like under the bright lights of the Monte Vista Elementary gymnasium? Would I wilt from the heat? Would conditioning come into play? Should I maximize my hydration?

The day of the big show finally arrived.

I was a wreck.

I could barely focus at school the day of the talent show. While Mrs. Baumgaertner went over multiplication tables, I was mentally running through my routine. During recess kickball, I flubbed several routine plays at shortstop. We lost — something we rarely did — to the other third-grade class. Afterwards, I got an earful from John Flush, our notoriously hot-headed pitcher, who loudly questioned my commitment to winning.

Then the school day was over. I rushed home and immediately laid out my dance clothes. At dinner, I poked at my food, unable to eat. The butterflies in my stomach felt more like pterodactyls. I gave up on dinner and tried to mentally lock in, which was difficult with my little brother Chris and his best friend James rehearsing their own act in the next room — a charming, slightly off-key rendition of "You Can't Get to Heaven (on Rollerskates)".

Eventually we all piled into the station wagon and headed to the school. I sat in the back seat, careful not to wrinkle my shirt, silent and stone-faced. Game face on.

Backstage, the performers were a buzzing hive of nerves and excitement. After a few perfunctory remarks from Principal

Duncan, the show kicked off.

The kindergartners went first. I remember nothing about them — I mean; they were kindergartners. It's not like any of them were going to drop some Chopin on the crowd.

Next came the first graders: my brother and James. They killed it with "You Can't Get to Heaven", adding woodblocks and maracas for extra flair. They even rewrote a verse to say, "You can't go to heaven in Mr. Duncan's car," which brought down the house. Those two definitely raised the bar early.

The second graders were a notch above the first. One girl played a song from *My Fair Lady* on violin. Another group of girls performed "Tomorrow" from *Annie.* They were good — but I didn't care. The third graders were next, and that meant me.

The order had been predetermined: I was going on right before Tracy and her pom-poms. That raised the stakes — already sky-high — exponentially. I had to nail this routine to counter the inevitable Tracy Thompson charm offensive. I was so focused on her I completely forgot what the other two third-grade acts were.

All I remember is standing to the side of the stage, clutching my newly purchased 45 of "You Should Be Dancing" (after the audition debacle, I wasn't taking any chances with the LP), and waiting for my cue.

Then my name was called.

I stepped out onto the stage in my platform shoes, the spotlight catching my slight frame. The lights were blinding. I was alone out there. The needle dropped.

A hiss and pop from the record's lead-in crackled through the speakers. Then the song kicked in — the thump-thump-thump of the percussion, the pulse of the bass, the icy shimmer of the guitar. "You Should Be Dancing" filled the gymnasium.

And I danced.

I danced like I had never danced before — completely in the zone.

Every move landed. Each spin was sharp, every turn effortless. Even the knee drops — the move I'd dreaded for weeks because of the hardwood stage — hit smooth, no pain. The "Greased Lightning" steps I'd grafted in? You'd swear they'd been part of *Saturday Night Fever* all along.

For those four minutes and seventeen seconds, everything clicked. It was, without question, the best I'd ever performed.

Then it was over.

Polite applause followed. I bowed, walked offstage, and was escorted to a seat in the audience beside my family, heart still hammering, sweat cooling, waiting to hear the results.

The rest of the talent show is a blur, with one exception — James's brother Larry, who performed "Peter and the Wolf" on piano. Larry was incredible, the kind of kid who made adults go quiet when he played.

When the final act ended, Mr. Duncan returned to the stage to announce the winners from each grade.

My brother Chris and James took first place for the first grade class. The second-grade winner was announced next. Then came third grade.

I sat on the edge of my seat.

Mr. Duncan called out third place, then second. Neither my name nor Tracy's. That meant one of us had taken first place. Mr. Duncan opened the envelope, looked out at the crowd, and announced the winner—Tracy Thompson.

I was shell-shocked.

I lost. To Tracy. Her pom-poms. Her blonde hair. Her cheerleader outfit. I didn't even place. Not second. Not third. Nothing.

So I did the one thing I didn't want to do: I burst into tears. Full-body, hiccuping sobs. The kind of crying that comes from someplace deep inside. All those hours of practice, the nervous energy, the hope of being recognized for my hard work were just crushed and every emotion poured out of me right there in the audience.

My mother tried to console me, but it was useless. Even Mrs. Cox, my no-nonsense second-grade teacher who I once saw shake a kid so violently I thought his head was going to pop off, came over and put an arm around my shoulders.

I just sat there, a quivering, blubbering mess. It wasn't my finest moment — I don't think I even applauded when Larry was announced as the fourth-grade winner.

After the sixth-grade results were read, Mr. Duncan's boss took the stage. I don't remember her name. She was there to present the last award of the night. The winner would receive a trophy and a five-dollar gift certificate to Straw Hat Pizza.

I barely registered what she was saying. My head ached from crying. I just wanted to go home.

The head judge walked up to the stage and handed her an envelope. She opened it, smiled, and announced:

"John Travolta, eat your heart out! From the third grade, Jesse Taylor is the winner of the 1979 Monte Vista Elementary School Talent Show!"

The gymnasium erupted in cheers.

Tracy—gracious and kind—rushed over to congratulate me. I stood, stunned, as the crowd continued to cheer. I walked up the center aisle to a standing ovation, my face still crimson, my eyes swollen from earlier, but this time I wasn't crying. I was grinning like an idiot.

I climbed the steps to the stage, where they handed me my trophy. I turned and held it up to the audience. More cheers.

As I walked offstage, the music teacher stopped me and said, "You can play any instrument you want next year — but I see you as a drummer."

I just nodded, not fully processing any of it.

There's a photo of that night — me with my brother, James, and Larry. My brother is wearing a white-and-blue polo and black slacks. James and Larry are in suits. And then there's me: tan bell-bottoms, a belt as wide as the Rio Grande, a maroon polyester shirt, and platform-soled Hush Puppies. My ears are beet red and I'm holding a gold-plated plastic trophy.

It's a ridiculous image, really — but it's a moment I'll never forget. Hard work had paid off.

"You Should Be Dancing" still pulls me back to my cousin Chirrin, my grandmother's living room in Mexico, and that little house on Flora Street in Montclair, California. It always leads me back to the stage at Monte Vista Elementary—the lights, the certainty that I'd lost, and the shock of realizing I'd won the whole thing.

I don't remember any of the moves now, and I'm certainly not the slender boy I was at eight or nine. Relearning them would be a challenge. But the spirit of that moment — that era — still lives in me every time I hear the opening beats of that song.

For a while, that was the happiest I had ever been in my life: there in Montclair, at Monte Vista Elementary. I'd made a name for myself, had friends, a routine — a sense of stability.

It would be short-lived.

MY SHARONA

By the time school let out for the summer of 1979, I had settled into a blissful routine in Montclair. I had my three trusty friends, Larry, Sean, and Raymond. The four of us would walk home from school together, occasionally stopping at Raymond's house for a quick game of pool.

The pool games were excruciating. None of us were tall enough to properly hold a cue or line up a shot, so we just knocked balls around until someone scratched.

We rode our bikes everywhere, building makeshift ramps out of plywood and milk crates we found behind the Circle K up the street. Then we'd launch ourselves over whatever we could find...firewood, discarded cinder blocks, Tonka trucks, even each other. Some jumps ended in spectacular crashes resulting in skinned up elbows, hands, and knees. Our mothers must have gone through a gallon of Bactine between May and September of that year.

Other jumps became the stuff of cul-de-sac legend, like the time Raymond sailed over me, Sean, and Larry on his Huffy Thunder Star bike. That thing had to weigh a hundred pounds if it weighed an ounce, but Raymond somehow pedaled hard enough to build up the speed to clear the three of us. If I close my eyes, I can still see the battered undercarriage of that bike sailing over me.

There were sleepovers and treehouses and the endless trading and bartering of Topps football and baseball cards. Tony Dorsett, running back for the Dallas Cowboys, was my favorite football player, followed closely by Roger Staubach. What can I say? The stars on the Cowboys helmets looked pretty damn cool to me. Sean knew of my Dorsett obsession and fleeced me out of Terry Bradshaw, Earl Campbell, and Walter Payton cards for one Dorsett card. Desperate times called for desperate trades, and I could not for the life of me draw a Dorsett card no matter how many packs I bought.

We would also chase the ice cream truck down the road, convinced the driver sped up as he approached Flora St. just so he could watch us sprint after him for a couple of blocks. Dimes in hand, we would buy Bomb Pops and Fudgsicles…except for Raymond. He inexplicably preferred Push-Up Pops, which were nothing more than orange sherbet served in a cardboard tube. Gross.

The Montclair house was more than just our home; it was also a gathering place for both sides of the family, where worlds collided.

My mom's family was, of course, very Mexican. My aunts and uncles may have settled in California, but they definitely brought a lot of Mexico with them. Birthday parties were total ragers, complete with pinatas, hogs roasted on a spit, tamales, pan dulce, and lots of dancing. And it didn't matter if it was a birthday party for a one-year-old or an eighty-year-old, the parties were insane.

Parties with my dad's family were equally raucous, but with much less dancing. Instead, there was a hillbilly version of karaoke. My dad would connect a microphone to his stereo system and he and my uncles would take turns singing along to Waylon Jennings, Tom T. Hall, and Merle Haggard. Badly. "Okie from Muskogee" was a particular favorite, fitting, as they were from Oklahoma. What they lacked in singing ability was made up for with drunken enthusiasm, fueled by Schlitz.

Now, take all of that and throw it into a small house, add plenty of Tecate and malt liquor, and you've got a combustible mix. There were never any fights or anything like that...just adults cutting loose and on the edge of losing control. Imagine a Jimmy Buffett concert if "La Bamba" era Los Lobos were the co-headliner. BBQ chicken, burgers, and hot dogs sat alongside steaming dishes of chile colorado, tostadas, and carne asada.

Glorious doesn't begin to describe it. The summer of 1979 was one big fiesta fueled by cheap domestic beer and even cheaper tequila.

Sean, Jason, and Raymond would sometimes come over when the house was raging. They'd be overwhelmed by the sheer number of people, but also the loudness of it all. Hank Williams alternated on the stereo with Vicente Fernández while my Uncle Manuel filled a tortilla with barbequed chicken and my dad added a mountain of roasted Anaheim peppers to his burger. For a visitor, it had to be a lot to take in.

I entered the fourth grade the fall of 1979, still basking in the afterglow of my talent show triumph. My reputation had only grown since: I'd become the clutch shortstop for our classroom's kickball team - nothing got past me. I was also racking up gold stars for perfect scores on the daily math speed tests. Life was good. Raymond was in my class now, while Sean and Larry were just down the breezeway, making lunch and recess meet-ups a daily highlight.

I was happy, secure, content. Then it all fell apart.

One evening over dinner, my parents announced we were moving—to El Paso. The very place we had fled from just a few short years earlier. There were supposed to be endless job opportunities waiting for my dad there. He had grown tired of his two-plus-hour commute to and from work every day and wanted a change. Still, I couldn't believe what I was hearing. How could we be going back to the place we had clawed our way out of?

Time slipped away in a numb haze as we packed for the move back to Texas. I couldn't make sense of it. I didn't want to. After school, I'd navigate my way through the maze of moving boxes stacked in the living room, shutting myself away in my barren bedroom. The walls were stripped bare, the bookshelves empty —books, toys, comics, and of course, my talent-show trophy, all stuffed into boxes.

I clung to my friends like a lifeline, fitting in every last minute of time we had together. On other days, I escaped into my Elvis records and the *Saturday Night Fever* soundtrack, letting the music block out the reality of the move closing in around me.

I remember walking into the school office with my mom, my stomach twisted in knots. Mr. Duncan spotted me from his office and came around to greet us. He rested a hand on my shoulder, his voice warm and sincere.

"Best of luck at your new school, dance king. We're going to miss you."

I managed a wan smile and nodded, fighting back tears—already knowing I would miss them, too.

Maybe more than they would ever realize.

The day of the move arrived. I said goodbye to Sean, Larry, and Raymond. My brother rode bikes with James one last time. That evening, we ate our final dinner in Montclair—a bucket of greasy KFC with all the sides—sitting on the floor of the empty living room. We slept in sleeping bags that night, the house around us stripped bare and hollow.

At 2 a.m., my dad—famous for wanting to get an early start on every road trip—woke us up. Groggy and heavy-eyed, we climbed into the back of his pickup truck. My mom had made a bed of blankets beneath the camper shell, and that's where we would ride for the duration of the trip to El Paso. My dad drove the U-Haul, packed with everything we owned and towing our station wagon behind it.

As we pulled away, I watched our house shrink in the small window at the back of the camper. One of our neighbors blinked their porch light—a silent, final goodbye. I pressed my face to the cold glass, taking it all in one last time, trying to memorize as many details as I could: Sean and Jason's front yard where we played countless games of touch football; Larry's front porch—dark in the early morning hours—where we sat and talked *Star Wars*; the Circle K where we bought Slurpees and candy; and, of course, Monte Vista Elementary School.

Then it was all gone—fading behind me, swallowed by the night. The tires hummed against the asphalt, carrying me farther and farther into a future I wasn't ready to meet.

We drove through the night, arriving in El Paso late the following evening. The fourteen-hour drive was a blur of endless desert once we crossed into Arizona.

It took a couple of days to settle into the new house, though *settle* didn't feel quite right. Gone were the lush, green avocado, fig, and orange trees of our Montclair backyard. In their place: agave, cacti, and desert willows.

Our front yard was little more than a patch of dying brown grass, framed by a low stone wall and a black wrought-iron gate. It felt less like a home and more like a sun-bleached desert mission.

My new school was directly across the street from our house. Glen Cove Elementary School was much newer than Monte Vista. Where Monte Vista, with its outdoor breezeways and stucco exterior, had a certain worn-in charm, Glen Cove—finished just a year earlier—felt cold and impersonal. The building was all brick and harsh angles, devoid of personality. Then again, maybe I was biased.

First-day jitters were manageable, but I was definitely nervous. After my mom finished the enrollment paperwork in the front office, I was escorted to my new fourth-grade classroom—located outside in a portable trailer. My teacher, a brash and proudly Texan woman named Mrs. Stillwell, introduced me to the class as "the California boy."

After the introduction, she boomed, "Don't worry, you'll learn everything there is to know about Texas...and you'll love it!"

I wasn't sure if that was a promise or a threat as I took the empty desk at the back of the room.

The day was mostly uneventful, that is, until I made a horrific mistake.

The week prior, Mrs. Stillwell had assigned the class a poem to memorize and recite. Now she was working her way around the room, calling on random students to stand and deliver. Maybe half the class managed to get through it; the rest stammered and stumbled. For some reason, the poem clicked for me almost immediately. It was short—just a handful of stanzas—and after hearing a few more failed attempts, I raised my hand.

Mrs. Stillwell looked my way. "Yes, California boy?"

"I'd like to give it a try," I said.

I stood up and absolutely nailed it—word for word, no hesitation. I might've even thrown in a hand gesture or two for extra flair. The class went silent.

Then Mrs. Stillwell unleashed her wrath on the room. "California boy has been here less than an hour and memorized the poem perfectly! The rest of you had a week!"

I sat back down, thinking I'd just earned some new-kid respect. Maybe I'd even impressed them.
See? I thought. *It's not that hard. You can do this.*

I was wrong.

At recess, I was asked to join the boys from my class to take on the other fourth-grade class in a game of touch football. Football of any kind had been outlawed at Monte Vista, so this was exciting. The quarterback, a kid named Francisco, asked if I could catch.

I answered with all the swagger of the Dallas Cowboys' Drew Pearson: "Yeah, I've got great hands."

That was mistake number two.

What I didn't know was that Eddie Aguilar, the fourth-grade

bully and self-appointed kingpin, had already conspired with the other class's team to "teach the California boy a lesson."

Francisco told me to line up at wide receiver. For the next twenty minutes, I paid for my poetry performance—hard. The game was supposed to be two-hand touch. Every time Francisco threw the ball to me, I was "touched" with full-on tackles. The two-hand touch rule didn't seem to apply to me. I got knocked down play after play, slammed into the dirt until my shirt was torn and my jeans were ripped at the knees. A bloody nose bloomed under the warm West Texas sun.

Still, I kept catching every ball Francisco threw.

After the game, as I limped back to class, Eddie walked up, smirked, and said, "Don't go showing off in class again."

I nodded.

Then something unexpected happened. Francisco clapped a hand on my shoulder and said, "Way to hang on to the ball."

And just like that, I was in—officially accepted as part of Mrs. Stillwell's fourth-grade football crew.

Every recess after that was spent playing football. Francisco and I developed a natural chemistry; he knew where to throw it, and I knew which route to run. Our offense was loosely modeled after the Dallas Cowboys' pro-style system, built around Francisco's dual threat as both a passer and a runner. The other receiver, Freddy Hernandez, was a speedster who could take the top off the other fourth-grade team's defense. Francisco excelled at leaving the pocket and then finding me in the flat—or launching a deep ball to Freddy downfield. It worked.

On defense, we again looked to the Cowboys for inspiration, running our version of the Doomsday Defense—which was really nothing more than playing deep and not giving up the long ball. The games were competitive and fun, and while I still missed my Montclair house and friends, Francisco and Freddy made coming to a new school easier, less lonely.

After school, I still listened to my Elvis records, but not nearly with the same devotion I once had.

A new sound emerged. I'd catch snippets of it from the car radio or drifting out of the jukebox at Pizza Planet. These new songs were vibrant, electric, crackling with a different kind of energy. There was an artificial sheen to some of the instrumentation, but underneath the polish, the grit of guitars cut through the icy synthesizers. *The Cars. Blondie.*

I was drawn more and more to these modern sounds. The world was changing, and music was changing with it.

Around that same time, Michael Jackson released *Off the Wall* —his first adult solo album, and a joyful declaration of independence from his brothers and his father. It felt like a perfect bookend to the disco era: funk, pop, rock, and soul braided into something sleeker, sharper, new. It was the first album I ever bought with my own money, earned by doing chores around the house.

These new songs formed the soundtrack of my life back in El Paso.

One day, my mom drove me and my brother Chris downtown to see the Hotel Linden—the welfare hellhole we once lived in. I remember standing on the sidewalk out front, staring up at the building. The front doors creaked open, and an older man shuffled outside. The faint, sickly smell of stale cigarette smoke and urine-soaked stairways followed after him.

Somewhere inside those walls, I felt a version of myself still roamed the halls—a ghost from another life. A life that felt as if it had been lived a hundred years ago but, in reality, was less than five. I remember a deep sadness, memories of cans of Chef Boyardee ravioli heated on a barely working hot plate, the constant yelling and screaming in the hallways, the disgusting bathroom we had to share with the rest of the floor. It all came rushing back—thick and suffocating.

Without thinking, I turned and tugged at my mother's hand,

pulling her away from that building that stood there, a desolate monolith of heartbreak and desperation from another life.

Over the following months, I began to settle in at Glen Cove, feeling secure and stable in this new environment.

Then, without warning, it all changed. Again.

For reasons still unclear to me to this day, we had to move across town to west El Paso. We packed seemingly overnight and were withdrawn from school at whiplash speed. In the blink of an eye, I found myself in my third fourth-grade class—once again, the new kid.

The neighborhood we moved to was older than the previous one, a little rougher. Not long after we'd arrived, I tried to make friends with some of the neighborhood kids. A group of them were playing basketball a couple of driveways down from ours. I walked up wearing a tank top, shorts, knee socks, and black patent leather dress shoes. My sneakers were still buried somewhere in one of the unpacked boxes in the house.

I must have looked ridiculous—standing there at the end of the driveway, waiting for someone to ask if I wanted to play.

"Man, get outta here with those shoes!" one of them yelled.

The others laughed and piled on.

"Have your mom take you to Kmart for some discount Keds!"

"Yeah, get some blue-light specials, boy!" another one cried out.

I walked back to the house, despondent but determined to find my sneakers.

A few minutes later, as I dug through boxes, the doorbell rang. It was David—the kid whose driveway was serving as the neighborhood basketball court. Standing beside him, arms crossed, was his mom.

He looked at me, sheepishly. "I'm sorry we made fun of your shoes."

His mother nudged him, and he continued, "You can come play if you still want to."

My eyebrows shot up. "Sure… gimme a minute!"

David and his mom turned to leave, but not before I heard him mutter, "What if he steps on us?"

I resumed hunting for my sneakers, rooting through boxes like a rabid raccoon in a tipped-over trash can. Once I found them, I bolted out the door and headed straight to the basketball game.

David and I became friends after that. I even made friends with Javier—the one who'd told me to "get outta here with those shoes." Javier was a little older than I was and had lost an eye the previous summer in a fireworks accident. David was a grade ahead of me, so I never saw either of them at school.

I honestly don't remember much about that second school in El Paso. My brother and I only attended it for the last two months of that school year. I just numbly shuffled to and from class, going through the motions. Then the school year was over.

The summer of 1980—yes, it was officially the '80s now—was a fun one, despite another move. I spent every day playing hoops with David and Javier. They became an extended part of the family. Neither of them had a dad that lived at home with them, so my dad became a bit of a proxy father to them - fixing bicycles, taking us all to see The Empire Strikes Back, organizing neighborhood wiffle ball games. It seemed like every morning began with the doorbell ringing, David standing there, asking if I wanted to play.

I got my first AM/FM radio that summer, and I played it constantly. My room was filled with the sounds of Billy Joel's *"It's Still Rock and Roll to Me,"* Blondie's *"Call Me,"* and yacht-rock god Christopher Cross's *"Sailing."* I was, of course, still spinning MJ's *Off the Wall.* David was a huge fan and liked to sing along to *"She's Out of My Life,"* eyes closed and head tilted back.

What I didn't know then was that my family was in a desperate financial situation—which may explain why we'd moved so abruptly from that first house. The job opportunities my dad had been promised never materialized. Though he was a talented and experienced welder, that particular skill set wasn't in demand in El Paso at the time. Maybe he could try Houston or Dallas, or one of the refineries farther east? So he did. Nothing.

Instead, my dad took a job delivering and repairing household appliances. In California, he'd made good money working at Todd Shipyard. In El Paso, I think he made less than eight hundred dollars a month at the appliance store. We were broke, though my parents didn't really let on.

My mom clipped grocery coupons with religious devotion, stretching every dollar as far as it would go. My dad worked long hours, his back aching from loading and unloading heavy washers, dryers, and refrigerators. The work was beneath his skill level, but he never complained.

I drifted through that summer blissfully unaware of how bad things were beneath the surface. For me, it was still basketball, bike rides, music, and *Star Wars* figures.

Then one afternoon, the phone rang.

My parents were outside, so I answered. A man's voice crackled through the receiver—he said he was calling from someplace called Puget Sound Naval Shipyard in "Bummertown," Washington. He wanted to speak to my dad. I asked him to hold, set the phone down on the counter, and went outside.

"Dad, a guy from the shipyard in Bummertown, Washington is on the phone," I said.

My dad shot out of his lawn chair like he'd been launched. I watched him sprint into the house. A few minutes later, he came back outside—beaming. He'd been offered a job. A good one.

The shipyard was in Bremerton, not Bummertown—but that's what I heard. And that's what stuck. Because that meant we were moving. Again. To Bummertown.

My dad left for Washington a couple of weeks later. Because we were broke, he stayed at the YMCA in downtown Bremerton when he first arrived. My mom, brother, sister, and I stayed behind in El Paso to pack and deal with the realtor.

We pinched pennies even harder during that time. My dad went almost a month without a paycheck and still had a mortgage to cover back in El Paso. He subsisted on whatever he could buy using his gas-station credit card. Back home, we ate a steady diet of egg burritos for breakfast and bean burritos for everything else.

I still played with David and Javier, but it was different. The days felt heavier, wrapped in a quiet sense of foreboding. We were moving again—to a part of the country I knew almost nothing about.

I knew Mount St. Helens had erupted earlier that year, but beyond that, Washington was a distant, blurry idea. For a while, I thought maybe we were moving to Washington, D.C.

That's not entirely true, though. I did know one other thing about Washington State. Thanks to a syndicated rerun of Leonard Nimoy's *In Search Of...*, I knew that's where Bigfoot lived.

And after watching that episode, I was absolutely terrified of Bigfoot.

One of the last afternoons before we moved, I walked up to Javier's house to see if he wanted to ride bikes to Circle K for a Slurpee. As I got closer, I heard a stuttering, syncopated guitar riff tearing through the walls—edgy, electric, raw. This wasn't like anything I'd heard that summer. The minimalist production made it feel like the band was right there in his living room. The sound was primal, cutting through the soft, glossy pop hits that dominated the radio.

I stood on the porch until the song ended, completely transfixed.

When the music stopped, I rang the bell. Javier opened the door, holding the 45 he'd just been spinning.

Clocking in at four minutes and fifty-two seconds, The Knack's *"My Sharona"* was considered long for a single. The punchy first half drives straight into a blistering, extended guitar solo. The arrangement is sparse, but the bass and drums fill every gap, giving it a live-wire energy. The melody hooks you instantly, and that chorus—*"M-m-m-my Sharona"*—is pure, contagious electricity.

The song marked a cultural pivot, bridging the rebellion of punk with the accessibility of new wave. Its jagged edges stood out against the soft-focus ballads like *"Sailing"* and anything Air Supply put out.

I asked Javier to play it again. He did. I sat cross-legged on his floor, completely enraptured. The urgency of the beat, the mind-blowing second guitar solo—it was all so alive. When it ended, I asked if we could hear it one more time.

He started the record again, but a few beats in, his mom burst into the room.

"Javi! That's enough!"

That was the end of that.

I went home, turned on my radio, and tuned to the Top 40 station, hoping to catch *"My Sharona."* I don't remember if I heard it that night, but every time it played after that, I cranked the volume as high as it would go.

Then it was back to packing.

The realtor brought a steady stream of people through the house until one day, a bright red *Sold* sign dangled from the For Sale post out front.

My dad flew back from Washington to drive the U-Haul north. Before we left, he arranged one last hurrah for me, my brother, Javier, and David. Using a two-for-one coupon for Pizza Planet, he took us out for dinner. Afterwards—with another coupon—we spent the night racing go-karts at the local track.

That night was our last magical adventure, a perfect way to close out my brief return to El Paso before heading out into the unknown.

Two days later, we left.

The last few items were loaded into the station wagon, and we climbed in. My mom started the car, and out of the corner of my eye I saw movement—Javier, running down the sidewalk with a paper bag in his hand.

He knocked on my window. I rolled it down.

Javier handed me the paper bag. Inside was the 45 of *"My Sharona."* I looked up at him, not sure what to say.

"To remember us by," he said.

Then we drove away.

The drive to Washington took a week. We spent a couple of days in California, visiting family. I asked if we could go to Montclair to see Sean and Jason, but my mom said they had moved to Oceanside.

Back on the road, I watched out the window as the scenery slowly changed. We crossed the Grapevine and dropped into Central California's endless fields of oranges, pecans, and almonds. It seemed to take ages to get to Redding. From there, towering evergreens guided us all the way into Washington.

We lived in El Paso for about a year, but like all of the other time I had spent there, it left a lasting impression. Mrs. Stillwell was right—I did learn to love Texas, and I found myself back there again in 1988, this time in San Antonio for Air Force boot camp. I didn't love the boot camp part, though.

I'll always remember Francisco and the way he would look down the line of scrimmage at me, telepathically communicating which route to run on crucial third-down plays during those epic football games. And, of course, David and Javier, and the summer of 1980 will live on forever in my memories—the basketball games, the bike rides, and especially the shaky beginning of our friendship when I showed up to play hoops dressed like an early Hispanic prototype of Steve Urkel.

"My Sharona" is, admittedly, a problematic song by today's standards. But still, when it comes on the radio, a streaming

channel, or shuffle on my phone, the volume is going up. All the way up. And we're going to rock out.

FANTASY

I didn't know it at the time, sitting there with my headphones on and thinking about the places and people that had shaped me, but I was standing at a kind of emotional crossroads.

Everything I had survived so far—the moves, the loneliness, the constant reshuffling of friendships—had only been the beginning. The next few years would be just as challenging.

At that age, though, I didn't have the vocabulary—or the perspective—to understand where my struggles ranked on the grand scoreboard of suffering. I wasn't fighting leukemia. I wasn't homeless. I wasn't living through the kind of poverty or violence that shatters childhoods. But you don't know that at eleven. You only know your own world, and mine felt unstable. Whatever you're dealing with feels huge because you don't have anything worse to measure it against. It's only with a few decades of distance, a few more miles on the odometer, that you learn to hold two truths at once: your problems weren't the worst in the world, but they were real to you, and they shaped you all the same.

I had already attended five schools in just two years. What I didn't realize was that I was about to add three more schools to that list, crammed into another turbulent two years.

Another move was coming, too—a local one, but it would still feel like an earthquake under already shaky ground.

And even before all that, I had quietly survived my earliest upheavals: two kindergartens, two first grades. The pattern had been set early. I just hadn't understood what it meant yet.

The music, the memories, the people I carried with me—they would have to be enough.

Because the road ahead wasn't going to get any smoother.

Not yet.

The early 1980s found popular music at a crossroads as well. The industry suffered a sales slump from 1980 - 1982, with sales dropping from 762 million units in 1978 to 594 million units in 1981, and further decline of 8% in 1982.

The major record labels placed blame on home recording, enabled by the rise of cassette tapes. The British Phonographic Industry (BPI) went so far to launch its "Home Taping Is Killing Music" campaign in October of 1981. U.S. record executives echoed this, with the CEO of CBS Records calling home taping "terrifying". The sales of blank tapes rose, suggesting consumers were taping music - off the radio, from each other - and not buying albums.

This is somewhat true, but there were bigger factors at play.

By 1980, disco was dead. The industry experienced a surge in sales of disco albums in the late 1970s, led by the immensely popular Saturday Night Fever soundtrack. With disco rapidly waning in popularity, there was no genre or band waiting in the wings to fill that void.

Gold albums (500,000 in unit sales) dropped from 153 in 1981 to 128 in 1982, platinum albums (1 million units) fell from 60 to 54. Only three albums hit mega-platinum (2 million units) in 1982, signaling a lack of blockbuster releases.

Big acts from the 1970s, Fleetwood Mac, the Eagles, even Paul McCartney, were still around, but most were either breaking up or retreating into safe, forgettable solo albums.

Disco - burned out. Punk splintered. Arena rock was beginning to feel bloated. Radio playlists were stale, and for a while it seemed as if the music business - and even bands themselves -

had run out of ideas.

The music industry was at a crossroads. This was a transitional moment for music.

It was for me too.

In the summer of 1981, I flew back to Michigan to visit my father. This would be the first time I would see him in over five years.

My mother, being my mother, made me wear dark blue dress pants and a light blue and white polo shirt that didn't fit me right. It was much too big. I also had to wear dress shoes, black and clunky. For some inexplicable reason, I topped this outfit off with a plastic Seattle Mariners batting helmet. My thick hair, looking like something between Epstein's from Welcome Back, Kotter and the late Freddie Prinze's from Chico and The Man, poked out wildly from underneath the helmet. Photo evidence of this tragic outfit exists. I looked ridiculous.

I entertained myself on the plane by reading comic books. My dad brought a stack of them home from work, left behind by sailors on board the ships he worked on. I was immediately drawn to Spiderman, The Avengers, and The Uncanny X-men. Without knowing it, my dad had sent me down another pop-culture rabbit hole. I became obsessed with the world of superheroes, the concept of dual identities, and the responsibility that comes with great power. But that's a different story for a different book. Maybe.

My father was waiting for me at the gate in Detroit. He was dressed casually, a t-shirt and jeans. He was accompanied by his wife and their toddler son. Awkward hellos and hugs were exchanged.

Our first stop on the way to his house was at my grandmother and grandfather's house. Or mom and pop's, as everyone called it.

When my mother would travel back to Mexico from Detroit, I was left in the care of my grandmother. My father had to work, so it made sense that I would stay with her and Pops. She was a big part of my life, even though I remember very little of it.

"Who is that I see?" my grandmother said as I walked up the path to her front door. Another awkward hug. I stepped inside the house and memories began to flicker. My mom sitting on the couch, completely mangling the words to "Bridge Over Troubled Water". My aunt Michelle, a couple of years older than I was, playing cars with me on her bedroom floor. The backyard where pops taught my father how to start charcoal briquettes without drowning them in lighter fluid. It was familiar and foreign all at once.

Over the next few days I met aunts, uncles, cousins I'd forgotten I had. There were sleepovers, cookouts, fireworks on the Fourth of July, and lots of questions:

Did I like school?

How is Chris doing?

Where the hell is Bremerton?

How's your mom?

That last question always seemed...loaded. The memory of my mother's time in Michigan loomed liked a ghost. The impression she made was lasting and deep. My aunt's told stories of how she struggled to fit in, how they tried to help her to adapt to life in Michigan. My uncle's had stories too, of how they teased her for speaking broken English.

Did she still make bean burritos?

Does she still sing, "Like a bridge over troubled, babies!" to Simon & Garfunkle?

My head spun trying to process their stories and answer their questions.

Most of all though, I found myself feeling something I was not expecting: envy.

I was envious of how tight-knit my cousins were, living just blocks from each other - some literally next door to one another.

They all had an easy camradarie, shared jokes, memories, experiences. They were more like a sprawling group of best friends rather than family.

I couldn't help but think of my house back in Bremerton - isolated, quiet, surrounded by trees - a lonely square in a vast ocean of Bigfoot inhabited woods.

I felt like a stranger at best, an intruder at worst. As much as I wanted to belong, I didn't. I looked different, dressed different. I didn't play hockey, whereas all of my cousins seemed to not only love the Detroit Red Wings, but played as well. My cousins were handsome, athletic, and lean. I was...dumpy, wore glasses, and smelled weird. They talked about things I knew nothing about; cabins 'up north', water skiing, birthday parties, and camping trips. I would offer my own experiences up, what Bremerton was like (rainy, woods, the very real possibility of a Sasquatch stalking through the trees behind our house), and they listened, asked questions.

In retrospect, my Michigan family did all they could to make me feel welcome, I was just a weird kid that was way up in his own head. They opened up their homes to me, took me places - I went into the entire experience guarded.

One area I could bond with my cousins was over our mutual love of The Beatles. We would take old tennis raquets and pretend they were guitars, using ace bandages as straps. In my cousin Joe's room, (or was it Keith's?), we'd pretend we were The Beatles, lip-syncing to the records my uncle Joe had purchased in the 1960's.

I spent the majority of my time on that trip with my father though. We'd start everyday with breakfast. I'd ride on the back of his motorcycle, giant helmet on my head, to his favorite restaurant - Denny's.

I was well aware of my father's epilepsy and knew that his riding a motorcycle was extremely dangerous—double so with me on the back. He had been in car accidents before after experiencing seizures behind the wheel. I'm not even sure he was legally allowed to drive at that point. I just held on tight and prayed he wouldn't have one as we weaved through traffic.

We'd sit at Denny's—in the smoking section—and my father would drink about a billion cups of coffee and smoke about two billion Marlboros. Breakfast was eaten in a haze of second-hand cigarette smoke. Then we'd plan out the day—what aunt we were going to visit next—and it was back on the motorcycle, me in that giant helmet, arms locked in a death grip around my father's waist.

There isn't one song that stands out from that trip, but music was everywhere. My Uncle Jim was a big fan of REO Speedwagon's *High Infidelity* album, and "Take It on the Run" was huge that summer. Juice Newton had a hit with "Queen of Hearts," and Kim Carnes was everywhere with "Bette Davis Eyes."

Mostly, though, I remember the time spent with my father. He looked older. The medication he took for his epilepsy aged him, made his bones brittle. The smoking didn't help. He was still charming as ever—able to elicit smiles from waitresses like before—but he'd lost the mystique I'd built up around him. He wasn't the cinematic version of a dad I'd imagined all those years—a mix of Danny Zuko and Steve McQueen in *Cool Hand Luke.* That trip burst the bubble and made my father real again and not a character created from childhood memories, but a flesh-and-blood man.

I flew home at the end of July feeling more isolated than ever. The rest of that summer was spent chopping and stacking wood in preparation for winter. Money was still tight, so we had to have plenty of firewood to heat our drafty house. Heating oil had gone up in price from the year before, and my dad made sure to remind us of that every day.

We went camping and fishing, so it wasn't all pioneer-style chores. I listened to music, rode bikes with my brother, and played in the woods—always keeping one eye out for Bigfoot. But we still ventured past the tree line.

I wished I had family nearby. Or friends who didn't live miles away.

At the end of August, we received a letter from the Bremerton School District. School zones had been redrawn, and we were no longer within Armin Jahr's boundaries. I'd have to attend Tracyton Elementary for sixth grade.

My heart sank when my parents told me. Another new school. My emotional state was still somewhat turbulent after Michigan; the thought of being the new kid again was too much.

Making matters worse, my brother and I began to drift apart. I was going to turn twelve that fall; he was ten, but the two-year gap felt like a mile. He was finding his place in every social hierarchy—confident, outgoing, alpha. I was none of those things.

I withdrew further into myself, counting down the days before school began. My life became headphones and Beatles records, daydreams of those lip-sync concerts with my cousins. I dove deeper into comic books, wishing I was Peter Parker. And every night, I lulled myself to sleep pretending I was Luke Skywalker taking on the Galactic Empire.

Anyone but me.

Tracyton Elementary was known as a rich, preppy-kid school. I didn't belong.

We were broke—and it showed.

The girls at Tracyton wore trendy local brands like Charly B and Normandy Rose—labels you could only find at The Bon Marché (now Macy's) or Nordstrom. The boys wore shirts and jeans from the Squire Shoppe, their hair perfectly feathered back.

I had one pair of jeans that weren't from Goodwill. They were husky fit, but at least they were new. So that was something.

My brother had two shirts that he alternated throughout the

week, and to him, it was no big deal. Chris wasn't just confident, he was asolutely immune to letting circumstance define him. He could walk into any classroom, any park, and act like he owned the place.

At eleven, I was still in the thick of it—self-conscious about everything: my clothes, my thick glasses, my cowlick-riddled hair, my total lack of anything remotely trendy. I felt like a thrift-store mannequin come to life.

That insecurity pressed against my ribs, thudding in my chest as the first day of school approached. I was desperate, scared, and anxious.

Then the first day of school arrived, and I completely lost my mind. I'm not kidding—I went absolutely batshit crazy.

My mom dropped me off in front of the main office. I checked in at the front desk, letting them know it was my first day. A very pretty girl was also there—it was her first day, too. Not that I had the courage to say anything to her, but still.

Then my mom burst through the door waving a very bright yellow sheet of paper. It was my application for reduced-price lunch tickets. Christ. She set it on the counter and walked out as fast as she'd come in. The pretty girl next to me glanced at the paper, then at me. She winced—not in cruelty, but in secondhand embarrassment.

An office assistant escorted both of us to our homerooms. Mine was already buzzing with conversation—kids reconnecting after summer break. Everyone seemed to know each other. Everyone seemed to belong. I found an empty seat and sat in silence, my brand-new, absolutely gigantic Trapper Keeper on the desk in front of me.

All the other kids had yellow Pee-Chee folders—thin, flexible, cool. My Trapper Keeper had a hard plastic cover and sealed with Velcro. Every time I opened it, a loud, tearing sound ripped through the air. Double Christ.

Then the classroom doors swung open and two boys entered like they owned the place. One of them, grinning wildly, shouted Richard Pryor's line from *Stir Crazy* as they strutted in: "We bad, that's right, we bad!"

The room erupted with laughter and cheers. James and Kelvin —Tracyton Elementary's resident superstars. The girls adored them. The boys nodded in admiration. Even our teacher, Mrs. Day, lit up when they walked in. It was a lot to take in.

The bell rang and the room settled. Mrs. Day stood at the front and introduced herself, then went around the class asking each student to say their name and share what they did over the summer.

The answers came quickly:

Camping. Swimming. Disneyland. Mount Rainier. The usual stuff.

Then it was my turn.

Looking back, any therapist could tell you exactly what was happening. I was trying to protect myself. I was the outsider —again. My eleven-year-old brain scrambled for something, anything, that would make me stand out. Make me interesting. Make me not me.

Because I didn't want to be me. I didn't even want to be in that room. I was just a lumpy, dumpy kid in husky jeans, a Goodwill shirt, and knock-off Pro-Wings. I shifted in my seat, panicked, heart pounding.

Then it happened.

I stood up, said my name—and did so in the worst fake British accent imaginable. Then I told the class I had spent the summer in Liverpool, England, writing a song called "Taxman."

Like I said, I went batshit crazy.

The class went silent. I don't think Mrs. Day bought my terrible accent, but the kids did.

At first recess, I wandered around the playground wondering how the hell I was going to get out of this British-accent predicament. Then a group of girls from class approached me, asking me to say certain words so they could "hear my accent."

Oh my. There was no easy way out of this now. I'd painted myself into a corner using the colors of the Union Jack.

I was going to have to keep this charade going for the rest of the school year. This was, of course, impossible. I'd be lucky to keep the fake accent going for the rest of the week.

First of all, my brother attended the same school—and he wasn't walking around talking like a Dickensian street urchin. It wouldn't be long before someone, anyone, put that together and outed me.

Second, my mom was very clearly Mexican, with a heavy accent. How exactly was I planning to explain that?

And third, open house was two weeks away. Surely Mrs. Day would say something to my parents about my "odd" accent, right?

But no one did—at least, not to my face.

I eventually became friends with a kid named Brian, a super sweet kid who could solve the Rubik's Cube in forty-five seconds and held the high score on several games at the Redwood Plaza arcade. We hit it off quickly, over a game of chess during a rainy indoor recess.

Before long, I was going over to his house after school, or he was coming over to mine. During those visits, I wasn't talking like an extra in a community-theater production of *Oliver Twist.*

Back at school, though, I kept the accent up. Again, I was batshit crazy.

What strikes me now, as I sit here writing this, is that I already *had* a compelling story to tell. By age eleven, I'd lived in six different states and attended eight different schools. I know people in their fifties now who've never left Washington State.

There was no need for me to invent anything—no fake accent, no claiming I wrote a song called "Taxman" (my apologies to

George Harrison). My reality was compelling enough.

Had I just been honest with myself, maybe even a little vulnerable, I could have lived more authentically.

I didn't know that then. I didn't even know *how.* Not yet.

The school year moved ahead, and I continued carrying on like an Englishman in Bremerton. Meanwhile, around the rest of the world, something was happening. There was a shift in the air.

The malaise of the early 1970s—political disillusionment, social fragmentation—had given birth to the flash and dazzle of the late-'70s disco era. But there was a skeevy, dark underbelly to it. The drug-fueled glitz and hedonism of that time were unsustainable. Disco may have been upbeat and bright, but it was still set against a background of grey.

Morale was low, reflected in the gritty realism of popular culture. Movies like *Taxi Driver* explored moral decay and urban rot...

Oops. In the intro, I promised this book wouldn't delve into political or socio-economic topics. I'll stop now.

The pop charts of 1981 and 1982 were an eclectic mix. Dolly Parton hit #1 with *9 to 5*, a song about a dead-end office job. Sheena Easton scored with *Morning Train*—a song about commuting. Air Supply and Christopher Cross were churning out soft-rock hits. We bitch-slapped the air to Kim Carnes's *Bette Davis Eyes* and played with the *Queen of Hearts* alongside Juice Newton. Rick James introduced the world to punk funk with *Super Freak.* Eddie Rabbitt—the inspiration behind my dad growing out a beard—was still getting airplay with *I Love a Rainy Night* over a year after its release. Heavy metal, particularly the new wave of British heavy metal, was starting to gain traction too. So, on any given day, you could turn on a Top 40 station and hear country, pop, soft rock, or Judas Priest telling you that you've got another thing coming.

Album sales may have been down, but music was alive again. Something brighter, more colorful—fun even—was taking root. Something called MTV had launched.

The first music video I ever saw wasn't even on MTV. It was on a Canadian station we picked up over the air. MTV wouldn't reach Kitsap County until September 1983, so we took what we could get, music-video-wise.

There I was, mindlessly flipping channels—manually, since our TV didn't have a remote—when it happened: *Aldo Nova's* "Fantasy."

I don't know why it stopped me cold, but it did. I stood a few feet from our nineteen-inch RCA, close enough to feel like I was soaking up the radiation my mom warned us about.

The video was absurd and thrilling all at once—Aldo Nova bursting onto the screen in a stupendous leopard-print jumpsuit, guitar slung low, confidence cranked to eleven. It didn't matter what was happening around him. Doors exploded. Riffs tore through the speakers. Reality bent to his will.

And then that opening lead line hit—sharp, melodic, impossible to ignore—and something in me snapped to attention.

"Fantasy" wasn't subtle. It didn't ask permission. It didn't explain itself. It just declared that escape was possible, that reinvention was allowed, that imagination could overpower circumstance.

I didn't have lasers shooting out of a guitar headstock or a rooftop waiting for me, but I understood the impulse immediately. I was already living in my own fantasy world—one where I could be anyone but the awkward, anxious kid I was becoming.

Music had done that for me before. Now it was doing it again—louder, brighter, and with a visual language I'd never seen before.

Fantasy would later be credited with blazing the trail for countless '80s hard rock bands. The fusion of arena-rock power chords, pop hooks, and synthesizer layers wasn't entirely new, but it had never been done quite like this.

Lyrically, *Fantasy* is about escaping reality through imagination—something I knew a little about. I wasn't living out the hedonistic adventures of Aldo Nova (I had zero access to guitars with lasers in their friggin' headstocks), but I *was* living in a fantasy world inside my head. There were no neon lights or city nights in there, just a sad-sack kid too uncomfortable in his own skin to live authentically. It was easier to pretend I was Paul McCartney's paperboy before showing up in Bremerton.

My grades were horrific that entire school year. I spent most of my time not doing homework and stressing out about my stupid fake accent. I just wanted it all to be over.

Sixth grade did, mercifully, come to an end. I had to scramble to bring my grades up enough to qualify for non-remedial math and science classes, which wasn't easy. I packed four months of schoolwork into two weeks—but I pulled it off.

Something was in the air as I walked out of Tracyton Elementary for the last time—hope. The optimism of Reagan's America was building momentum. Maybe, just maybe, I'd catch a break and move on to junior high with the rest of my classmates.

Who am I kidding?

Seventh grade would be even more tumultuous.

WHY DON'T YOU LOOK INTO JESUS?

In 1981, my family began attending First Church of Bremerton. My mom had always been a seeker when it came to religion. Between 1976 and 1981, we had been to Catholic churches, nearly converted to Mormonism, and flirted with the idea of becoming Jehovah's Witnesses. When we moved to Bremerton, we attended several congregations before finding First Church.

It was there that I would find a lifelong friend.

First Church sat up on a hill, overlooking downtown Bremerton and a portion of Olympic College. It was an imposing building, brick exterior, large footprint, and a bell tower that was both dramatic and understated.

The main chapel was vast, with red carpet running between two long aisles of wooden pews. At the front of the chapel stood a simple pulpit, flanked by a choir loft and a plain wooden cross that looked out across the congregation.

It was an old building, structurally speaking, but it was alive and thriving, especially in the basement.

That's where the youth group met every Sunday morning, in the sprawling lower level that held a kitchen and a carpeted gym where ACLs went to die.

It was in that gym that I met Mark.

There's no single moment I can point to, no origin story. I don't even remember what was said, who spoke first, or even what we were doing. We just became friends.

We shared a love of video games and spent hours playing *Asteroids* and *Space Invaders* on the Atari 2600. Mark also knew how to get to the secret room in *Adventure*, credited with being the first video game Easter egg, which was mind-blowingly cool in 1981. There was also a mutual admiration that we had for pro athletes...Magic Johnson, Larry Bird, Marvin Hagler, and Jim Zorn and Steve Largent of the Seahawks.

Mark loved Star Wars as much as I did too, and we counted down the days until *Return of the Jedi* (still titled as *Revenge of the Jedi* at this point) would be released.

Most of all, though, we shared a love of music. I introduced him to Michael Jackson, the Beatles, and whatever pop gems I heard over the radio airwaves. He opened the door to an entirely new world for me—Christian rock.

I know what you're thinking. *Christian rock? Isn't that just a watered-down version of real rock music, only worse?*

You wouldn't be wrong. Christian rock was pretty awful in the early days—treacly, preachy, and unimaginative. But in 1972, one man asked, *"Why should the devil have all the good music?"*

That man was Larry Norman.

Mark played me Larry's answer to that question one night during a sleepover. He handed me a cassette, and on the cover was a photo of a man walking down an L.A. street, dressed head to toe in denim, his long blond hair cascading down past his shoulders. Across the top, in simple font:

Larry Norman–*Only Visiting This Planet*

This had potential.

Mark queued up song three. An acoustic guitar riff kicked off —nothing special. If anything, it was overly simplistic and amateurish. Then Larry sings:

"Sippin' whiskey from a paper cup / you drown your sorrows 'til you can't stand up..."

Well now, this is different.

"Yellow fingers from your cigarettes/your hands are shaking while your body sweats..."

This is most definitely not Kumbaya territory.

"Why don't you look into Jesus, He got the answer."

The song is a direct plea to the strung out, the burned out, the disillusioned. There is no shaming in the song, no judging, just unconditional reaching.

Verse two pulled no punches and made Christian radio stations squirm:

"Gonorrhea on Valentine's Day (VD)/and you're still looking for the perfect lay..."

This was raw, confrontational, a gritty dispatch from the remnants of the 1960s where free love, drug use, and spiritual emptiness exacted a heavy toll.

Here's what I wasn't expecting to hear: Beneath the weathered vocals, early-'70s rock aesthetic, and pointed lyrics was something I didn't expect - empathy.

Larry Norman isn't condemning the people he sings about. He understood who they were - flower children and hippies disillusioned by the government and even the church. He's providing a solution, a way out of addiction and despair. He's offering hope.

Mark kept the tape rolling.

Norman bounced from bluesy confessionals to end-times dread to sharp, Dylan-esque cultural satire, openly singing about sex, addiction, broken idols, and spiritual burnout. For a Christian music scene built on politeness and reassurance, it was confrontational—and a little terrifying.

But Mark wasn't done. He dug out Randy Stonehill's album *Welcome to Paradise.* Released in 1976, *Welcome to Paradise* is another pivotal Christian rock record. Stonehill blends folk-pop and rock with introspective songwriting. It's less gritty and more accessible than *Only Visiting This Planet,* but the themes are similar—human frailty, grace, and redemption.

Like Norman, Stonehill also faced a backlash from Christian radio. His music was deemed too rock, too real. But there was no denying its brilliance.

Norman and Stonehill quickly became my personal Christian rock Lennon and McCartney. Larry Norman was the introspective soul-searcher; Stonehill was the clever storyteller. That doesn't mean they couldn't switch roles, though. Norman was more than capable of dropping a tune full of witty wordplay, like "Watch What You're Doing", just as Stonehill could hit you with deeply personal songs like "First Prayer".

I leaned into their music quite a bit as a confused and wildly insecure kid. There was comfort in those words—they made me feel like I wasn't wandering alone. Navigating adolescence is hard enough, but it's even tougher when you believe no one understands what you're going through. I may not have been struggling with addiction, but wrestling with low self-esteem and feeling like you don't fit in or belong are heavy burdens for a kid to carry. Now I felt like, with God, I wasn't bearing that weight all on my own.

In the summer of 1982, my parents concluded I was highly susceptible to the corruption and evil influences lurking in the halls of the Bremerton public school system. My mom saw a boy from my sixth-grade class—Clint—wearing a black Blue Öyster Cult concert T-shirt and smoking a cigarette outside of Value Giant. This set off a low-grade Satanic panic in our house. Suddenly, my mom saw and heard the devil everywhere, and he was coming for my soul via "Burnin' for You" and "Don't Fear the Reaper".

Wait—I have to backtrack a bit here. When we were kids, my mom would tell us stories about the multiple times she had seen the devil. Not metaphorically. Literally.

The first time she laid eyes on him was as a young girl at a carnival in Ciudad Juárez. She was waiting in line to ride the carousel when a ripple moved through the crowd—not fear, but awe. A man was making his way down the midway, the most handsome man my mom had ever seen. She described him as "more beautiful than an angel, but dressed in a black suit and tie." Women swooned; men stepped aside, almost reverently.

Then she looked down, expecting to see silver-tipped cowboy boots or polished dress shoes. Instead, protruding from the cuffs of his trousers were cloven hooves, thick, filthy, and matted with something dark and tar-like.

Her eyes shot back up, and in that instant his face had changed. The handsome stranger was gone. In his place was a grotesque goat's head, the horns glistening as if slicked with blood. His eyes burned red. She said they looked like flames trapped behind glass. His mouth hung slightly open, revealing teeth that didn't belong to any earthly animal.

And then there was the smell. She always mentioned the smell. She said he smelled like sulfur and death.

She screamed. The spell was broken. The crowd scattered, and my mom ran all the way back to her sister's house without looking back.

But wait, there's more!

The next sighting was a year later, near my grandmother's house in La Mesa, Mexico—a small village about thirty minutes from Chihuahua. It was late, and my mom was walking her drunk brother home from a cantina. He heard what sounded like a baby crying inside a small cave across from the village church. He went in and came out carrying an infant bundled in blankets. The full moon, hidden behind clouds, suddenly broke through.

That's when my uncle peeled back the blankets and saw that he wasn't holding a baby—at least not a human one. According to my mom, this "baby" had lizard-like eyes, a forked tongue, and hissed and growled at her brother. He dropped it. My mom said the thing then scurried back into the cave "like an evil little spider."

Until then, my uncle could best be described as a degenerate drunk—the kind who spent what little money he made at the cantina instead of taking care of his family. He stopped drinking after that night.

Whenever my brother and I were misbehaving, my mom would tell us that the devil was going to appear to us that night as a goat with flaming eyes. This usually got us to straighten up—until one time I pushed back on the logic of it all.

It just didn't make sense to me.

"Why would the devil want us to be good?" I asked. "Doesn't he want us to be bad so we'll go to hell? Isn't people being bad what he wants?"

She had no response other than to up the ante.

"You want to be like that *Exorcist* girl?" she snapped. "That's what will happen if you and your brother keep fighting."

This, of course, triggered my *Exorcist* PTSD—a condition that lingered well into adulthood. One mention of Pazuzu and I'd be folding all the laundry and cleaning my room at a record-breaking clip.

So, my mom's fear of the devil went way back and ran way deep—pre-dating Blue Öyster Cult. They just happened to be the catalyst for my family's Satanic Panic of '82.

That panic drove my parents—our shaky financial situation be damned—to decide that I would *not* attend Fairview Junior High in the fall with the other kids from Tracyton Elementary. Oh no. Kids at Fairview smoked pot, sold pot, maybe even did cocaine.

I protested, insisting that none of the kids I knew from Tracyton smoked pot or even drank. My mom reminded me she saw Clint in a "devil shirt." Somehow, that equated to every kid at Fairview being a mini Pablo Escobar in training.

I was going to attend Bremerton Christian School—BCS—the ninth school I'd attended in less than four years. All because my mom saw a kid I'd maybe exchanged four words with all year, firing up a heater while wearing a Blue Öyster Cult T-shirt outside of Value Giant.

I can only imagine what her reaction would've been had Clint been wearing an Iron Maiden *Number of the Beast* shirt. She probably would have sent me off to a monastery.

The one and only good thing about going to BCS was that Mark's parents had also decided the devil was out looking for him. He would attend BCS too.

We arrived that fall, and our paths immediately diverged—at least academically. I struggled to adapt right out of the gate, falling behind almost immediately in my schoolwork. Mark was a familiar face and a friend, and there were other kids from First Church attending BCS as well, but it was still a new school.

If Tracyton was the school of rich kids and preppies, BCS was the school of trust-fund babies and old money. At least, that's how it felt to me. My mom took on babysitting jobs to help pay for my tuition, while other kids' parents owned car dealerships, convenience stores, or held high positions at banks or the shipyard.

My inferiority complex immediately kicked into high gear. This meant further withdrawal into music, comic books, and video games—while doing absolutely zero homework. I just couldn't get out of my head that, once again, I didn't belong.

Making matters worse, I was now entering the most awkward physical phase of my life. I had weapons-grade BO—the kind deodorant could mask but not contain. It was an entity unto itself, alive, radiating from me in visible waves of funk.

I also developed terrible acne that marched across my face and forehead like an invading Mongol army. Then there was the dandruff. My hair was already problematic—cowlicks, home-brew haircuts, and an ever-present sheen of grease. Now I had to deal with dandruff that fell from my head as if my scalp were a broken snow globe.

Last, but definitely not least, were my glasses. I had finally moved on from the *Flintstones*–branded frames, swapping them out for metal ones. Plastic frames weren't structurally sound enough to support the sheer weight of my prescription lenses. I needed frames made of good ol' American steel. Gold-plated steel. I looked like the prototypical early-'80s movie nerd—only with Dahmer glasses.

There were other kids going through their awkward puberty phases too, but my situation was dire. I wasn't going *through* puberty—I was being violently *transformed*, like a werewolf in a horror movie.

Gym class was a special form of torture. Mark was a graceful and natural athlete, able to master any sport in a matter of minutes. I struggled to run in a straight line.

The relay races were the worst. My team would openly scheme—right in front of me—about how to mitigate my clumsiness and lack of speed. The strategy was always to let me run first so they could spend the rest of the race making up the ground I'd lost.

That meant I had to run against the fastest kids, and by "run," I mean *lumber*. My legs simply wouldn't cooperate. No matter how hard I tried, they refused to move faster than a labored stomp. The end result looked less like sprinting and more like seismic activity in slow-motion. My feet thudded loudly against the wooden gym floor, and by the end of my leg, I'd be twenty yards behind the closest kid.

It was embarrassing.

More embarrassing were the basketball layup relays. Again, Mark would glide around the gym, effortlessly rolling in layups like George Gervin. Me? I dribbled like I was trying to smash the air out of the ball, pounding it into the hardwood. My layups were an unmitigated disaster. I'd hit the bottom of the rim, the side of the backboard—sometimes I even launched the ball *over* the backboard.

Whatever team I was on was guaranteed to lose. I dragged my

team down like a boat anchor tied around the neck of a mafia snitch.

The consequences of my poor performances in gym class were immediate. My team would lose, I'd sulk, everyone wished I wasn't on their team.

The results of my academic failures lagged. I'd not turn in a homework assignment, and two days later a detention notice would appear on my desk.

Detention notices were sent home with the student and had to be returned the next day with a parent's signature. Failure to return the notice on time resulted in a second detention. It was entirely possible to have one detention notice cascade into two or three.

Trust me—I know.

At BCS, detention was served immediately after school, and no bus service was provided. My dad would pick me up after my debt to society had been paid in full for not doing my homework. Detention let out at 4:00 p.m.; my dad worked until 4:30. That meant on days I served detention, I was at school from 7:30 a.m. until almost 5:00 p.m.

You'd think I would have used that time to complete overdue homework. I didn't. Instead, I read comic books I had hidden inside my Trapper Keeper—the same one from sixth grade. I suddenly found all those pockets and folders handy.

For that hour, I escaped into worlds inhabited by Wolverine, Spider-Man, and Daredevil when I should have been working on algebra or completing a book report.

Detention wasn't a punishment I served in isolation; it affected my dad too. The drive home from school was a half hour long. On days he picked me up—and there were a lot of them—that meant we wouldn't get home until 5:30 in the afternoon.

By law, Washington State requires students to attend a minimum of 180 school days each year. In seventh grade, I served detention on 114 of those 180 days. This may be some kind of record. Not a good one, but still a record.

My parents were consumed with their own issues so they didn't seem to have the energy to hold me accountable for my unwillingness to do my homework. I wasn't a dumb, but I was lazy and more interested in living inside the fantasy world in my head than in the reality of the present. That was just easier.

The one person who would call me out was Mark. I can still hear him today:

"C'mon, Jess… you gotta buckle down and get this done."

I wouldn't buckle down, and I wouldn't get it done—but Mark would still implore me to apply myself.

"Jess, c'mon… this is easy."

Then came the day, late in the school year, when I brought home yet another detention notice. My dad took it from me, and as he was signing it said, "I'm disgusted with you. You're useless."

Harsh words to hear—and if he could take them back, he would. But he was frustrated, not just with me, but with phone bills, long hours at work, and an unhappy wife. A kid choosing to fail at a private school he was paying for was the icing on the world's worst-tasting cake.

I made it to the end of another school year, but not before one last humiliation: field day. We were required to participate in two individual events and one team event. I looked over the signup form, trying to find something that matched my lack of athletic prowess. Nothing.

Mark took the form from me and checked off the 400-meter run and shot put. Those would be my events.

"Pace yourself on the 400-meter run. Hang back, then sprint at the end. Use your legs on the shot put—you're strong. That's an easy one for you," he said, offering encouragement.

Field day arrived. Students wandered around the track with snow cones and sodas, having a great time. Not this guy. I was hanging back, hiding, trying to avoid my events. But I couldn't. Mark—and a girl named Felicia—found me and dragged me to the track.

Mark offered one last bit of advice. "Don't sprint early. Save it for the end."

I nodded and took my place on the line.

The starting pistol fired, and we were off. I immediately struggled as the pack pulled away. By the time we rounded the first turn, I was already twenty-five meters behind. At the halfway point, I heard Mark yell, "Now! Now! Now!"

It was time to sprint.

I tried. My legs felt as if they were encased in concrete; my feet were cinder blocks. The harder I tried to sprint, the slower I went. The pack surged ahead, runners kicking into their final sprints.

I crossed the finish line. Dead last. My lungs felt like they were filled with wet dirt. I could barely breathe.

Mark sauntered up. "You were supposed to sprint at the end. What happened?"

Gasping, I looked up. "I *did* sprint."

Oh.

And that was that.

The shot put was just as bad. I may have had thick legs, but they were doughy and weak. For the team event, we tossed water balloons. The last team with an intact balloon won. Easy enough —if you didn't drop it. Which I did. Early.

Sigh.

Final report cards arrived in the mail about two weeks into summer vacation. Mine came in an envelope a little thicker than the others. Inside was a letter detailing all the reasons I could not attend Bremerton Christian School the following year.

Poor grades. Failure to apply myself. Multiple dress-code

violations—including hair length and style (my hair didn't grow long; it grew *big*, and it was impossible to keep it from touching my ears or shirt collar).

The main one, though, was my "inability to adapt to the culture at Bremerton Christian School." I was not chiseled from timber suitable for BCS.

Honestly, they could've stopped with the poor grades. The rest just felt like the administrators were piling on.

That was it. My parents had paid a decent amount of money to keep me away from the legion of devil-worshipping drug dealers roaming the halls of Fairview Junior High—just so I could fail.

I was actually relieved that I would not be going back. Junior high is hard enough without having to worry about dress codes, morality clauses, attending chapel, and memorizing Bible verses. I, of course, made this even more difficult by refusing to put forth any effort with any of it.

Mark and I spent quite a bit of time hanging out that summer. We played a lot of video games, hung out at church sponsored events, and discovered new music. He was being drawn more and more to heavy metal; I leaned more towards pop. Through it all, we still found ourselves listening to Larry Norman and Randy Stonehill.

Looking back at it all, it's easy to see a mopey, self-absorbed kid that was focused on everything wrong to the point of being blinded by what was right. I was more interested in escaping reality than in taking advantage of the opportunities in front of me. While my mom and dad were trying to save me from the devil, I was wrestling with demons of my own making right in front of them.

I wasted a lot of time feeling sorry for myself.

Those thoughts, those...demons, still come knocking on my door from time to time. I just ignore them now, they are boring and tedious. I've also learned to give that messed up kid that still lives inside me some grace and forgiveness for doing what he felt he had to do, no matter how ridiculous it was.

A few months before I started writing this book, I was browsing at a local antique store. There, in a crate chock-full of used Little Feat and Grand Funk Railroad albums, I found a copy of Randy Stonehill's *Welcome to Paradise*. I immediately set it aside. I flipped through more records. Nothing. I moved over to a stack of cassettes, and there it was; *Only Visiting This Planet*. I picked it up, opened the case and looked at the sun-yellowed cassette inside. The faded print. But I could still make out track three, "Why Don't You Look Into Jesus".

In an instant, they transported me back to Mark's room sometime in 1981...or was it 1982? Does it matter? I can see him pop the cassette into his Magnavox tape deck, rewind the tape, and then hit play. The acoustic guitar strum, underwhelming at first, then Larry Norman's reedy tenor hits, "Sippin' whisky from a paper cup..."

I carried the record and cassette up to the front counter. It was the best eight bucks I've spent in a long time.

OPEN ARMS

If you attended a junior high or middle school in the early 1980s —especially in a town with limited entertainment options—the odds are high that you went on a field trip to a roller rink. Roller rinks offered entertainment at a reasonable rate, a major bonus for any school with a modest operating budget, public or private.

Near the end of the 1983 school year, Bremerton Christian School took the seventh-grade class to Skate Land, the one and only roller rink in Kitsap County. There was a special irony in this: Skate Land played *secular* music, and just a few weeks earlier, we'd been lectured on the evils of secular pop music.

Every Wednesday, we attended chapel for one hour. This required wearing shirts and ties—usually of the clip-on variety, but ties nonetheless. The girls were required to wear skirts or dresses of "appropriate" length (below the knee, naturally). It was all very prim and proper.

Most chapel days were forgettable. We sang a hymn or two, then one teacher would speak. Sometimes we'd hear a life lesson drawn from the New Testament, other times it was a straight Bible study. Occasionally, we had a guest speaker.

On one of these Wednesdays, the guest speaker was an "expert on Satanism." Well now. This was going to be different.

He was a serious man with serious glasses and a serious suit. He was also quite young—maybe twenty-four or twenty-five—which gave him a bit of "street cred," I suppose. For the next forty-five minutes, he lectured us about the evils of popular music and how any exposure to it opened the door for Satan to possess our souls.

We all squirmed in our seats, especially me. All I listened to was secular music—the only exceptions being the times I listened to Larry Norman or Randy Stonehill. Even those two were sometimes chastised by the church for being *too close* to the secular scene, especially Norman.

In the early 1980s, a cultural phenomenon known as the "Satanic Panic" swept the nation. It was a time of heightened moral and religious anxiety when concerned parents and self-appointed moral watchdogs scrutinized pop music—particularly hard rock and heavy metal. These groups alleged that certain lyrics and album covers promoted Satanism, occultism, and moral decay.

This hysteria was fueled by a couple of nitwits named Paul Crouch and Michael Mills, who claimed that songs like Led Zeppelin's *Stairway to Heaven* contained Satanic messages when played backward. The theory was quickly debunked, but by then it had already settled into the culture as misinformed folklore.

Our guest speaker cited Crouch and Mills as the inspiration for his "studies." Which other bands, he asked, were secretly trying to lure kids into devil worship via backward masking (or even frontward masking) of satanic messages in their music?

We were about to find out.

He started with low-hanging fruit—KISS—before shuffling on down the highway to hell to AC/DC.

In the late '70s and early '80s, KISS always seemed to be at the center of one controversy or another. With their face paint, Gene Simmons's blood-spitting antics, and boneheaded yet provocative lyrics, KISS was constantly part of the conversation when it came to "devil music." It didn't help that Simmons's stage persona was literally called *The Demon*.

I was never a KISS fan. Even as a young kid in the mid-seventies, I thought their music kinda sucked. I *was* an Ace Frehley fan, though—mainly because his "Spaceman" makeup and persona were cool, and the star painted over his eye looked like the one on the Dallas Cowboys helmet. That was enough to impress me.

I distinctly remember a kid from Montevista Elementary named John Flush—who always introduced himself by saying, "I'm John Flush, like a toilet"—telling me that KISS stood for either "Kids In Satan's Service" or "Knights In Satan's Service." Either way, I'm sure the band preferred the more noble and regal-sounding latter to the former.

Now here was our guest speaker, repeating the same claim. The less worldly students murmured nervously among themselves.

Then he moved on. AC/DC, he warned, had *nothing* to do with electrical current. Oh no—"Anti-Christ Demon's Children," or sometimes "Anti-Christ Devil's Crusade," was the *true* meaning behind the name, depending on which playground theologian you consulted.

I'd already heard both versions back at Tracyton Elementary. Angus and Malcolm Young, the brothers and founders of AC/DC, had long since laughed off the accusations of Satanism—but that didn't stop parents, pastors, and self-proclaimed experts from clutching their pearls every time someone cranked up *Highway to Hell.*

Next slide: the cover of Blue Öyster Cult's *Spectres* album. Now we were getting somewhere. BÖC, as they were commonly called, was one of the reasons I was sitting in the chapel of BCS that morning.

The speaker explained that the cover showed the band mid-seance, summoning the devil. The dead giveaway, he said, was the ghostly hand on the right side of the image—reaching in from beyond.

"This," he warned, "is why *Blue Öyster Cult*"—he really leaned into the word *Cult*—"does not fear the reaper. They believe in reincarnation and the power of black magic."

I found it clever, even then, that he managed to tie in the band's biggest hit—a song nearly a decade old—to make the case for why Blue Öyster Cult should be feared *today.*

Next slide: Black Sabbath's *Sabbath Bloody Sabbath.* The album, he explained, was reportedly written in the bowels of Clearwell Castle within the Forest of Dean in England. Rumor had it the band was routinely visited by a female ghost while staying there.

Sabbath Bloody Sabbath is considered by some to be Sabbath's finest album. This "some" would include my dad. He was a huge Black Sabbath fan and loved this record. I'd hear him blasting it at skull-crushing volume while working in the garage. He was also a devoted Led Zeppelin fan. Make of that what you will.

I made a mental note: should I warn him that listening to *Killing Yourself to Live* while changing the oil in our car might open a portal to hell? A demon could escape the fiery underworld—or worse, I could get sucked in. Maybe when they took me to see *The Exorcist* at five years old, it wasn't meant to be viewed as fiction, but as a documentary. The mind boggles.

To be fair, the *Sabbath Bloody Sabbath* cover *is* a bit much. It depicts a man writhing on a bed, tormented by demonic figures, surrounded by skulls, an inverted pentagram, and a not-so-subtle "666." The image drew audible gasps from both faculty and students.

He pressed on.

The cover of Iron Maiden's *The Number of the Beast* drew audible gasps from the faint of heart. "You'll see," he said, "Eddie, the band's demonic mascot, is shown manipulating the devil like a puppet."

He paused for dramatic effect. Then, in a low and grave tone, asked, "So... who's really in control?"

Silence.

Ozzy Osbourne was next, earning a rare split-screen slide - on one side, the album cover for *Diary of a Madman*; on the other, *Blizzard of Ozz.* Both covers show Ozzy doing Ozzy things: upside-down crosses, a crucifix in hand, goat skulls scattered across tables and floors. Except on the *Diary* cover, Ozzy's wearing a ridiculous tasseled outfit. He looks like the kid who had to throw his costume together just as Spirit Halloween was closing for the season.

"Ozzy Osbourne," the speaker bellowed, "is a devotee of Aleister Crowley, infamous British occultist and follower of the devil!"

This, of course, we already knew — Ozzy sang about him on the song "Mr. Crowley." And by "we," I mean Mark and myself.

The guest speaker moved through more slides — some bands we recognized, like Judas Priest. "It's all in the name!" he thundered. "The betrayer of Christ! Held in the highest esteem — the clergy — by these practitioners of British metal!"

The delivery was that theatrical, chopped into an odd, staccato rhythm.

I always found Priest — as the kids called them — to be on the milder side of the New Wave of British Heavy Metal that had crashed onto U.S. shores. Band name aside, *Livin' After Midnight* is a real toe-tapper. I didn't see or hear anything wrong with it.

Other bands were completely unfamiliar to us. Venom, anyone?

Sensing he was losing the room, he pushed ahead with Mercyful Fate. Their lead singer, King Diamond, claimed to be a member of the Church of Satan. None of us seemed to care. They were too obscure.

He had to hit us where it hurt.

And that's exactly what he did.

The coup de grâce, you ask—the kill shot? Journey's *Escape.*

Journey was *massive* in 1983. Songs from *Escape* were still in heavy rotation on AOR and Top 40 stations, even though the band had released *Frontiers* earlier that year. It wasn't uncommon to hear "Open Arms" and "Faithfully" back-to-back during "Two-for-Tuesday" radio sets.

Frontiers is a solid record, but *Escape* catapulted the band into the stratosphere. The album is an arena-rock juggernaut—packed with sing-along anthems, soaring power ballads, and echoes of the band's early prog-rock and fusion days. It had something for everyone.

I had no idea how "Who's Crying Now" tied into the occult or the devil, but this guy was going to connect those dots for us.

The *Escape* album cover shows a spaceship bursting out from the center of a planet—Earth, perhaps. No landmasses are visible, so if it *is* Earth, it's the *Waterworld* version. Honestly, the cover looks like an airbrushed sci-fi scene you might find on the side of a skeevy 1975 Chevy van.

Where things took a turn toward the demonic was in the details. The spaceship wasn't just a spaceship—it was a rocket-propelled scarab beetle. That scarab was the smoking gun.

During the height of the Satanic Panic, some claimed the scarab beetle was an occult symbol tied to the Egyptian god Khepri—the deity tasked with rolling the sun across the sky. Naturally, someone connected Khepri to Satan. There was no evidence for this. No ancient text, no scrolls of dubious origin tied Khepri to Ol' Scratch.

The speaker's voice boomed through the chapel: "As you can see, Journey is promoting occultism! This scarab-shaped *rocket,"*—yes, he actually said *rocket*—"is tearing open the Earth itself, creating an unholy doorway that allows demons a means of escape from their hellish underworld domain!"

A classmate named Rick cried. He was a huge Journey fan. A girl named Felicia tried to comfort him.

They would marry shortly after high school.

We were then told that not even Christian rock was safe. The speaker brought up Larry Norman specifically.

"He hangs out with Jerry Garcia of the Grateful Dead," he warned, "one of the SICKEST and most DEMONIC bands around!"

This, of course, was a wild exaggeration—and a lie. The Grateful Dead were a lot of things: boring, overindulgent, noodly, and terrible—but not because of Satan. That was just who they were. Also, Larry Norman liked to say he was pals with Paul McCartney, not Jerry Garcia—though no evidence exists to support that claim.

By the end of chapel, I didn't even know if Amy Grant was safe to listen to. Still, I wasn't about to give up The Beatles or Michael Jackson... but I wasn't too sure about my dad's Sabbath albums.

The school was buzzing afterward. Rick remained inconsolable for the rest of the day, but he and Felicia continued to trauma-bond. Mark and I debriefed about what went down in chapel, both skeptical of most of the claims, though admittedly wary. Maybe we'd cool it with some of the more "overtly Satanic" music, but we weren't about to give up the Go-Go's, Joan Jett, John Cougar (he hadn't gone back to John Mellencamp yet), or Van Halen—even if they were runnin' with the devil.

Besides, it would be impossible to avoid all the bands they had warned us about while playing *Dig Dug* or *Ms. Pac-Man* at the Punk Palace. We accepted that some devil music was going to creep into our lives, and there wasn't much we could do about it. It was the cost of doing business.

As the school year wound down, I kept serving time in detention while actively avoiding anything resembling homework. The buzz from the Satanic Panic chapel session faded, though it still came up occasionally during lunch table conversations.

We also had something to keep us distracted.

Anticipation built for the end-of-year skate party. On this sacred day, we could wear jeans—even the girls! Short skirts were banned, of course, and jeans had to be clean and free of holes. T-shirts were acceptable but only in solid colors; any graphic tees required pre-approval. We might have been venturing into the secular wild, but the administration wasn't about to let us appear feral.

We took school buses to Skate Land, the name *Bremerton Christian School* proudly stenciled on the sides. Other schools were unloading at the same time. We could see their students pointing and snickering at us private-school weirdos, as if we were Amish kids granted a break from barn-raising duties for the day.

Entering Skate Land was like stepping into the *Star Wars* cantina. The music was loud. The kids from other schools looked wild, with their unkempt hair and ripped jeans. Some boys wore muscle shirts and bandanas around their necks. The girls had shorts and skirts that scandalously fell *above the knee.* It was an ocean of mullets and feathered hair.

We may not have been Amish, but we were probably the closest thing to Puritans these kids had ever seen.

We lined up to get our rental skates, taking it all in. Skates in hand, we hit the rink. I wasn't a great skater, but I could stay upright. Other kids were whizzing around—skating backward, forward, sideways, pulling off spins. One kid even jumped over one of his classmates, earning an immediate rebuke from the skating-rink safety monitor.

After a few wobbly laps, I gave up and made my way over to the arcade.

Skate Land had a solid lineup of games: *Zaxxon, Pac-Man, Tempest,* and *Donkey Kong.* I placed a quarter on the *Donkey Kong* cabinet, signaling I had next. The kid ahead of me was good. *Really* good. I was going to be waiting a while—which was fine.

The DJ announced that couple's skate was coming up soon and instructed everyone to "find that special boy or girl" to skate with. Yeah, that wasn't happening.

Finally, my turn. I pulled my quarter down from the cabinet and got to work. *Donkey Kong* wasn't a game I was good at. I could usually make it five or six screens in before it all fell apart. But today felt... different.

I cruised through the first couple of screens without losing a life

—er, *Mario*. I was definitely on track to top my personal high score.

Kids began gathering around the *Donkey Kong* cabinet. They could sense something special was happening. I breezed through the second iteration of the "pie factory" screen using my first life. I was locked in; the barrels seemed to move in slow motion. It felt like I could anticipate the fireballs' movements before they even appeared.

The game and I were one.

In the background, I heard murmurs—"all-time high score," even "kill screen." The *Donkey Kong* kill screen was the stuff of legend. Rumor had it that if you hit level 22, the game would glitch and end. Someone always knew a kid who knew a kid who *swore* they'd seen it happen once at an arcade in Oklahoma City or something.

I kept climbing, level after level. The surrounding crowd grew quiet, reverent even, as if I were putting for the win at Augusta National.

From the corner of my left eye—movement.

A girl pushed through the crowd gathered around me. She was trying to get my attention.

Marty, one of my classmates, shushed her, but she was persistent.

"Jesse... Jesse!"

I ignored her, laser-focused on my kill-screen quest.

She tugged at my sleeve, "Jesse, I have to talk to you."

First Mario down.

"What?" I asked, impatient during the brief pause between lives.

"Kari wants to skate with you," she said. "For couple's skate."

Wait—what?

She repeated herself.

"Kari wants to skate with you. The couple's skate is about to start."

Kari. The girl I'd had a crush on since the first day of school. We caught the same bus every morning—and would've ridden home together, too, if I hadn't always been in lock-up.

She was beautiful, stylish, and impossibly smart. It was an open secret that I liked her. Honestly, every boy in seventh grade did.

And she wanted to skate with *me*—the boy with the thick glasses, unfortunate hair, husky-boy jeans, crooked teeth, and Goodwill shirt. The boy so filled with self-loathing he would later cut his picture out of the seventh-grade yearbook.

I wasn't buying it. I'd seen too many sitcoms where the nerdy kid got tricked into thinking the popular girl liked him.

"Give me a break," I said. "I'm not falling for that."

"For real! I'm not making this up! She's waiting for you!"

Her voice was sincere, almost pleading. And this was one of the nicest girls in school—she wouldn't be part of a cruel prank.

I was torn and tried to stay composed as I navigated the increasingly difficult rivet level.

What to do?

The DJ's voice boomed over the speakers: "Clear the floor for couple's skate—couples only!"

Here I was on the verge of video-game immortality, inching closer and closer to the kill screen. I would be *the kid* some other kid heard about while talking to another kid.

Or I could go skate with Kari.

I stepped away from the *Donkey Kong* console. "Marty, take over," was all I said.

The crowd gasped in disbelief as I awkwardly rolled to the edge of the rink.

And there she was—Kari in her Normandy Rose jeans, a ruffly blouse buttoned to the neck, and a smile on her face.

A light seemed to glow around her. It was probably just the

reflection off the disco ball. But still.

Cautiously, I approached her as the opening notes of Journey's *Open Arms* played over the speakers.

She held out her hand. I took it, and we entered the rink.

For three minutes and twenty-one seconds, I was the envy of every seventh-grade boy at Bremerton Christian School. We skated, hand in hand, to Journey—the same Journey we'd been told were agents of the devil.

It was sublime.

The song ended. She smiled, thanked me, dropped my hand, and returned to her friends.

I drifted back to the arcade. *Donkey Kong* was empty. Marty stood nearby, defeated. "Sorry," he said. "I couldn't make it to the kill screen."

On the bus ride back to school, I learned Kari had skated with me "to be nice." She knew I had a crush on her and wanted to do something kind. Out of what, exactly—pity? Compassion? I didn't really care.

It was a sweet gesture from a nice girl. I appreciated it. Not in a romantic way — even then, I knew there was no universe in which she actually *liked* me. I appreciated it because it would've been so easy to be mean to me, or worse, to ignore me altogether.

She never did. Every morning at the bus stop, she'd ask how my night was. I'd tell her about music or the latest episode of *Knight Rider* until the bus came. Then she'd sit with her friends, and I'd sit alone—or with another awkward kid.

Seventh grade ended—mercifully. My only year at Bremerton Christian School was over. Eighth grade would mean another move, another new school.

I never saw Kari again.

You're probably thinking I think about her every time I hear *Open Arms*.

You'd be wrong.

Journey makes me think of that guest speaker who tried to scare a bunch of impressionable Christian-school kids. Of *Donkey Kong* and kill screens. Of my friend Mark and rental skates. And then, yes—of Kari. Because she was nice to me, and she asked me to skate to music that, apparently, was also playing in the devil's fiery underworld.

Sometimes that's enough to be remembered.

FOOLIN'

The summer of 1983 was, hands down, one of the best. I wasn't going back to Bremerton Christian School in the fall, and honestly, that was a relief. Instead, I was going to Fairview Junior High, the school my mom swore was overrun by pot smoking Blue Öyster Cultists. I was going to be the new kid again, but not really. Brian was attending Fairview, and not only surviving but absolutely thriving. This gave my mom hope that I too could navigate the Satanic halls of Fairview without being thrashed within an inch of my life by heavy metal vomit heads or lured into the dark, slithery, underworld of easy drugs and rock & roll.

Spending all of seventh grade away from the Tracyton kids also gave me the cover I needed to arrive at Fairview without the fake British accent. I could just claim to have lost it, now that I was a good and proper Yank, you know?

Return of the Jedi hit theaters in May and instantly became the movie of the summer. Brian, my brother, and I must have watched that movie at least five times, maybe more. We'd walk to the Redwood Plaza Theater for a matinee, then hit the arcade next door to watch Brian dominate Dragon's Lair. If we were lucky, our mom's gave us a couple of extra bucks to hit Pizza Hut. Back then it was a sitdown restaurant with red vinyl booths, plastic stained glass lamps at every table, and the iconic dark red textured soda glasses.

In July, the First Church youth group took a two-night camping trip to Lake Ozette. It had everything: capture the flag, campfire songs, and a long, winding hike through mossy forest to the coast.

The hike was one of my favorite memories. Sunlight lit up the moss-covered trees, turning the woods into our own forest moon of Endor. The trail ended at the beach, where we explored tide pools and scrambled over rocks.

Lunch, though, was unforgettable for other reasons.

My brother and I were on sandwich duty. The menu? Egg salad. We had never seen egg salad before. Our mom didn't believe in sandwiches. She said they were made by White moms who didn't love their kids. We got burritos or empanadas, caldo or menudo in our thermoses. While other kids had PB&J and Capri Sun, I was picking out cow tripe. Sometimes I'd trade an apple empanada for a Wonder Bread and peanut butter sandwich, thinking I won. I didn't. Her empanadas were amazing, but kids are dumb. Or at least I was.

Back to the egg salad. We had no clue how much to use. Some sandwiches barely had any, others oozed globs from the sides. It was hot, and a few adults questioned whether egg salad was even a good idea. But the youth pastor's wife had made it, so we were stuck.

By lunchtime, complaints were loud and immediate. Some sandwiches were mush, others were dry. Most ended up in the Pacific. A few kids powered through, knowing dinner was hours and miles away. It's a miracle nobody got food poisoning.

Overall, that camping trip with the youth group remains one of my favorite memories. Returning home, I expected the regular long list of chores my dad created for us so we wouldn't be "bored". But something felt off. My parents were acting weird —tense, distracted. I didn't know what was coming, but deep down I knew it wasn't good.

A couple of days later, late morning, I was still in bed—it was summer, after all—when I heard it: the roar of chainsaws and the low rumble of heavy machinery. It was coming from the woods behind our house. I threw on clothes and followed the noise.

What I saw stopped me cold.

The woods behind our house—the woods where I thought Bigfoot roamed—were being cleared with ruthless efficiency. A huge swath of trees was already gone, bulldozed into a giant tangle of stumps and branches. The air, normally filled with the scent of pine and cedar, was now heavy with the smell of diesel exhaust and smoke from the piles of branches that were smoldering like funeral pyres.

I ran back to the house and asked my dad what was going on, but his answers were vague.

I kept pressing. Finally, over a dinner of Banquet fried chicken and mashed potatoes, he broke the news: the landlord had sold the property to a developer. The trees were being cleared to make way for a new shopping center. Our house was next. We had thirty days to move out.

What we didn't know—me, my brother, my sister—was that our parents had already been looking for a house. In fact, they'd already started the buying process. That explained the tension, the short tempers, and all those late-night whispers behind closed doors.

A few days later, they piled us into the station wagon and drove us out to see our new place.

It didn't take long to realize we were moving *out* of Bremerton.

We drove down Wheaton Way, through the fading downtown corridor, past the shipyard, around the bend on Highway 16 through the still unfortunately named town of Gorst, and into Port Orchard.

The new house sat near the top of Mile Hill Drive, bordered by a small patch of woods in back and an empty field beside it. Unlike the Bremerton house, we'd have neighbors—but they were a hundred yards away on either side. The house itself was small: three tiny bedrooms and one bathroom. But it sat on nearly two acres, dotted with apple trees and one massive walnut tree that would later become the bane of my existence.

During the drive, the reality sank in—I wouldn't be attending Fairview with Brian in the fall.

Now I was really going to be the new kid again, in a new town, in a new house.

To top it off, I'd have to share one of those tiny bedrooms with my brother.

"We'll keep going to First Church for now," my mom said, "but I'm looking for something closer."

Fantastic. New everything.

The rest of that summer blurred into a rush of packing—not just boxes, but time. I was determined to squeeze in as much as possible with Brian. We played endless video games, hit the movies, and even hitchhiked to downtown Bremerton once... and lived to talk about it.

In the early '80s, everyone knew hitchhiking meant you were probably going to end up dead. We'd missed the bus and really wanted to get to *Buy, Sell & Trade,* the record shop that always smelled like weed and incense. All caution tossed aside, up went our thumbs—and a nice couple let us ride in the back of their pickup into downtown.

That summer felt endless, loud, and alive. Maybe that's why it's so vivid in my memory—like God was giving me one last highlight-reel summer in Bummertown before everything changed again.

When moving day arrived, the woods behind our house were gone—reduced to giant piles of broken limbs, stumps, and underbrush that looked like funeral pyres. I stood outside the garage, staring at what used to be a solid wall of trees. I remembered standing in that same spot three years earlier, certain Bigfoot was watching us move in.

Now it was just an empty lot.

Our house looked lonely and exposed—sad, even—the way houses do once they've been emptied out.

We'd only lived there three years, but it felt longer. Maybe because it was the longest I'd ever lived anywhere. The move from Texas had been hard, as was attending four different schools in under three years. Inside those walls, I'd found comfort. Refuge. It was where I buried my head in comics, trading cards, and music. Where I sat on the living room floor with my headphones on, listening to The Beatles, wishing I was anywhere but there—anyone but me.

Now, as we were leaving, I wished I'd appreciated it more.

The slam of the moving truck's door jolted me back to the present. My dad climbed into the driver's seat. The rest of us piled into the station wagon.

Another house. Another town. Another adventure as the new kid at a school I hadn't asked for.

By late summer, life in Port Orchard had started to take shape. Unpacking gave way to exploring the neighborhood, and a narrow trail in the woods behind our house led straight to a small strip mall with a grocery store, a Ben Franklin, and a tiny pharmacy. I ended up spending a lot of time at the pharmacy—not for candy or comic books, but for its surprisingly eclectic magazine section.

That's where I found *Star Hits*, the U.S. version of the U.K. magazine *Smash Hits.* This discovery cracked open an entirely new world of pop music for me. *Star Hits* featured bands ignored by mainstream American magazines.

Rolling Stone—run by boomers—was stuck in the past, endlessly recycling stories about the Stones, The Who, and Eric Clapton. Every now and then they'd try to seem relevant by throwing Talking Heads on the cover, but even in 1983, *Rolling Stone* felt like a tired, out-of-touch, second-rate rag.

Other magazines like *Creem* and *Kerrang!* were wall-to-wall stories about Mötley Crüe, Quiet Riot, and Iron Maiden. I wasn't a metalhead, so they didn't do much for me. *Smash Hits*, and by extension *Star Hits*, were something else entirely. Through them I discovered The Cure, New Order, Bananarama, Depeche Mode, Adam Ant, and The Smiths. There were also longform features on Duran Duran, Culture Club, and The Police—usually with glossy fold-out posters I'd carefully tear out and tape to my walls.

The pharmacy staff didn't always stay on top of rotating old issues, so on my first visit I scored three months' worth of *Star Hits*. I buried my head in those pages during the days leading up to the new school year.

Sharing a room with my brother was strange; we were in different phases of adolescence. At thirteen, I still loved *Star Wars*, but my toys were boxed up. My brother had moved on to G.I. Joe. Our room became a mash-up of those two worlds—his action figures lined the shelves, while my freshly torn-out *Star Hits* posters of Duran Duran, Billy Idol, and Culture Club decorated the walls.

My dad set up his reel-to-reel system in the basement, which could only be accessed from outside. It wasn't as creepy as the cavernous basement in Bremerton, but it was still a basement. He spent hours down there working on home-improvement projects, the thunder of Zeppelin and Sabbath rumbling up through the heating vents.

Thankfully, my dad found a receiver and a pair of cheap speakers at Goodwill, so I was able to set up a small system of my own in our room.

Then came the first day of school.

My mom pulled into the drop-off loop while I sat in the passenger seat watching kids shuffle through the doors. It seemed like every other boy was wearing a black Mötley Crüe or Iron Maiden concert tee. Some of the girls were too.

I took a deep breath, opened the car door, and stepped out into the fray.

If my mom thought Fairview was bad because she'd once seen a kid wearing a Blue Öyster Cult shirt, then the front doors of Marcus Whitman looked like a direct portal to hell. Yet she remained relatively calm.

As the new kid, I started the day like all new kids do—checking in at the front office, picking up my schedule, and getting assigned a homeroom. Paperwork in hand, I navigated the chaotic halls of Marcus Whitman Junior High. Lockers slammed. Kids shouted greetings. I kept my head down and followed the numbers.

Second deep breath of the day.

I stepped into the room and immediately second-guessed myself. Had I walked into the wrong class? The woman at the front looked barely older than we were. She smiled and welcomed me. This was Ms. Jill Gross.

Her classroom was unlike any I'd ever seen. No portraits of presidents. No inspirational quotes. Instead, it was a shrine to pop music. Posters of Culture Club, Billy Idol, The Romantics, and Thomas Dolby covered the walls. It looked more like a record store than a homeroom. It was awesome.

I found an empty seat next to two harmless-looking kids named Doug and Greg. Well—Doug was harmless-looking. Greg had curly blond hair that fell well below his collar. He definitely would have earned a detention slip back at Bremerton Christian School.

Behind me sat Jason and Eric. The room buzzed with chatter. When the bell rang, Ms. Gross introduced herself with bright, contagious energy. She was young, maybe early twenties, and unapologetically into pop. Every poster, she told us, came from Tower Records in Seattle. No, she wouldn't be playing The Police during attendance.

Then came the dreaded introductions. You'd think I'd have had a go-to speech by now, but I didn't. I stood, mumbled my name, got a few polite nods, and sat back down. Honestly, that counted as a win.

The bell rang again. We spilled back into the noisy hallways, trying to find our next classes.

Lunch was its own kind of anxiety. No classroom sanctuary here —just the full cafeteria experience. I stood in the hot-lunch line, scanning for an empty table, already resigning myself to eat alone like the sad-sack kid in Rush's *Subdivisions* video.

Lunch tray in hand—square pizza, fries, carrot sticks, chocolate milk (my standard order for the next nine months)—I walked toward the commons. No empty tables. *Shit.* I weaved through the maze of tables, careful not to bump anyone. Unfamiliar faces glanced up, then turned back to their friends.

I drifted to the outer rim of the commons galaxy. There, in a back corner, sat Greg, Jason, Doug, and Eric from homeroom. Third deep breath of the day.

I approached and took a seat. It was that easy. Intros were exchanged again, conversation restarted—mostly about music.

Doug was a huge Beatles fan. We compared favorite albums. His was *Let It Be,* which I didn't own. He brought me a dubbed copy on cassette the next day. Doug was also Mormon—a detail that may seem random now, but will matter later.

Jason was a dungeon master obsessed with Malcolm McLaren's "Buffalo Gals." He was looking to recruit new adventurers for his Dungeons & Dragons campaign. I hesitated. D&D had become a target during the great Satanic Panic—accused of promoting witchcraft, demons, and other questionable habits like drinking gallons of Mountain Dew, eating your body weight in Funyuns, and never talking to girls.

What the hell, I thought.

"Sure, I'll join your campaign," I said. I had no idea what I was getting into.

Eric was quiet, with a dry sense of humor and a unique sense of fashion—dress shirts tucked into parachute pants. He loved Hall

& Oates so much that when he saw them live with his dad, he stuffed cotton in his ears "so I could better hear the words." He also liked Billy Joel and drew a comic strip about a machine-gun-toting sheep named *Basil.* That was...different. He'd be joining Jason's D&D campaign too. I didn't know it that day, but Eric would become my best friend for the next forty years.

Greg was the wild card. His hair was longer than any of ours, and he was wearing a ¾-sleeve Def Leppard *Pyromania* tour shirt —white torso, black sleeves, the album cover silkscreened on front, tour dates on back. Those shirts were *the* thing in the early eighties. Greg's looked brand-new, as it should have: Def Leppard had played the Seattle Center Coliseum on August 27, 1983, just a week before school started.

This lunch crew would remain intact through a majority of the school year, only being broken up when Eric came down with a nasty case of mono that winter. He spent a majority of the second semester being home schooled as he recovered. Still, the friendships and music conversations had staying power.

That fall, a new kind of language took hold. It had started over the summer—July 29th, to be exact—when *Friday Night Videos* debuted on NBC. That ninety-minute block of time would change how we talked about music for years to come.

Before that, my only exposure to music videos came in fleeting clips on *Solid Gold* or *American Bandstand.* That was it. We didn't have cable, so I couldn't even watch *Night Tracks* on TBS. MTV was still several months away from reaching our area. I was living in a music-video desert—until *Friday Night Videos* came along.

And it was seismic. I can't overstate its impact, not just on me, but on pop culture at a granular level. We'd heard songs like "Every Breath You Take," "Sweet Dreams (Are Made of This)," and "I'll Tumble for Ya" in our little corner of the world, but seeing them was something else entirely.

Music suddenly gained a new dimension.

Rock stars moved beyond glossy promo shots for *Rolling Stone*, *Smash Hits*, or *Hit Parader*. Now we got to see their stage personas—and sometimes, glimpses of who they really were. Suddenly, conversations about music had to include discussions about the accompanying videos.

On September 30th, 1983, *Friday Night Videos* aired Def Leppard's video for "Foolin'." Def Leppard wasn't getting airplay on the stations I listened to, but they were savvy enough to realize the power of music videos to expand their reach beyond FM AOR radio. I'd already discovered them earlier that summer through the videos for "Photograph" and "Rock of Ages."

Their videos were low-budget affairs—usually just the band on a soundstage, flanked by lights and punctuated with pyrotechnics—but they worked. Especially "Photograph." Still feeling the aftershocks of the Satanic-panic chapel presentation, I watched it with a wary eye. No scarab beetles, no skulls, no inverted crosses. So far, so good.

I did, however, feel some trepidation about "Rock of Ages." We'd discussed 1 Corinthians 10:4 in youth group that summer: *"And all drank the same spiritual drink. For they drank from the spiritual Rock that followed them, and the Rock was Christ."* In short, Jesus is the Rock of all ages.

The video opens with the members of Def Leppard dressed as druids—because why not? Then there's an owl. A druid plays chess with a woman. The woman ends up tied to a tree. Then guitarist Phil Collen shakes his ass at the camera. And that's just the first thirty seconds.

Eventually, lead singer Joe Elliott rescues the woman with an oversized cardboard sword that looks stolen from a Shakespeare-in-the-Park prop closet. And the overpowering majesty of rock provides the soundtrack to it all. "Rock of Ages," indeed.

Def Leppard were labeled a *heavy metal* band, but to me, they never fit that mold. I considered them—and still do—a *hard rock* band. A very, very good one. Their songs had hooks and melody. Some lyrics veered into boneheaded, misogynistic territory, sure, but others hinted at genuine vulnerability.

By 1983, metal bands were starting to adopt glam's trappings—think Mötley Crüe with their leather, studs, makeup, and teased hair. The guys in Def Leppard looked more like the dudes at Skate Land. Joe Elliott may have worn leather pants, but he also wore leg warmers. He had style that went beyond the leathered-up faux-tough-guy act popularized by Vince Neil and Rob Halford.

I became a bona fide Def Leppard fan on September 30th, 1983—the night *Friday Night Videos* aired "Foolin'."

That video looks like it was filmed on the same soundstage as every other Def Leppard video, with some subtle differences. This time, Joe Elliott is chained to a giant neon triangle instead of a tree. No druids. No owls. Drummer Rick Allen wears nothing but a pair of Union Jack dolphin shorts. Three members sport white jeans, except bassist Rick "Sav" Savage, who goes for red. Joe Elliott's pants reach his armpits, and his tissue-thin tank top reads *Le Club.* There are flames, there are giant skulls, and none of it makes a lick of sense.

But the song—*the song*—rules. "Foolin'" is a masterclass in early-'80s hard rock. It opens softly, Steve Clark on acoustic guitar as Joe Elliott plaintively sings, "Lady luck never smiles." The verse gains momentum, then crashes into the chorus like a sonic tidal wave. Everyone remembers the stuttering hook —*fa-fa-fa-foolin'*—but it only works because of the quiet-loud-louder-quiet structure Mutt Lange built into it. His production elevated *Pyromania* into something transcendent.

The following Monday, "Foolin'" dominated lunchroom conversation. Eric hated it, calling the chorus "stupid" and the video a "low-budget train wreck." Jason was ambivalent; his tastes were already shifting toward the Dead Kennedys, Black Flag, and, of course, Malcolm McLaren's "Buffalo Gals." Doug liked "Foolin'" but stayed neutral on Def Leppard. Greg, however, was all in. He reminded us—repeatedly—that he'd been a fan since *On Through the Night*, had seen them live that summer, and had the concert shirt to prove it.

The Great Def Leppard Debate raged all week. I dug in, passionately defending their hooks and melodies. Okay, what I actually said was, "Def Leppard songs rock—and they're catchy!" Not my most nuanced argument, but it worked for Greg. He backed me up, though he insisted they were metal. I held firm. They were hard rock. We agreed to disagree.

Looking back, those debates didn't matter nearly as much as what was forming underneath them. In that noisy lunchroom, over trays of square pizza, fries, and chocolate milk, the seeds of friendship were planted—friendships that would span decades.

It's funny how quickly that kind of connection can take root. One shared cassette. A quick joke about D&D. An argument about a music video. And suddenly, you're part of something. I found my people at that lunch table. We had no idea then, but those small moments were the start of something lasting—through good times, heartbreaks, even tragedy.

I could've sat at any other table that day. Or eaten alone on the stairs. But I didn't. I chose the table that led to lifelong friends.

IS THERE SOMETHING I SHOULD KNOW?

In January of 1984, a nasty case of strep throat landed me in the hospital for an emergency tonsillectomy. My mom cried as I was wheeled away for surgery, loudly praying that I'd wake up from the anesthesia, which wasn't exactly comforting. My dad stood stoically next to her as she wailed. It was quite the scene.

Everything I knew about tonsillectomies came from TV—mainly *The Brady Bunch.* I thought recovery meant lounging in bed, eating ice cream, and not talking for a few days. In reality, it was two weeks of blinding pain radiating from my throat up into my ears and a neck so swollen that sipping water felt like swallowing glass. The *Brady Bunch* tonsillectomy narrative was bullshit. I spent those first two weeks in a Percocet haze, living on Jell-O and generic vanilla ice cream—the only things I could get past the stitches without blacking out.

A few days into recovery, a miracle happened: my dad broke down and got us cable. MTV arrived like a beam of light through the murky pain fog.

Watching hours of MTV can really mess with your self-esteem when you're a fourteen-year-old kid that owns a total of three shirts, two pairs of jeans, one too many pairs of double-knit action slacks left over from your Christian school days.

The endless parade of charismatic and stylish male singers left a mark. Sting, with his intense stare, ethereal presence, and blonde locks, brooded at me from our nineteen-inch TV. David Bowie, always immaculate in tailored suits and bold colors, was pure sophistication. Billy Idol blended punk swagger with pop accessibility, topped off by that signature sneer.

But no one made me feel dumpier than Simon LeBon of Duran Duran. He had it all—moody good looks, carefully tousled hair, a sharp jawline, and that New Romantic flair that made him look like he lived permanently on a yacht. Christ, all the guys in Duran Duran were impossibly good-looking.

Duran Duran's videos were like nothing I'd ever seen. Shot in exotic locales and directed by talents like Russell Mulcahy and Godley & Creme, they were cinematic, narrative-driven, and ridiculously stylish. The songs were already great, but the videos elevated them to another level. Duran Duran were made for MTV —and MTV, in turn, launched them into the stratosphere.

It was a lot to take in.

Now, one positive feature of having your tonsils removed is weight loss. Since I literally couldn't eat anything firmer than yogurt until the incisions healed, I was noticeably less lumpy after a week. By the end of week two, I was downright svelte. My shirts weren't quite as snug. My pants fit looser. Even my face, usually puffed out behind metal framed, sad photo-grey lensed glasses, had hollowed a bit.

I returned to school with a tragically fresh haircut, courtesy of my mom, where the sides and bangs were lopsided and every cowlick was accentuated. My friends noticed the weed-whacker hairdo, then the weight loss. Ms. Gross said I looked "healthier." Doug asked what happened to the rest of me.

Eric was still out with mono, but Greg welcomed me back by proudly showing off a full-page Kahlúa ad taped to his Pee-Chee. During the two weeks I was gone, he'd developed a taste for Kahlúa and milk, courtesy of a bottle his older brother procured for him. Several months later, we'd learn the hard way that you had to drink a gallon of the stuff to even get within shouting distance of being drunk.

My last class that trimester was choir. Greg was in it too, which surprised me—he didn't exactly scream "choirboy." He had way too many Def Leppard and Iron Maiden t-shirts.

One afternoon, while Mr. Allen, our late and beloved choir teacher, worked with the sopranos, Greg and I got into a heated argument about Culture Club. Greg insisted they were a reggae band. I vehemently disagreed. Culture Club was pop with a touch of blue-eyed soul. He doubled down, and I reminded him he'd also thought Quiet Riot's song "Metal Health (Bang Your Head)" was called "Mental Health (Bang Your Head)." He swore the song was a literal cry for therapeutic intervention, not a play on words.

Things escalated. There was a shove, the volume of our voices rose. I soon found myself in a screaming match in the middle of the choir room over Culture Club and Quiet Riot as the sopranos were trying to work on their section of *Ave Verum*.

Just as Greg dropped into a karate stance, I felt a beefy hand on the back of my neck. Mr. Allen yanked me back and then grabbed Greg by the collar. He tossed us into two separate practice rooms to cool off.

We stayed in lockdown until class ended.

When the bell rang to end the school day, Mr. Allen dragged me and Greg out of solitary confinement. He wanted to know what we had been arguing about.

I started to explain, but halfway through I lost it. "It was about Culture Club," I said, trying not to laugh. Greg started snickering, too. When I got to the part about *Metal Health* versus *Mental Health,* we both burst out laughing. Mr. Allen did not.

When we finally pulled ourselves together, he said, "If either of you pull something like that in class again, you'll both fail the trimester. No exceptions."

And that was that.

After school, we hit the record section of the small drug store where I bought my music magazines. I yanked the Quiet Riot album from the bin, pointed to the track list—"Metal Health (Bang Your Head)" in big, bold letters—and waited for the apology.

Greg scoffed. "Typo."

He then insisted that the record company had obviously shipped that misprinted copy to the drugstore, hoping no one would notice. Or, that the drug store had created a bootleg version of the record.

In his mind, it was easier to believe that the executive team running CBS Records shipped misprints to a strip mall drug store in Port Orchard, or that the pharmacist was churning out bootleg heavy metal records in between filling prescriptions of antibiotics, than admit he was wrong.

The next day in choir, a girl approached me. A cute girl. A *popular* girl. She wanted to know what the argument with Greg was about the day before. A quick rundown later, and we were in a deep conversation about pop music. When I told her I didn't own any Culture Club records, she promised to let me borrow *Colour By Numbers*.

"You'll love the song 'Victims,'" she said. She was right.

This girl was a huge Duran Duran fan, a true Duranimal. Her jean jacket was covered with Duran Duran buttons, and her Pee-Chee was plastered with photos of the band. I pointed at one and said, "Hey, that's from *Star Hits*! I've got that issue too!"

Just like that, we were friends.

We talked every day in choir. Then one day she asked if I wanted to go see *Footloose*—like, as a date. I may have blacked out for a moment, but managed to finally get out, "Yeah...of course. I'll pick you up Saturday."

That afternoon, as Greg and I walked home, I told him everything. He let me borrow his jean jacket so I'd "look kinda cool." It smelled like incense and stale pot smoke. But whatever —it *was* cool.

My mom had to drive us in our blue Ford Fairmont wagon with the dead stereo, so I brought along a clunky thrift-store FM radio to fill the silence and prevent her from launching into stories about me or all the different times she saw Satan. My date looked impossibly cool in that "effortless eighth grader" way. Bench seats and nonexistent seatbelt laws meant we sat shoulder-to-shoulder both ways. We saw the movie, wandered around downtown Bremerton after, hit Peaches Records & Tapes and the drugstore soda fountain, and by the time my mom picked us up, I was floating.

A few days later, she came over to my house to hang out and listen to music. We sat on my bedroom floor while the radio played. At one point, as Sting sang about a dead salmon in a frozen waterfall, she leaned in and kissed me.

For three glorious weeks, we talked on the phone at night and passed notes in the halls—her loops and hearts versus my serial-killer block letters. I couldn't believe it: a real, live, popular Duran Duran fan liked me. Me. The kid with the uneven haircut, three shirts, and glasses that could pick up distant radio stations.

And then came the afternoon everything shifted.

We met up at the South Kitsap Mall for what would turn out to be our last date. We hit Mr. C's arcade, where I played Dig Dug and she annihilated some vector-graphics game I can't remember the name of. She looked calm and confident, completely in her element.

Her friends appeared out of nowhere, and I felt a change in the air. Not anything dramatic—just the subtle sense that I was suddenly holding a smaller piece of her attention than I had the day before. They closed in with the effortless confidence of kids who already knew their place in the eighth-grade social hierarchy.

And I… did not.

She shifted a half-step toward them without even thinking about it, and I felt myself fading to the edge of the frame. They formed an instant orbit around her, and I felt something shift. Her voice got brighter, her laugh more performative. I tried to join in, even offered one of her friends a few of my quarters and suggested she try Punch-Out. I reached into my pocket, and that's when she saw them.

My shoes.

"Oh my god," she said, staring at my feet. "Are those Velcro shoes? Don't you know how to tie your shoes?"

Her friends burst out laughing.

I yanked my hand back, fist clenched without thinking, and turned my pocket inside out. Quarters spilled onto the sticky arcade carpet like the world's saddest slot machine payout.

By the time I gathered up my pile of quarters, the moment had moved on. She wasn't cold or dismissive, just... distracted and pulled back into the gravity of her group.

"Hey," I said, trying to sound normal. "My mom's picking us up outside Godfather's in a few minutes."

She hesitated, eyes flicking toward her friends. "I think I'm just going to ride home with them, okay?"

It wasn't. But I said, "Yeah. Sure."

She wasn't trying to hurt me. She was just a kid caught between two worlds inside a mall arcade. Still, it stung.

I stood on the sidewalk outside Godfather's with the bulge of about four dollars worth of quarters in my pocket. They suddenly felt very heavy. My mom pulled up, took one look at me climbing into the Fairmont alone, and knew something was wrong. I told her it was no big deal. It absolutely was.

A day or two later, the official breakup arrived in the form of a neatly folded note dropped in my lap during choir—my name on the front in her perfect handwriting, no hearts, no flourishes:

"This has been bothering me all weekend, but this is not

working out. We should just be friends."

And with that, I was banished to the shadow realm.

I took it about as well as any fourteen-year-old kid who flew a little too close to the cool-girl sun. I was devastated. The next few days passed in a blur of self-pity and the kind of intense introspection and self-loathing that would have made Morrissey cringe.

In the wake of my emotional annihilation, I drifted between school and my bedroom like a low-budget Dickensian ghost. I came downstairs only when my mom forced me to eat. I had no appetite. When I wasn't sleeping, I replayed our month-long romance like it was the Zapruder film, hunting for clues.

Every time, I wound up back at Mr. C's arcade, the quarters spilling out onto the floor—back, and to the left... back, and to the left. Her friends hadn't approved of me — my clothes, my hair, my face. If I wanted her back, I decided, I'd have to change all of it.

The end-of-year dance was only a couple weeks away. That would be my moment — not just to win her back, but to win over her friends, too. All I needed was... everything I didn't currently have.

So I turned to MTV. Specifically, Duran Duran videos. She was obsessed with them, so obviously I needed to become them. Whenever a Duran Duran video came on, I studied their wardrobes and took notes like I was prepping for the bar exam. I needed skinny ties, fitted shirts, leather pants, stylish shoes, a haircut from an actual stylist, and — if this full-body reinvention was going to work — contact lenses.

List in hand, I presented my case to my parents over dinner.

My dad was skeptical and brutally honest. "She didn't dump you because of your clothes," he said. "She just doesn't like you anymore."

Thanks, Dad.

My mom balked at paying for a proper haircut, insisting she could fix the very hair she'd been butchering for years. Then came her verdict on contact lenses: "They're too expensive. And contacts are cosmetic, not medical…insurance won't cover them."

Yes, Mom. *Cosmetic.* That's exactly the point. Sigh.

We *could*, however, shop for new clothes. My dad handed me a modest budget to assemble a "dance outfit."

My mom and I had done this once before—the infamous talent show ensemble. But this time, we weren't going for Tony Manero or the Brothers Gibb. No, I was aiming for Bryan Ferry and John Taylor: sleek, stylish, vaguely British, maybe even slightly moody. There was only one store that could even pretend to deliver that: Jay Jacobs in downtown Bremerton.

Jay Jacobs was the Seattle area's mecca for anything remotely cool or hip in the early-to-mid 1980s.

Not so cool or hip? Going there *with your mom*, who happily announced our tight budget before we were even fully through the door.

The moment we stepped inside, I was hit with sensory overload. Everything was bright and mirrored—absolutely the last environment I wanted to encounter my own reflection in. Part of me wanted to bolt across the street and hide in the husky-boy section of J.C. Penney, but I was a man on a mission.

A cheerful Jay Jacobs employee approached and asked what I was looking for.

I told her. *All of it.* I over-explained in excruciating detail. She listened patiently, nodding. Her eyes may have glazed over the third time I emphasized that I needed to look like I was in Duran Duran.

When my sad-sack soliloquy finally ended, she gave me a sympathetic smile, turned, and motioned for me to follow.

She helped me pick out clothes for the next several minutes. I pointed to a mannequin that was decked out in a sleek sleeveless maroon shirt that were tucked into a pair of white tight-fitting jeans. "That's what I'm going for," I said, nodding my head up and down as I admired the slim silohuette of the mannequin.

The salesperson pursed her lips, then smiled and said, "I think you'll be happier with fuller fitting clothes." Translation: she didn't want me looking like Philip Seymour Hoffman squeezing into that "imported Italian nylon" shirt in *Boogie Nights*.

She picked out a black-and-white zippered polo that was collarless and the appropriate amount of billowy for my frame. It kind of looked like a baggy football referee jersey than something Simon LeBon would wear, but the price was right and that was all my mom needed to hear.

Now, for the pants. What I wanted were leather pants, like the ones John Taylor wore in "The Reflex" video. Our budget did not allow for actual leather pants, but Jay Jacobs carried faux ones. They were nothing more than a polyurethane shell glued over a cotton and polyester lining. When I tried them on, the salesperson said, "You've got enough meat on your bones to make them look good."

I'm still not sure if that was a compliment.

The pants may have been budget friendly, but not cheap enough to leave room for shoes. I'd have to wear my old black dress shoes, a size too small. I'd make them work.

Mission... somewhat accomplished.

That school week crawled. I tried to make small talk with her in choir, but it went nowhere. Of course it didn't. I was still the old me.

Friday finally arrived. The dance ran from six to eight. I walked home with Greg, who planned to skip it. Eric wasn't going either, but Doug would be there with his posse of Mormon friends.

I was too nervous to eat dinner, so I went upstairs, laid out my clothes, and prepared to blow her mind with my makeover. After a shower, I tried to tame my bushy Mexi-fro with mousse. That went poorly. All it did was mat my hair into a sticky, stiff mess.

I may or may not have practiced a few ice-breaker lines in the mirror, too. "Oh, these pants? Yeah, they *are* cool. Jay Jacobs in Bremerton. Maybe we should, uh…check it out sometime."

Even as I said it, I knew nobody in recorded human history had ever swooned over someone in polyurethane pants and a ref-shirt polo, but I was committed.

When it was time to go, my dad took one look at my "dance outfit," gave me a tight-lipped smile, and went back to his paper. My brother laughed and said my clothes were stupid. I fired back that his G.I. Joes were stupid. Little did I know he was less than four months from becoming one of the most popular kids at Marcus Whitman.

I was silent on the ride to the school, trying to get my game face on. My mom pulled up to the main entrance. A group of kids I vaguely knew were hanging outside in regular school clothes. She shook her head in disbelief at how sloppy and slovenly the boys looked in their black concert tees and jeans.

"You're dressed for a dance. They aren't."

I got out and walked to the door.

I'd love to say that when I stepped into the commons, the whole room stopped, the DJ dropped the needle on "Sharp Dressed Man," and a perfectly choreographed dance routine broke out, ending with me sweeping her off her feet.

None of that happened.

I walked through the commons, scanning for her in my fake leather pants. I heard snickers as I passed, and one of the metal burnouts in a faded April Wine shirt called me a "fag." I ignored him. (I had to, he was like seventeen and still in ninth grade, practically a grown man.)

Then I spotted her.

She and her friends were dancing to Wham!'s "Wake Me Up

Before You Go-Go," all bright colors and bigger smiles than I could compete with. I gathered every shred of confidence I had and started toward her. Her back was turned, but one of her friends noticed me approaching. She burst into laughter—loud, delighted, and unfortunately contagious. Another girl gave me a look that was mostly disgust with just enough pity to keep it from registering as full-on cartoon-villain cruelty.

She turned around.

Her brow furrowed as she looked me up and down. She put a hand to her chin, tilted her head, and her eyes traveled upward as if she was trying to understand what, exactly, she was looking at. Our eyes met for half a second. She smiled—polite, strained—and then turned her back and walked off with her friends.

She wasn't being mean, she was just caught off guard in that eighth-grade way where you don't know how to react, so you retreat to the safest place: your friends. Plus, she probably needed space to process the felony level fashion crime I was actively committing in that get-up of mine.

I was left standing in the middle of the commons as George Michael's voice boomed over the PA. I'm not sure exactly what I felt in that moment. Humiliated, for sure. Heartbroken, obviously. But mostly, I felt defeated.

My dad was right. She didn't dump me because of my clothes. She dumped me because she didn't like me anymore. And all the fake leather pants in the world weren't going to change that.

"Rock You Like a Hurricane" exploded through the speakers, and the New Wave girls scattered while the dance floor filled with vaguely terrifying denim-clad rocker chicks.

I slunk over to where Doug was hanging out with his Mormon gang. They were too polite to laugh. Instead, they quietly dispersed, leaving me alone with Doug.

"You tried," he said, patting my shoulder.

I wanted to cry, but I knew if I did, an already nightmarish evening would descend into full Biblical hellishness. Plus, there is no dignity in crying while clad in fake leather pants. None.

I walked out the front doors and headed home. It was a warm night, and those pants were basically a personal wearable sauna. Rivulets of sweat ran down my legs before I was even halfway to my house. Even though it was getting dark, I cut through the woods wherever I could just to avoid being seen in my ridiculous outfit.

Honestly, at that point I didn't care if a werewolf, a pervert, or Bigfoot himself jumped out from behind a tree and attacked me. It would've been a mercy killing.

When I got home, the back door was locked. I knocked, and my mom opened it. She started to say something about me being early, but one look at me—sweaty, wilted, five pounds lighter from dehydration, visibly defeated—told her everything she needed to know.

I tried not to cry as I walked past my dad at the dining room table. He stood and put his arms around me, and all the heartache and humiliation I'd been holding in just...poured out as he patted the top of my head with one of his rough, leathery hands.

When it was over, I went upstairs, peeled off my dance clothes, tossed them in the back of my closet like evidence from a crime scene, and crawled into bed.

Looking back, I know this whole thing wasn't really about her, or the dance, or even the ridiculous fake leather pants that had me sweating like a wrestler trying to make weight. It wasn't as extreme as the fake British accent, but it came from the same place. I thought if I dressed a certain way, acted a certain way, looked a certain way—maybe I'd finally be enough. Whatever flaws I had weren't going to be fixed by a budget wardrobe upgrade and polymer-based hair product.

Those desperate makeovers never really work. And I'm reminded of that every time Duran Duran's "Is There Something

I Should Know?" comes on. I turn the volume up and listen, half-smiling, half-wincing at the memory of those polyurethane pants and that goofy referee-looking zip-up polo.

Somewhere in a parallel universe, there's another version of me still chasing someone else's idea of cool. In this one, thirty-five years later, she and I met for beers. We laughed about the fake leather pants for maybe five seconds, then talked about our actual grown-up lives. Turns out neither of us stayed trapped in eighth grade.

And I still love Duran Duran.

WHEN DOVES CRY

On May 16, 1984, Prince released "When Doves Cry" as the first single from his upcoming *Purple Rain* album. I remember hearing it on the radio and being immediately drawn in by the song's unconventional structure. The production was stark and minimalist, no bass line, no warmth. It was just that relentless drum machine and stabbing synths after a wild guitar intro. It almost sounded like a demo.

There were wild, completely unfounded rumors that Prince had lifted the song's opening guitar solo from Jimi Hendrix. This infuriated my buddy Greg, who was a die-hard Hendrix fan and took any comparison as blasphemy.

From what I've gathered, this Prince/Hendrix rumor was a uniquely Pacific Northwest phenomenon — possibly cooked up by a DJ at KZOK, Seattle's classic rock station. Jimi Hendrix being a local hero probably fueled the completely unfounded rumor.

But I digress.

Prince's voice then cuts through the rhythm, raw, emotive, and haunting. His vocals sounded despondent, heartbroken even, which was perfect for me because I had, of course, just been unceremoniously dumped. And I wasn't taking it well.

At fourteen, everything feels like the end of the world even when it obviously isn't. I didn't have the emotional experience or vocabulary for it then. I just knew the song matched my mood perfectly. And that the skin on my legs was still irritated from the chemicals in the fake leather pants.

How can you just leave me standing, alone in a world that's so cold?

Indeed.

The video for "When Doves Cry" worked as a long-form trailer for Prince's much-rumored biopic *Purple Rain*. Clips from the film were spliced between shots of Prince crawling out of a bathtub and staring pensively into a mirror. The video also introduced his new band, The Revolution.

The song and video moved Prince squarely in the middle of the pop music universe.

"When Doves Cry" wasn't my first exposure to Prince, I discovered his music on Friday Night Videos way back in the summer of 1983.

I can still hear the host's intro: "Here's a 24-year-old who writes, produces, and plays most of the instruments on his albums. It's Prince with "1999.""

At first, what grabbed me wasn't even Prince — it was Jill Jones and Lisa Coleman on keyboards, laying down that iconic opening riff. To thirteen-year-old me, Jill Jones was the foxiest woman alive. Each member of the band had their own unmistakable style: Dez Dickerson with his rising-sun headband and Vox Explorer guitar, Brown Mark in a leather vest with his bass slung low, Dr. Fink in surgical scrubs, and Bobby Z in a suit, looking like he'd wandered in from DJ'ing a wedding. They all looked different, yet somehow completely in sync.

Then there was Prince in a purple sparkly trench coat, white ruffled shirt with a deep V-neck, and black high-waisted dress pants. He had a Madcat telecaster guitar slung over his shoulder, and with his eyeliner and voluminous permed hair, he looked cooler, grittier, and more magnetic than anyone else on that stage.

I caught the video for "Little Red Corvette" a week later. Same basic setup as "1999," but this time Prince skipped the guitar and showed off his dance moves while Dez handled the solo. Jill Jones was (sadly) nowhere to be seen.

I didn't understand the metaphors about jockeys or rides as smooth as a limousine; I just knew the song was incredible.

1999 is a double album, which put it out of reach of my allowance, especially since most of my money still went to comic books and music magazines. I only heard Prince when a local station played "1999" or "Little Red Corvette," or when I caught a video on Night Tracks. He got lost in the jet wash of all the other bands I was obsessed with. I didn't forget about him; there was just too much music competing for the same airtime and the same teenage brain.

This all changed with "When Doves Cry." The single sold out as fast as the local record store could stock it. I recorded it off the radio — it was static-filled, and the DJ talked over the intro, but it was still better than nothing. Luckily, the video was in heavy rotation on MTV and Night Tracks.

The song and video for "When Doves Cry" made *Purple Rain* one of the most anticipated films of the summer of 1984. As the movie release date approached, MTV, Night Tracks, Night Flight, and even Friday Night Videos started airing clips from Prince's earlier albums — not just "Little Red Corvette" and "1999" (with Jill Jones!), but also older videos from *Controversy* and *Dirty Mind*. It was my crash course in Prince's musical history.

But the summer of 1984 wasn't all Prince all the time. Two other songs also provided musical fuel to stoke my misery. Not long after the Dance Disaster & Fake Leather Pants Debacle of 1983, I sequestered myself in my room and filled a 90-minute cassette with two songs: Duran Duran's "Save a Prayer" and Def Leppard's "Bringin' On the Heartbreak," alternating back-to-back for the entire tape.

Looking back, it was the musical equivalent of Elias and Barnes fighting for control of Charlie Sheen's soul in *Platoon*. Only I wasn't dodging tripwires or bullets from Viet Cong snipers in the jungles of Vietnam. I was just a dumb ass kid who couldn't cope with the end of a junior high relationship that lasted less than a month.

"Save a Prayer," with its lush, layered arrangement, serves as the Sgt. Elias of this admittedly dodgy analogy. Elias approached war with compassionate rebellion and introspection — he longed for meaning amid chaos — and that's the same energy this song carries.

"Bringin' On the Heartbreak" is the prototypical power ballad. Joe Elliott's anguished vocals amplify the song's emotional weight. In *Platoon,* Sgt. Barnes is ruthless, pragmatic, and morally compromised — he embraces the brutality. "Bringin' On the Heartbreak" echoes with the sounds of someone who's accepted pain as the new normal.

I know I'm reaching here, but I really just wanted an excuse to write about one of my favorite movies and two of my favorite bands. Moving on.

School had let out in early June, and I spent the first couple of weeks moping around the house. My parents were concerned at first, saying and doing everything they could think of to snap me out of it. My recovery from the spectacular flame-out at the end-of-year dance was, to put it mildly, non-existent. We went camping and fishing — I was there physically, but not really present. Concern turned to annoyance, then frustration. My mom thought I was being dramatic. My dad thought I needed to toughen up.

By the end of June, my parents had had enough of my Junior Morrissey routine. They shipped me to California to stay with my aunt and uncle for a week in hopes I'd get my shit together. I'm not sure they knew why I'd been exiled, but they spent the whole week trying to cheer me up — Straw Hat pizza, Venice Beach, even the cavernous Westminster Mall.

That's where I made two life-changing purchases with my forty dollars of spending money: *1999* and the *Purple Rain* soundtrack. With those tapes, the Duran Duran/Def Leppard doom loop was broken. I spent the rest of the trip deep-diving those two albums, reading liner notes, studying photos, and basically imprinting on those records like a newly hatched velociraptor.

Purple Rain was the easier record to digest — nine tracks, each one memorable. From the chaos of "Let's Go Crazy" to the vulnerability of "The Beautiful Ones" to the infamous "Darling Nikki," it felt like a greatest-hits album even before the movie came out.

1999 was more sprawling. It opened with the title track and "Little Red Corvette," one of the greatest one-two punches in pop history, then veered into rockabilly and synthpop before dropping two songs — "Let's Pretend We're Married" and "Lady Cab Driver" — that introduced me to levels of sexual frankness I did not know could exist on vinyl.

Yeah.

On my last night in California, my uncle rented Eddie Murphy's *Delirious.* I'd never seen anyone command a room like that. It wasn't the jokes as much as the certainty—this sense of owning who you were. I didn't know it at the time, but that confidence, combined with Prince's audacity, would become a kind of blueprint for me.

That was the night the heartbreak loosened its grip.

The next morning, walking to return the tape with "Baby, I'm A Star" blaring in my knockoff Mexican swap meet Walkman, I kept thinking about Eddie — and Prince. They were nothing alike, but they shared one thing: they were bold. They didn't apologize for who they were.

I returned home to Washington a new kid, confident and armed with a sense of humor rooted in sarcasm and edgy social commentary. Well, as edgy as a fourteen-year-old could be. I mainly just started cursing more, out of earshot of my parents, of course.

My folks noticed the change right away, and were thrilled that I had broken out of my funk. They weren't too thrilled at my sudden Prince obsession though.

Early reviews of *Purple Rain* started hitting newspapers and talk shows, and every parent in America seemed to lose their collective minds. Prince was being called out for the movie's sexual content, and suddenly his entire back catalog was under a microscope. Songs like "Head," "Sister," and "Let's Pretend We're Married" were treated like coded messages from Satan and the Marquis de Sade. My mom read at least three editorials out loud to me during dinner that warned parents about his "moral depravity."

Still, I nagged my mom nonstop to take me and Mark to see *Purple Rain* at the Charleston Theater in Bremerton. It was rated R, so we needed an adult. I knew that my mom's constant looking for negative Prince articles meant she was interested. After a week of pleading and promising to do chores I absolutely never intended to do, she finally caved.

The Charleston Theater had... a history. It opened as an adult theater (read: porn palace) that catered to fellas in the Navy in the years before home video killed that particular business model. It had sat empty for a while, then new ownership tried to rehab its image with a remodel and a bold "We're totally not a porn theater anymore!" marketing push. It didn't stick, so to speak. Over the decades, the place has closed and reopened more times than I can count.

But in 1984, it was just the former porn theater where my mom took me and my best friend from church to see *Purple Rain*.

The sexual content in *Purple Rain* is downright tame compared to what earns an R rating today. But in 1984, watching it in a former porn theater made it feel like the Charleston was back in its original line of business. My mom was scandalized — not by the sex scene, oddly enough, but by the F-word. My mom can tolerate the most depraved sexual acts being depicted on screen, but as soon as someone drops an F-bomb and she turns into a one-woman FCC.

She did, however, love Morris Day and The Time performing "Jungle Love" and "The Bird." Small victories, but their collective charisma and comic timing offset Morris's use of the dreaded F-word early in the movie.

Mark liked *Purple Rain* too — but he also liked The Time more than Prince, although he considered himself a fan of both. I flew completely over the edge. I went from obsessive to whatever comes *after* obsessive. I needed to know everything: Prince, The Time, Apollonia, the whole Minneapolis sound. My allowance didn't stand a chance. It all went straight into posters, magazines, unauthorized biographies, and Prince's entire back catalog — which, at that point, was only six albums, but felt like a universe.

Before the school year started, my dad "converted" part of the basement into a bedroom for me. His renovations consisted of gluing contractor-grade carpet over bare cement (no padding) and building a few shelves into the cinderblock walls. There were no heat registers, so when winter hit he brought home a Navy-surplus space heater to keep me from freezing to death.

I could only access the basement from outside, which meant that if I had to use the bathroom at night, I had to walk around to the back door — or duck behind a tree. Not ideal, but it was my space, and that was enough. Naturally, I tried to turn it into a replica of Prince's basement bedroom in *Purple Rain*.

I bought incense at the used record store in Bremerton and covered the walls with Prince posters and weird tapestries from thrift stores. My bed was the gutted remains of an old waterbed frame topped with a squeaky queen-sized mattress and a gigantic headboard that could've killed me if it ever tipped forward.

For entertainment, I had an ancient console TV with a built-in record player, speakers, and an AM/FM receiver. Later in high school, once I finally had a job, I used part of a paycheck to hook up a cassette player to that monstrosity.

All things considered, it was a pretty sweet setup.

That basement room became my refuge — for better or worse. It was great having a place to hang out with Eric, Greg, and Mark, but it allowed me to disappear into my head when things weren't going well. Still, it was my first taste of independence, even if the bathroom was still upstairs.

The new school year was coming, and for once I was excited. For the first time since second grade, I'd be at the *same* school two years in a row. No new-kid anxiety. I couldn't wait to see Eric and Doug again. Greg and I had drifted apart during the summer, but once school started we snapped back into our usual routine.

A couple days before classes began, my mom took me to JC Penney. My dad had been promoted, which meant new school clothes — and a haircut from an actual stylist. Contacts were still out of reach financially, but the haircut alone was transformative. The stylist worked magic on my uneven bangs and rogue waves, and suddenly I had the classic mid-'80s feathered look. She even taught me how to use mousse like a civilized person.

On the first day of school, I walked through the doors of Marcus Whitman in a bright red polo and Levi's 501s, feeling something I hadn't felt in years: confident. Ms. Gross greeted me warmly in homeroom — The Romantics and Madonna had replaced the Culture Club posters — and I took my seat next to Eric. Greg wandered in soon after. Doug sat with a church friend, but we still met up at lunch. For the first time in a long time, I felt like I belonged.

It didn't take long for the "new me" to get noticed. The shy, quiet kid had been replaced by someone talkative, sarcastic, and actually funny. Teachers noticed. Students noticed. My circle grew fast: Glen, Duane, Roland, the Mendiola brothers from Guam; Chris and Arelando, two of the few Black students; Arnold, Richard, and George, who were Filipino. No one talked about diversity — it just was — and it ruled.

My humor and self-deprecation made it easier to talk to girls. I was safe, approachable, harmless. I took up permanent residence in the friend zone, sure — but the friend zone was a hell of a lot better than no zone at all.

Of course, providing the soundtrack to all of this was Prince.

My Prince-covered Pee-Chee became a conversation starter and even got me invited to my first kegger by a girl named Cassidy. I didn't go — Greg couldn't, and the thought of showing up at a party hosted by scary metal chick Cassidy with no backup was too much for me. I may have had more confidence than the year before, but not enough to handle *that.*

Ninth grade ended up being the happiest I'd been since Montclair. I finally felt like I belonged. I had a solid group of friends, and I spent hours on the phone with girls who listed me firmly categorized in the "safe to talk to" category. We chatted about movies, school, and of course, music. It was a genuinely magical time, no social media to distract from actual human interaction and communication.

Pop historians love to claim kids in the '80s lived in constant fear of nuclear war. Not us. We lived next to a naval shipyard full of aircraft carriers and nuclear subs — a hard target guaranteed to get vaporized first — and we still didn't care. We were too busy having fun and living life in Port Orchard.

On April 22, 1985, Prince released *Around the World in a Day,* an album that marked a dramatic shift from the rock, funk, and pop fusion of *Purple Rain.* Prince leaned into a more eclectic, borderline psychedelic sound inspired by The Beatles and Jimi Hendrix. This, of course, sparked plenty of discussion and debate within my friend group. I loved the album — it showcased a different side of Prince as a songwriter. Songs like "Pop Life" and "Paisley Park" had *Sgt. Pepper* vibes to them. Prince with a dash of The Beatles? I was in. With this record, Prince lost many of the fans he'd gained from *Purple Rain,* but he had clearly moved on to the next phase of his artistic journey.

Once again, Greg didn't appreciate any mention of Prince's name alongside that of Jimi Hendrix. In his mind, Hendrix existed on a different level than any artist who had ever lived. Prince "aping" Hendrix would not stand with him. His dislike of Prince grew into a white-hot hatred that lasted for decades.

That hatred eventually cooled, but it took the death of George Harrison to douse the flames. Prince's epic solo at the end of "While My Guitar Gently Weeps" during Harrison's star-studded memorial concert finally convinced Greg that Prince was, in fact, an amazing guitarist.

The standout track from *Around the World in a Day* was "Raspberry Beret," a universally praised pop gem. Its bright, jangly sound painted a vivid story that highlighted Prince's gift for words.

That album became the soundtrack for the spring and summer of 1985, and it set a pattern — Prince seemed to release a record every year, each one different from the last.

I struggled when we moved to high school in the fall of 1985. The friend group I had been so tight with at the end of junior high splintered. New circles of friends were formed and new interests discovered.

Even Greg and I, great friends through all of ninth grade, grew apart. He found his tribe, as people say today, and began evolving into a more complete version of himself. One day we were nearly inseparable, the next we were barely acknowledging each other in the hallways. These things happen.

Then I was walloped with a brutal case of bacterial pneumonia right after Christmas break. The infection threatened to go septic, so I was briefly hospitalized. At time of my illness, I was failing six of my seven classes. Like I said, I was struggling. To keep me on track to graduate, I was forced to complete the second trimester through home study. I was a ghost.

On February 5, 1986, as my mom drove me home from a follow-up hospital appointment, Prince's new single "Kiss" came on the radio. It sounded nothing like the psychedelic pop of *Around the World in a Day*. This was straight-up James Brown funk. Even half-delirious with pneumonia, I was floored. Prince had moved on to a new sound again.

I returned to school in April, and it kind of felt like being the new again. Some people had assumed I'd moved away. Everything felt reset.

But by the summer, I had my driver's license and, thanks to my father, I finally got contact lenses. The metal framed Dahmer glasses were relegated to the dustbin forever.

Prince released his second movie, *Under the Cherry Moon, in* July. The critics hated it and honestly; they weren't wrong. The soundtrack album, *Parade*, was so good it made the movie feel almost beside the point.

Under the Cherry Moon was the first movie I ever drove a date to. I brought a girl who'd had recently showed interest in something more that friends, which was early evidence that ditching my binocular-strength glasses was the most successful glow-up of my teen years. Eric brought a date too, his neighbor who also had him listed as "someone to talk to." Maybe seeing Prince on the big screen would spark something more.

I didn't realize it then, but a pattern had formed with *Purple Rain*: Prince dropped a record every year of my life for the next three and a half decades.

Some records stamped themselves onto entire seasons. *Sign o' the Times* was the sound of the summer of my junior year: tennis with Carlton and Eric, afternoons at the lake, and the first hints that maybe I was finally getting my feet under me. *Lovesexy* arrived in a blur of late-'80s color and confusion — critics hated it, but "Alphabet St." still drops me right back into the last months of high school. And when the *Batman* soundtrack came out, I was recovering from ACL surgery in the Mojave Desert; its return to pop-funk was the only upbeat thing during the grind of rehab.

Prince's output over the following years could be baffling, brilliant, and frustrating — sometimes all at once. *Diamonds and Pearls* was released in October of 1991, and I played it incessantly that fall and winter. A year later, Prince put out the sprawling "Love Symbol" album. He then went silent for almost two years before returning with the inconsistent *Come* and *The Gold Experience* albums. I bought them both, but they were quickly relegated to my CD shelf. I was late for work the day he went on Good Morning America to promote *Chaos and Disorder*. I had been looking forward to this album, but the record was just okay, and I was expecting more.

Emancipation was the last album I bought on release day.

I ran to Warehouse Tapes & Records on my morning break, determined to be at the door when they opened, hoping it would be a return to form. In a way, it was—but it was also a bloated mess of a triple album. Less was never more for Prince. He had to pour everything out because he didn't know how not to.

After that, I stopped chasing each new release the moment it dropped. Life got louder and priorities changed. His catalog became increasingly uneven, and his experimentation with non-traditional distribution methods made finding new material difficult to find. I picked things up later, sometimes out of discount bins, and sifted through each track hoping to find a hidden gem.

And then on April 21st, 2016, Prince died.

I didn't cry, but it felt like the ground shifted from under me. An artist who'd been the soundtrack to over thirty years of my life had left the stage forever.

How can you just leave me standing, alone in a world that's so cold?

All the memories came flooding back that day — the jolt of hearing "Let's Go Crazy" when I needed it most, late-night debates with Greg and Eric about *Around the World in a Day*, having *Diamonds and Pearls* on repeat during the long drive to Port Orchard from Edwards AFB.

Suddenly, there would be no more anticipation of what his next album might sound like. No more surprise club shows. No more late night talk show appearances to show off his new band.

He was gone.

Posthumous releases of anniversary editions of *Sign O' The Times, Around The World In A Day*, and *Purple Rain* have somewhat made up for the reality that there will be no new music. Those releases are always good for a walk down memory lane and for discovering tracks that didn't make the final cut of those records. There will be more anniversary editions of his entire catalogue, but that doesn't change the fact that he died and will never perform live again. And I miss not having the anticipation of that possibility.

In the summer of 2022, my wife and I drove cross-country with my daughters. We stopped in Minneapolis, where I stood outside First Avenue — the club immortalized in *Purple Rain*. I lingered by the box office, imagining the nights Prince played there, the electricity of being inside when the lights went down and the band kicked in.

Then we visited Paisley Park.

Inside, I felt sadness, gratitude, and something like peace. I thought about all the years his music had been there with me — too many to count — and had to step away so my daughters wouldn't see their dad tearing up. I found a quiet spot in front of the small stage he'd performed on, eyes fixed on his guitars and amps, and said a small prayer of thanks.

Until that trip, I'd never really explained to my daughters why I was such a Prince fan. They knew I liked the music, but maybe now they understand: it was never just the songs. Each record holds its own era of my life — joy, heartbreak, awkwardness, reinvention. Those memories have been pressed into vinyl grooves and frozen in time.

As Prince changed with every new album, so did I. His music left watermarks on my life, subtle reminders of who I was and who I

was trying to become.
And for that, I will always be grateful.

SINGLES GOING STEADY

If you've read this far in my book, you're probably thinking I'm a mopey sad sack. Honestly, I'd probably think the same thing if I were you. But I'm not. While I can be prone to deep introspection when certain songs come on, there are others that make me nothing but happy when I hear them.

For real.

Especially the songs from 1984–1985. Each one is tied to a specific moment that still makes me smile. That stretch of time was pure joy — hanging out with friends, going to the movies, junior high dances, and the legendary backyard apple fights with Greg and Eric.

Apple fights were exactly what they sound like. We'd pick up fallen apples and throw them at each other as hard as we could. The ripe ones left bruises; the mushy ones exploded on impact, covering us in sticky apple shards. By the end of a battle, we smelled like a fermenting mop used to clean a cider mill. Later that summer, we upgraded to hunting each other down with BB guns in the woods.

And of course, there was the music that was a part of it all.

"Glory Days" by Bruce Springsteen is one of those songs. When I was fifteen, my friends and I listened to it ironically—not that we knew that's what we were doing. Hearing a thirty-something Springsteen wax nostalgic about "days gone by" —

the very days we were in the middle of living — didn't fully register. I remember sitting in the dugout during a Pony League game, dissecting the lyrics with my teammates. We should have been paying attention to what was happening on the field, but weren't. That could be why we only won a handful of games that season. None of us understood why Bruce sang "speedball" instead of "fastball." We knew what a "speedball" was, thanks to John Belushi's overdose a few years earlier, and it seemed like a strange choice.

We also joked about how much drinking there was in the song. Bruce's character did nothing but get hammered, and the woman from verse two didn't exactly seem like Mother of the Year. She may have even still been married when Bruce came calling.

Of course, twenty years later, some guys from that baseball team had gone through their own divorces, spent plenty of time inside of road side bars, and more than likely sat around thinking 'bout the old times.

Irony can be a cruel mistress.

Any song by Huey Lewis & The News is almost guaranteed to make me smile, especially any of the big hits off of their second album "Sports". Although it was released in 1983, that record had serious legs and spent a whopping one hundred and sixty weeks on the charts. It hit number one in June of 1984, almost a full year after its initial release.

The first top ten hit off the album, "Heart and Soul", was my introduction to the band. Even though I had heard "Do You Believe In Love" on the radio years before, I didn't put it together that both songs were released by the same band.

"Heart and Soul" was accompanied by a quirky video that captured the band's personality as regular guys in a bar band that had kind of hit it big. It's your basic rock & roll song with a quiet-ish verse and a big bombastic chorus that had a killer guitar riff. This is also one of the few songs that me and my brother both agreed kicked ass.

The follow-up singles, especially "Heart of Rock & Roll", struck a chord with us at Marcus Whitman junior high. It's a celebration of regional music scenes and name drops various cities at the end. The song mentions Seattle right before San Francisco, and this was a big deal to us.

In the early 1980s, Seattle was considered a backwater logging town that was just beginning to crawl out of a crippling economic depression. The city was constantly praised by bands that came through on national tours for having the most enthusiastic fans in the country. This is because we were considered to be a bunch of culture starved hicks desperate for outside attention from the world of pop culture. Anytime a band rolled through town, especially heavy metal or hard rock bands like Judas Priest or AC/DC, we put down the chainsaws and rocked out harder than any fans in the country. At least according to the bands. Then again, radio was regional back then, so for all we know they could have been saying the same thing about fans in Spokane or Wichita.

Anyway, hearing Seattle mentioned in "The Heart Of Rock & Roll" was a big friggin deal to us. It put our then small corner of the world on the map. The irony (there's that word again) is that in less than a decade, Seattle would become the center of the music and technology worlds.

While I doubt that Huey Lewis's shout out had anything to do with that, it's still nice to know he was thinking about us in 1983.

If there was ever a song that captured what it felt like to be a kid in the 1980s, it's Simple Minds' "Don't You (Forget About Me)." It distills the quiet angst of an entire generation. Yeah, it's a cliché take—but it's true. I'll go further: this is the definitive Gen X anthem.

Part of that is because it's forever tied to *The Breakfast Club*, John Hughes's portrait of suburban teenage life. Five archetypes thrown together, realizing they're more alike than different, then sent back into the world mostly unchanged. That felt familiar.

The song was offered to Billy Idol, Bryan Ferry, and Chrissie Hynde. All passed. Even Simple Minds were hesitant, worried it sounded "too American." It became their biggest hit. That feels fitting. No one quite knew what to do with us either, but we turned out okay.

To me, the song has always sounded like moody defiance. Those opening "hey, hey, hey, hey" lines ring out like a call to arms—a declaration that even if no one was paying attention, we were still here, figuring things out. As first-generation latchkey kids, we learned self-reliance out of necessity. We lived with conformity pressure, sure, but also with a stubborn independence that shaped us.

We were the first generation told we might not do better than our parents, and our collective response was basically, *And?* We kept moving.

I'm getting a little deep here, but when I hear those opening chords—Jim Kerr's voice cutting in—I'm instantly back in the hallways of Marcus Whitman Junior High. We had the whole world ahead of us and met it with a shrug.

Moving along.

Hall & Oates had songwriting down to a science. Take classic Motown song structure, blend in a little blue-eyed soul, add some guitar crunch and synth-pop flourishes, then top it off with eye-catching videos — that's a recipe for multi-platinum success. Even before *Big Bam Boom* came out, Daryl Hall and John Oates were already part of my musical landscape. They were inescapable in the early '80s, filling the Top 40 with "Private Eyes," "Maneater," "One on One," and "You Make My Dreams

(Come True)."

My favorite pre–*Big Bam Boom* track was "Family Man," with its jagged guitar lines and bass line that sounded like it was lifted straight out of an arcade cabinet — pure *Spy Hunter* swagger. It's a brilliantly crafted piece of pop tension.

With *Big Bam Boom*, Hall & Oates crossed fully into superstardom. "Out of Touch," released in August 1984 as the first single, hit number one in December. The music video — the band performing and sprinting around an oversized drum kit — foreshadowed everything about the new record: huge production, huge hooks, and huge programmed beats courtesy of the LinnDrum. That single (and the album's overall direction) ended up splitting the fanbase: too new wave for some, not R&B enough for others, too much guitar, not enough classic Hall & Oates harmonies.

"Out of Touch" ended up being the duo's fifth and final number one, and later singles didn't connect as strongly with casual or longtime fans. But to me, the chart position is almost irrelevant. "Out of Touch" is hard-wired to my ninth-grade friend group — Eric, Greg, Kathy, Lanelle, Becky, Doug, Jeff, Glen, and the rest of the cast. The video alone was a week's worth of conversation starter. Everyone had an opinion: John Oates's ridiculous watch-check on the word *time*, Daryl Hall's massive lion-mane hair, the animal-print suit, and of course — his dancing. So many opinions on his dancing. Good, bad, unclassifiable. We didn't care. It was *fun*.

This was the kind of song that became a cultural touchpoint, even if it sometimes gets lost in the avalanche of great mid-'80s singles.

And then there was Eric, who went to see Hall & Oates on the *Big Bam Boom* tour with his dad. They brought cotton for their ears — not to protect their hearing from the volume, but so they could hear the lyrics *better*. Apparently, they didn't want to miss a single nuance or bit of subtle innuendo in "Adult Education."

News of a 40th-anniversary deluxe release of *The Power Station's* 1985 self-titled album made me downright giddy. I loved this record when it first came out—especially the debut single, "Some Like It Hot."

The Power Station was a supergroup in the truest sense: Duran Duran's Andy and John Taylor, Chic's powerhouse drummer Tony Thompson, and the incomparable Robert Palmer on vocals. Produced by Bernard Edwards, the album somehow sounded both spacious and huge at once. Thompson's drums detonated through the mix, while Edwards coaxed Andy Taylor's guitar into that perfect balance between restraint and edge. Andy was always a tasteful "less-is-more" player, but here you can hear the tension in his playing, his wanting to do more but being held back, and it's fantastic. (And a wise choice, considering some of his later solo output.)

John Taylor laid down those trademark funk-pop bass lines that made even the coldest groove feel alive. And tying it all together was Palmer—smooth, soulful, and on the brink of superstardom.

Every track felt like a collision of worlds. The Taylors were still riding the Duran Duran tsunami even as the band was splintering behind the scenes. Thompson, already a legend from Chic, hadn't yet been rediscovered by a new generation of drummers. And Palmer, still known mostly for "Bad Case of Loving You"—was considered a bit of a musical relic of the late 1970s by 1985.

Then came *The Power Station.* And soon after, *Riptide.* Suddenly Palmer wasn't just back, he was the suited-up, unflappably cool and elegant elder statesman of the MTV era.

The second single was a cover of T-Rex's "Get It On (Bang A Gong)". Where the original was a mid-tempo sultry slice of glam rock strut, The Power Station's version is a high-octane funk infused rocker. Thompson's drumming hits like a howitzer as John Taylor's bass provides the steady ground assault. Andy Taylor's guitar soars in, cutting through it all like precision air strikes. Palmer's baritone growls through the verses before exploding into the chorus. My dad, a T-Rex fan, heard this song blaring from my room the summer of 1985. He walked in and asked me who it was and I told him it was The Power Station. He shook his head up and down a few times, taking it in, then asked if I could make him a copy of the song for him to listen to in his truck. His exact words were, "This is how I always thought this song should sound." Another small moment that grows in stature as time rolls on by.

For me, *The Power Station* still represents one of the great what-ifs of the '80s—a flash of musical chemistry that was so combustible that maybe it shouldn't have worked, but it did. Even now, when I hear those opening drum hits of "Some Like It Hot," I'm right back in it, hearing it all like it was the first time.

There are so many other songs I could write about, like Wang Chung's "Dance Hall Days," and the small moral panic it caused for me, Mark, and Marty who was another survivor of Bremerton Christian School. We were all probably still carrying a little psychic residue from the "Satanic Panic" chapel session.

We were convinced lead singer Jack Hues was singing *"we were cruel on Christ"* as the verse built toward the chorus. It was... concerning. Were the members of the ridiculously named Wang Chung *in league with the devil*?

We hashed this out over sodas at the downtown Bremerton McDonald's, our seriousness wildly out of proportion to the situation. Finally, Marty—the most impulsive of the three of us—slammed his cup down, stood up, and announced, "I'm finding out right now."

He stormed across the street to JC Penney's record section, grabbed a copy of the album, and tore open the plastic. He yanked out the record sleeve, scanned the lyrics, and then froze.

A grin spread across his face.

"He's saying *'we were cool on craze,'* not *"we were cruel on Christ!'"

Mark and I huddled around him. Sure enough—*cool on craze.*

Wang Chung were not satanists after all. Marty tossed the album back into the bin and the three of us walked to the Punk Palace to play video games. We had one less thing to worry about.

Bryan Adams was a big part of our musical lives. His fourth album, *Reckless*, was packed with arena-rock hits like "Somebody," "It's Only Love," and "Summer of '69." But "Heaven" was the one junior high slow dances were built for.

At every junior high dance, the moment those opening chords hit, the gym floor filled with pairs of fourteen- and fifteen-year-olds swaying awkwardly, arms looped loosely around necks, hands hovering at hips. Chaperones patrolled like tiger sharks in the shallow surf, making sure nothing became *too* familiar.

Reckless became the first Canadian album to sell a million copies domestically. Holster that bit of knowledge, it may come in handy for you during music trivia night.

Other slow-dance staples included Paul Young's "Every Time You Go Away" — a song originally written and recorded by Hall & Oates. Young's raspy, pleading voice was perfect for conveying the things we wanted to say but couldn't. Those dances were really just musical Morse code, each of us hoping the person we were dancing with received the message.

We put a lot of pressure on Paul Young and Bryan Adams to speak for us.

But the crème de la crème was Madonna's "Crazy for You."

Goddamn, this song still sounds fantastic. The words perfectly capture what it feels like to be completely infatuated with someone at a young age. It's all right there, plain as day: *"If you read my mind, you'll see I'm crazy for you."*

There's a yearning innocence to it and there is nothing overtly sexual or explicit, just pure emotion. Young love is crazy; you don't know what to do with all those big feelings swirling around inside you.

Madonna's vocals here are expressive in a way they never quite were again. Later, she'd become more self-aware, more in control of her image and sound, more lewd even. But on "Crazy for You," she sounds vulnerable and sincere and we believed every word.

For anyone who came of age in the mid-'80s, this song *is* teenage love. It's the sound of nervous hearts beating, sweaty palms, cautious steps onto the dance floor, and the moment you finally found the courage to ask that girl to dance, hoping she'd say yes.

By the end of 1985, the world — and our playlists — were changing fast. The innocence of junior high gave way to bigger sounds, bigger dreams, and the first cracks in the surface of everything we thought we knew. But for a while there, in that window between innocence and independence, every song still felt like it belonged to us.

LITTLE DRUMMER BOY

Christmas is my favorite holiday of the year. Thanksgiving comes in a distant second. I could honestly do without Halloween and New Year's Eve. I go all out at Christmas. The interior of the house gets decorated, and the outside gets the Clark Griswold treatment with lights, LED candy canes, and animatronic reindeer.

I start listening to Christmas music on November 1st. I may not like Halloween, but I respect the traditions, so I don't start with Christmas tunes until it has passed. Plus, I don't need angry ghosts and spirits haunting my house because I cut off "Monster Mash" at 11:52pm on October 31st just so I could get a quick fix of the Barenaked Ladies version of Jingle Bells.

It probably looks a little excessive from the outside, but that's because my love of Christmas goes all the way back to a time when there wasn't much to love about anything, back to a welfare funded daycare.

I don't remember too many physical details about the daycare, except that it was near a large Catholic church. The church was built from red brick, its stained-glass windows ornate and incredibly detailed. They looked like illustrations out of a storybook—just with a lot more crucifixion imagery. When the sun hit those windows, colors of emerald, sapphire, and red washed across the pews and the drab brown carpeting. That much I remember. Oh, and the chapel looked a lot like the one they tried to drag Damien into in *The Omen*—but I guess a lot of Catholic churches looked that way in the 1970s.

Our meals were the same every day. For breakfast, we were given a small bowl of Cream of Wheat. If we were lucky, we got a small pat of margarine on top. Otherwise, it was as bland and flavorless as the paste we used for arts & crafts. Actually, the paste tasted somewhat salty. I know because there were days I was so hungry I'd scoop out a gob with my fingers and eat it. Anything to make the hunger pangs go away.

Mid-morning, we got a snack, which was always half of a graham cracker, and a small Dixie cup of that weird orange drink that was so popular back then. It was served out of a giant orange cylinder cooler with a white spigot that was forever stained with whatever dye was used to give that stuff its distinct hue. After our snack, it was nap time, where I'd pretend to sleep as I listened to my stomach, and the stomachs of the surrounding kids, groan and growl.

Lunch was always one plain boiled hot dog, no bun, no mustard, no ketchup. Some days we had milk, some days we got watery milk, and other days we just got water.

That was my day-to-day life.

We lived in a cramped room inside the Hotel Linden. Our room rent was eleven dollars a month, state welfare subsidized the rest. The hotel also served as housing for disabled veterans, and we all had to share one bathroom per floor. Stairwells and common areas reeked of urine and cigarette smoke and trash littered the dimly lit hallways. It wasn't uncommon to walk past someone passed out in their wheelchair by the front door.

My mom is a proud woman who worked hard. Accepting government assistance wasn't easy for her, but she had to. My father was rarely timely with the child support checks, if he sent them at all.

We had to rely only on food stamps to get by, that meant nothing extravagant. And because our room at the Hotel Linden had a barely working hotplate and a tiny refrigerator, cooking was nearly impossible. We lived mostly on my mom's homemade tortillas, pinto beans, and the occasional egg burrito.

The months my father sent a child support check, though, felt like holidays. My mom would splurge and buy us small treats—a little jar of maraschino cherries and a half pint of chocolate milk for me and my brother. Sometimes she'd buy herself a borillo roll or *pan dulce* from the bakery, but those moments were rare. Most of the money she tried to save, hoping one day she'd have enough for us to get out of there.

Since we didn't have a car, we had to take the city bus to the nearest grocery store.

One trip in particular is burned into my memory.

We were waiting to cross a busy intersection on the way back to the bus stop. My brother Chris had just learned to walk, and he was fearless—and strong. My mom was carrying all our groceries in one arm and trying to hold his hand with the other.

Cars were whizzing past us. I can still hear the whoosh of them speeding by, smell the exhaust, feel the blast of displaced air as a bus rumbled past.

Suddenly, Chris wrenched his hand free of my mom's and darted into the intersection. A car swerved, missing him by inches. He kept running toward the other side of the street, undeterred and unaware of the chaos he had caused. My mom screamed and dropped our groceries. I watched a cantaloupe hit the sidewalk and roll into the gutter. A loaf of bread flopped onto the hot blacktop. The rest of our groceries—cans of Chef Boyardee ravioli, a bag of flour that burst on impact sending a plume of white into the air, and my mom's *pan dulce*—lay scattered in the street.

I stood frozen, watching it all unfold.

My mother darted between cars, desperate to reach my brother. A bus driver saw what was happening and sprang into action, risking his own life by jumping out of his bus and into the street to stop traffic. I can still see my mom running and snatching Chris up out of the intersection, clutching him tight as she raced back to the sidewalk where I stood. Strangers helped us gather what groceries hadn't been crushed or ruined. The cantaloupe was gone, so was my mom's *pan dulce*, but somehow the jar of cherries—the only glass container—had survived.

We moved to a bench at the bus stop and sat there, my mom sobbing and holding my brother close. He was blissfully unaware of the panic he'd caused. A police officer eventually showed up and made sure we were okay. Luckily, no one was hurt, but we had lost most of our groceries for the week.

Once she calmed down, my mother opened the jar of cherries and gave one to me and my brother. It was the only comfort she could think to offer after all that had just happened. A kind lady brought us one of those woven plastic shopping bags that were popular back then. She salvaged a few cans and even scooped a decent amount of flour back into the torn sack.

For a while after that, all our tortillas came with a gritty dash of asphalt.

As the holidays approached, I was old enough to realize that we weren't exactly in a position to enjoy a festive Christmas. My mom cried, worked, and worried a lot. She had two small boys to provide for. Still, she made do. She found some leftover tinsel at the diner she worked at and brought it home to decorate our dingy hotel room. It was red and silver and hung around our window that looked out at nothing. It brightened the place up.

Every morning was the same. We'd wake up, walk to the bus stop, ride to the daycare, then do it all in reverse. I remember looking around at all the stores downtown, decorated for Christmas. Toys were displayed in the window, alongside other things we couldn't afford like proper winter coats. El Paso may be in the desert, but winter mornings and evenings can get cold. The three of us would stand close together for warmth as we waited for the bus. One afternoon, a bartender came outside as we stood at the bus stop in front of his place and gave me and my brother two small candy canes. My mother thanked him with tears in her eyes. It was a sliver of cheer on an otherwise dreary December day.

Christmas Eve started out like any other day. I ate my bland Cream of Wheat while Chris wreaked havoc in the toddler room. His specialty was stealing bottles from other kids and hiding under the cribs to chug them like a tiny fugitive. The staff was not amused. It got so bad that during bottle time they literally locked him in a closet so the other kids wouldn't starve. He was that much of a menace.

After our mid-morning snack and nap, they gathered us up and ushered out of the building and into a church gym. Long tables were set up, and we were all instructed to find a seat.

They then served us turkey, mashed potatoes, and Hawaiian Punch. It was the best food I had ever tasted. For dessert, they gave us a chocolate chip cookie, and I'm surprised I didn't fall into some kind of food coma afterward. I savored every bite of that cookie and sipped my punch extra slow. It was delicious.

When lunch was over, we all sat on the floor and watched *The Little Drummer Boy*. It was projected onto a screen hanging above the stage. The story mesmerized me and I instantly connected with the drummer boy. He kind of looked like me—skinny, with unruly black hair and brown skin.

I loved the song. The words and melody were haunting and poignant. When the drummer sang that he was just a poor boy too, with no gift to bring the baby Jesus, I felt it. I thought of our sad hotel room with the red and silver tinsel, the barely working hot plate, the small refrigerator that sat empty. Maybe that tinsel would make a good gift.

The movie ended, but the biggest surprise was yet to come.

There was a commotion at the back of the gym, and all of us turned to see what was happening. Some of the daycare workers had put on ill-fitting, colorful felt vests and were walking down the aisle singing *Jingle Bells*. At the back of the procession was Santa! Santa had arrived—and he had gifts. He moved down the aisle, ho-ho-ho'ing the entire way, and sat at the front of the gym.

He was handed a clipboard and studied it with a serious look on his face. Then he looked up and asked, "Have you all been good boys and girls this year?"

A chorus of yesses rang out. I stayed silent, somehow thinking my brother's incursion into speeding traffic disqualified me from the "good" list—but I remained cautiously optimistic.

After the room settled down, Santa began calling out names. One by one, kids walked up and were handed a wrapped gift.

When my name was called, I walked toward Santa, nervous and unsure. He had blue eyes, but I could see dark hair under the white wig and fake beard. He must be one of Santa's helpers, I thought. Then he handed me my gift. I thanked him and carried it back to the spot on the gym floor where I'd been sitting. The other kids gathered around to see what I'd received.

It was a Fisher-Price school bus, complete with a handful of Little People figures. I was beyond happy. I cradled that box in my arms the entire bus ride back to our room, where I finally opened it.

I played with that school bus for hours. My brother had received a bag of plastic dinosaurs, and when he fell asleep, those dinosaurs became part of my school bus world. They would attack, and the kids would have to run back to the bus to escape.

The bus driver—like the real-life driver who had helped my mom—was always the hero. It was the lowest of low-budget *Jurassic Park* scenes, but to me, it was magic.

Inside the box was a catalog for other Fisher-Price toys. I remember the words *"Add these to your collection today!"* in bright letters that popped off the page.

I knew there was no way we could afford those toys, but in the days and weeks after Christmas, I would flip through the colorful pages of that catalog and dream. One day, I told myself, I'd have the Fisher-Price airport—or the parking garage.

It took me decades of reflection and self-analysis to realize that the Fisher-Price catalog was the catalyst for my borderline obsessive collecting behavior. If something came in a set or a series—Star Wars figures, records, CDs, books—I had to have them all.

This behavior went into overdrive after my daughters were born. I tried to buy them every Playmobil and Calico Critter set available. I didn't want them to feel like I did—to not have something they wanted, or to have an incomplete set of toys or books.

I was overwhelming them with toys because part of me was still living in that rundown El Paso welfare hotel room. Burying them in stuff was just me trying to exorcise a ghost from a place I'd left years before but hadn't really escaped.

But it's those small moments that shape us all. I can't look at a jar of maraschino cherries in a grocery store without remembering the day my brother ran out into traffic, or see retro Christmas displays draped in cheap tinsel without thinking of the red and silver strands hung around that hotel window.

Every holiday season, the first Christmas song I fire up on my playlist is the Harry Simeone Chorale version of *The Little Drummer Boy.* The moment the tenors and baritones kick in with that vocalized drum roll, I'm taken back to that church gym floor — staring up at the screen, listening to the tinny sound from the projector speaker fill the room. I can still taste the Hawaiian Punch, the chocolate chip cookie, and hear the tearing of wrapping paper from boxes of donated toys.

I'm not sad when these memories return. I'm grateful — to whoever donated that Fisher-Price school bus. Yes, that gift may have sent me into a frenzy of unhinged collector behavior later in life, but it also made a sad boy very happy that Christmas. And I'll never forget it.

I hope that when my daughters read this, they'll understand why I gave them more toys than they could ever play with. It came from a place they've never seen or experienced. That doesn't make it right — it's just means some of us take longer to leave the places we left behind years before.

SONGS FOR THREE GIRLS

The first time I held my daughter Maddy, something broke open inside of me. I can remember looking down at her, swaddled in her baby blanket, and thinking I have loved nothing this much, this fast.

When we drove her home, I refused to take the freeway. People drove like maniacs, and I wasn't about to risk my newborn on I-5. We took the side roads instead, creeping along at twenty miles per hour. I slowed to a crawl over bumps, steered around pot holes, did everything I could to not jostle Maddy as she slept in her car seat.

The first three months blurred together in a fog of long work commutes that began before dawn and ended at dusk. Maddy's mom was counting down the days until she had to go back to work, and we were both dreading daycare—the thought of leaving our baby with strangers felt unbearable.

On the Friday before she was set to go back to work, I was laid off.

At first, I was crushed. Then, about ten seconds later, I was elated. I hated that job—the company was awful, the commute worse, a majority of my co-workers unbearable—and suddenly, I didn't have to go back. More importantly, it meant I could stay home with Maddy while I looked for a new job.

Our first day together was rough. Really rough. Maddy cried a lot and I couldn't figure out how to get her to calm down. She wasn't hungry, didn't need to be changed, she was just upset. I tried her baby swing, pushing her in the stroller, carrying her, all to no effect. The only time she wasn't crying was when she was asleep, but the moment she woke up she started crying all over again.

Her constant crying became such a concern that I even called the consulting nurse at the hospital, asking if I should bring her to the emergency room. The nurse chuckled kindly and said, "She's probably fine, babies can be fussy. Have you tried a car ride?"

After a half hour of wrestling to get the base of the car seat properly installed in the back seat, we were off. I drove all over the south end of Pierce County, with Maddy wailing in the back seat the entire time.

Back home. Exhausted.

There was only one thing left to try - the Baby Björn. I'd avoided it because I couldn't figure out how the thing went together. When I dumped it out of the box, it flopped onto the floor like a dead squid. I had no idea what buckled into where. The directions weren't very useful. In fact, they looked like Ikea directions, but instead of building a Billy shelf system, I was trying to assemble a Swedish baby-carrying contraption.

As I struggled with the Baby Björn, Maddy cried uncontrollably in her baby swing. Then the moment of truth. I lifted Maddy from her swing - still crying - and gently eased her into the Baby Bjorn. I was hesitant, nothing about the Baby Bjorn screamed "load bearing". It seemed flimsy. I wasn't too confident in my build, but I clipped the straps, held my breath, and let go.

It worked. She was secure up against my chest. Her tiny face looked up at me, her eyes wide and calm.

From that moment on, the Baby Bjorn became an extension of me. I became an expert at scooping Maddy out of her crib, car seat, or swing, and strapping her into the Baby Bjorn. We did everything together—laundry, dishes, grocery runs. They were all done with Maddy strapped to me, napping against my chest. I felt like I was exactly where I was supposed to be.

That was our life for six months. Then I got a job offer.

It was good news, of course—steady income, security—but it also meant the end of our little world. I was relieved, but gutted.

The day before I started the new job, Maddy was unusually fussy. She cried all morning, and nothing I did helped. Maybe she felt what I was feeling—the quiet dread of separation. I strapped her into the Baby Björn and walked the house, humming nonsense songs, but she kept crying.

My humming wasn't working, so we walked over to the shelf that held my bazillion CDs. I picked out The English Beat's *Special Beat Service* and skipped to track seven, "Save It For Later".

Maddy stopped crying. Over the next three minutes and thirty-four seconds, I danced around the living room with her. She smiled and laughed when I would swing her around a bit during the chorus or dipped when Dave Wakeling sang, "your legs give way and hit the ground".

When the song ended, I stood in the middle of the room and looked down at my baby girl. I felt the same way I did the first time I held her, complete and total uncomplicated love.

Then I played "Save It For Later" again.

And again.

And again.

Before I was a dad, "Save It For Later" was a favorite track of mine to play on the juke box at The George & Dragon, an English bar nestled in a Seattle suburb. I spent countless nights there with my friends, drinking pint after pint of Guinness and cider - black velvets - John Lennon's go to drink as an art school student. We'd talk work, sports, life, girls. It was a carefree and irresponsible time in my life filled with laughter with nothing more burdensome than surviving the next workday morning with a skull-crushing hangover.

"Save It For Later" was written by The English Beat's lead vocalist and guitarist Dave Wakeling. In interviews, Wakeling has said this about the song:

"Two kids monkeying around on a Saturday morning, one of them realizing it's time to grow up and face responsibilities, while the other just wants to keep playing."

He wrote the song when he was nineteen as his first serious girlfriend began to emotionally mature faster than he was ready to. The title is in reference to her trying to be polite in brushing him off, "not now; maybe when you're ready and more mature."

It took me a while to figure out what Wakeling meant when he sang, "sooner or later, your legs give way, you hit the ground", but the symbolism is clear to me now- life forces maturity, you can't run away from growing up forever.

When I hear that song now I'm taken back to that gloomy day in Spanaway, WA with my daughter giggling and laughing as we danced around the living room. With each replay that morning, a small part of my wildly irresponsible side began to fade. Not all at once — I still had plenty of self-destructive behavior ahead of me — but that was the beginning.

Life does indeed force maturity, and not always with a soft touch.

Life has a habit of knocking you sideways at exactly the wrong time. When my second daughter, Jossy, was born, I was unemployed again — not technically laid off, just "contract not renewed," which is corporate lingo for the same damn thing.

I'd like to say that I was better prepared for the stay at home dad life the second time around, but I wasn't. Having a new born to care for and a toddler are two very, very different and difficult jobs, especially when being performed concurrently.

Where Maddy had been a very, very easy baby to take care of, after I figured out the Baby Bjorn she was basically a human koala bear, Jossy was different. She wasn't difficult, she was just incredibly curious, determined, and strong.

Her first week home was a bit of a challenge as she would not nurse, and when she did, she would spit up quite a bit. We brought her in for a check-up with her pediatrician to determine what the issue might be. The doctor marveled at Jossy's muscle tone and strength. He slid a hand under her tummy and gently lifted her off the exam table. Jossy then held a very basic plank as he pointed out the definition in her lower back muscles, saying he'd never seen an infant so coordinated or strong. "She's fine," he laughed. "Just switch to formula until her stomach catches up to the rest of her."

Once Jossy started holding formula down, she was off to the races. Putting her in the Baby Bjorn was a challenge. She was a live wire and would squirm as soon as I tried getting her legs through the straps. And she absolutely hated not being able to face out and would push and kick against me in protest. She wanted to see what was going on, so even though she was technically too small to be facing outward, I would put her in the Baby Bjorn with her little face looking out at the world.

One of her favorite things to do was to watch the TV screen whenever I played Guitar Hero. She liked the colors that represented notes on the guitar neck as they scrolled up the screen and the crazy animations of the avatars. I'd stand in the middle of our TV room, fake guitar strapped to me just below her legs as they dangled from the Baby Bjorn.

Whenever she was fussy or upset, a couple of tries attempts at beating my high score on Black Sabbath's "War Pigs" would calm her down.

Life, of course, isn't just Guitar Hero and Baby Bjorns. I had to get a job. When Maddy and Jossy would nap, I would be online submitting what felt like hundreds of resumes, writing cover letters, and filling out applications. I was getting next to nothing in responses and a genuine panic began to set in as the date of my unemployment benefits expiring loomed.

Then, out of nowhere, I got a call. I interviewed. I nailed it. I got the offer. Like Morrissey, I was looking for a job and then I found a job... and heaven knew I was miserable now. Going back to work after Maddy was born had been hard. Doing it again — and now leaving *two* little girls behind — felt twice as heavy.

The day before I had to return to work, Jossy and I were home alone. Maddy was off with her mom at the store, so this was a rare occassion where it was just the two of us. We were in the living room, me sitting on the floor as Jossy lay on her blanket next to me. The TV was tuned to a music channel that I forget the name of, playing Elvis songs.

When "Can't Help Falling in Love" came on, Jossy began to push herself up off the blanket, determined to crawl. I sat there, watching. Her little brow furrowed as her arms struggled to hold her up as she worked to tuck her knees under her. She failed once, twice, three times, her arms giving out. She started to cry, so I tried to help her, which only seemed to make her more upset. I backed off, gave her room, and she tried again.

She lifted her head, tears of frustration in her eyes, pushed herself up off the floor, worked her legs underneath her, and then crawled towards me. I inched away from her, watching as she seemed to grow stronger each tiny push forward.

When she reached me, I scopped her up and held her close. She was exhausted. We laid down on the couch, Jossy on my chest. She fell fast asleep as I listened to her breathing as the last soft notes of "Can't Help Falling in Love" faded out.

That moment, that song, are tied together forever.

Sixteen years later, we were in a movie theater in Richland, WA watching Baz Luhrman's fantastic *Elvis* movie. "Can't Help Falling in Love" began to play. Jossy leaned in close to me and whispered, "Is this Kacey Musgrave?" I nodded. She rested her head against my shoulder for a moment before turning back to the movie.

I don't know if she remembered that first time she crawled toward me.

But I did.

Roles were reversed when my daughter Katelyn was born. I had steady employment, but her mom had been laid off from Washington Mutual. Every morning I would be the one going off to work as she stayed home and took care of the girls. Maddy was in school, but Jossy had not even turned two yet. Having two kids still in diapers is a lot to contend with.

My job was located in downtown Bellevue and there were no easy commuting routes from our house. Everyday I'd sit in traffic, sometimes up to two hours. It made me think of my dad doing the same when we lived in Montclair and he had to drive to Long Beach everyday.

Katelyn was different from her sisters - as an infant, she was already headstrong and determined to do things her way. Where most newborns are content to sleep on their backs, and should sleep on their backs, Katelyn wanted to sleep on her tummy, knees tucked up under her. This made me nervous and I would check on her incesstantly when she napped. She was fine, of course, and any attempt to turn her over was met with instant crying.

Her eyes were darker too. Maddy and Jossy's eyes were bluish as babies, but Katelyn's were a deep, rich brown. And she was born with hair, dark and full. Her sisters were both born basically bald.

The Baby Bjorn, a life-saver with the other two girls, was not appreciated by Katelyn. She hated it. Attempts to place her in it were met with a flutter of kicks to the face and chest. She wasn't having it. What Katelyn did like though, was riding in the backpack. So that's where she would go when I got home. I'd cook dinner and do dishes with her on my back, my own baby Yoda. She would pound on the top of my head and as she grew she'd push her feet into my back and push down on my head in an attempt to escape the backpack. To this day, my neck sounds like a cement mixer when I turn my head to the right.

Emotions ran high with Katelyn as well. She wasn't afraid to let everyone know how she was feeling at any particular moment. I spent a lot of nights walking her back and forth in the upstairs hallway, holding her close as she cried and cried, upset about... something.

There were times when it seemed nothing could or would calm her down - not the backpack, not holding her, not trying to soothe her with a bottle or binky. She'd just cry, a torrent of tears running down her sweet face. Her mom and I felt powerless when this happened. Eventually, she would fall asleep, physically spent from her emotions. Then she'd wake up, remember whatever it was that upset her, and would cry again.

One of these crying episodes happened during a trip to visit family. We were loaded into the SUV when Katelyn began to fuss and began to struggle to get out of her carseat, a baby Houdini squirming against the restraints. Then came the trembling bottom lip, the first tear, then the wailing that would impress a screeching banshee. Jossy and Maddy tried to calm her down with toys. Her mom turned in her seat to see if there was anything she could do to stop the crying. Nope. If anything, Katelyn cried harder. I sat behind the wheel, knuckles white and feeling helpless. In desperation, I turned on the radio. It was tuned to a country station just as Billy Currington's "Love Done Gone" came on. I reached for the volume knob and increased the volume. The first "ba-badda-badda-ba" filled the cabin of the SUV. The crying stopped instantly, replaced by a smile. Whatever it was that had made Katelyn so unhappy was instantly forgotten when that song started playing.

For the rest of that trip, Katelyn was a happy, smiling baby. When we got back home, I burned a CD with "Love Done Gone" as the first track. We kept it in the SUV, chambered up and ready to go for whenever Katelyn needed to be soothed.

As Katelyn learned to talk, she was always quick to share with us, and anyone else willing to listen, how and what she felt about things. Early on, she showed a quick wit and sharp sense of humor that is still there today. And she'll certainly let you know when she's upset or displeased with something.

Always an early riser, Katelyn would sometimes climb out of her bed, march down the hallway and open our bedroom door and yell, "Pancakes!" She'd then slam the door shut and wait for me to get up and make her breakfast. Pancakes, of course. If they weren't made up to her standards, she'd let me know about it. Ba-badda-badda-ba, indeed.

Three girls, three very different songs that remind me of particular moments in time with each of them - English ska, Elvis, and bro-country. In a way, each song fits them perfectly, and in a way, each fits in perfect with the memories tied to them. Maddy is an adult now, at the start of her teaching career, but she will always be my little koala baby, strapped tight to me as we dance around to "Save It For Later".

No matter how much success Jossy has as an athlete, I still see that baby girl struggling to lift herself up off the floor, determined to crawl.

With Katelyn, she'll always be the headstrong baby that didn't keep her feelings to herself. She's true to who she is, with a fierce independent streak and integrity.

They couldn't be more different from each other, but I love them all the same.

BE COOL OR BE CAST OUT

In 1982, Rush released *Signals,* an album that opened with one of their most haunting songs: "Subdivisions."

It's about not fitting into any of the accepted norms of suburban life—something a lot of us knew all too well.

The video perfectly captures that sense of quiet alienation. The main character moves through the halls of his high school like a ghost, always walking against the current of students who all look vaguely identical. He's got thick glasses, a haircut that looks like it was done in the kitchen, and a body that hasn't quite figured out what to do with itself yet. After school, he retreats to his room to escape into Rush's music, but his father shuts off the TV and orders him to study. On weekend nights, he wanders the empty streets, eventually finding solace in the glow of the *Tempest* arcade game.

Where *The Breakfast Club* gave us five familiar archetypes—the jock, the princess, the brain, the criminal, and the basket case —"Subdivisions" reminded us there was a sixth: the nerdy loner. Hughes tried with Ally Sheedy's character, but she was too attractive, too stylized in her weirdness. And Anthony Michael Hall's Brian, while endearing, still had a network—academic clubs, study groups, other kids like him.

The kid in "Subdivisions" had *no one.* He didn't fit in with the athletes, the outcasts, or even the brains. He lived in the in-between spaces—those endless suburban cul-de-sacs where every house looked the same and every driveway had an identical, non-descript sedan parked in it.

"Subdivisions" was about the invisible social grids we were all forced into—cliques, expectations, invisible boundaries you crossed at your own peril. For some of us, the song hit uncomfortably close to home.

Rush wasn't cool in 1982, not by any teenage metric. They were the band your older brother listened to while studying *Dungeons & Dragons* rulebooks. But to kids who felt unseen, they offered validation—and something more profound than a catchy hook. They told us it was okay to exist outside the lines of the map.

In the suburbs, conformity was currency. Rush made it okay to opt out.

IT TAKES TWO

Being a basketball fan in the 1980s meant you belonged to one of two camps — you were either a Los Angeles Lakers fan or a Boston Celtics fan. Sure, you could root for your local team, like the Seattle Supersonics, but the decade belonged to the Lakers and Celtics. From 1980 through 1989, at least one of those teams appeared in every NBA Finals, with the Lakers winning five titles to the Celtics' three.

I was a Lakers fan because they drafted Magic Johnson, who played college ball at Michigan State. I felt an odd allegiance to Magic because of his Michigan roots — I still had family there — but also because I was living in Southern California for part of his rookie year. His no-look passes, herky-jerky YMCA-rec-league-looking shot, and clutch play made him not just my favorite basketball player of all time, but my favorite athlete ever. (Tom Brady, another Michigan alum, is a close second.)

Eric was a big Celtics fan because of Larry Bird. As a teen, I thought Bird was an overrated doofus. It wasn't until I watched his gutsy performance against a much younger Indiana Pacers team in the 1991 NBA Playoffs that I changed my mind. Bird's back was a wreck and required traction after games just so he could walk the next day. When he returned in the decisive Game Five after smashing his face on the parquet floor earlier in the game, I had to tip my hat to the guy.

We played a lot of basketball in Eric's driveway or on the asphalt courts at Orchard Heights Elementary School. Out there, under the open sky, we were unstoppable. It didn't matter who showed up — older kids, college guys home for the summer, random dads in tube socks — we ran them off the court. We were a genuinely good group of pickup players, quick, scrappy, and confident.

But for some reason, all that skill evaporated the moment we stepped into a gym. During our senior year, we put together a rec league basketball team, and it was a disaster. We didn't have a coach, so Carlton and I volunteered. Our offensive "system," if you could call it that, was inspired by the Uptown Crew's "Uptown's Kickin' It."

The premise was simple: play tough defense, and as soon as the other team put up a shot, our guards would leak out to half court while the forwards and centers crashed the boards. Once we secured the rebound, the guards would shout "Uptown, uptown!" and the ball would get passed ahead to start what was supposed to be a Showtime-era Lakers fast break. Easy baskets. Fast tempo. Flashy play.

In theory.

In reality, our defense was awful, and we rarely grabbed the rebound when the other team missed, which wasn't often. When we did, we usually turned the ball over before anyone could yell "Uptown." Personally, I played like an absolute spaz in those rec league games — missing easy layups, clanking open jumpers, and dribbling like my hands were made of bricks. On the asphalt, though, I was a different player entirely — deadly from the elbows, automatic from the top of the key, draining fadeaways like a mini Bernard King.

The vaunted "Uptown Offense," as I called it, powered us to exactly two wins that season. We lost one game 76 to 14. But we had fun. I think.

The games at Orchard Heights were intense and competitive, sometimes to the point of being overly physical. Fights rarely broke out, but plenty of hard fouls were dished out.

During these games, someone always had a car stereo blaring

from the parking lot, tuned to a local station. The airwaves were still full of Lionel Richie, Cyndi Lauper, Madonna, and Prince, but a new sound was emerging.

In 1986, Aerosmith and RUN-DMC teamed up on a remake of "Walk This Way," and everybody lost their collective minds. Old-school rockers were appalled that Aerosmith would let their classic be turned into a hip-hop track. Rap fans, meanwhile, were baffled by the sight of two guys dressed like carnival fortune tellers screeching on RUN-DMC's latest release.

The collaboration was the brainchild of Rick Rubin, who had long wanted to merge hard rock and rap. He played RUN-DMC the 1975 Aerosmith track—and they hated it. At first. Then they realized the drum break from the original had already been sampled in hip-hop.

In 1986, Aerosmith were in a full-blown career death spiral. Addiction had gutted the band, albums had tanked, and they were on the verge of being a punchline. Steven Tyler and Joe Perry were each paid eight thousand dollars to re-record their vocals and guitar parts.

The rest is history.

"Walk This Way" didn't just introduce rap to a mainstream audience—it resurrected Aerosmith's career from the boneyard. The song hit number four on the U.S. charts and became the first rap video placed into heavy rotation on MTV, where it now ranks among the network's top five videos of all time.

I already knew about RUN-DMC thanks to Glen Flores, who made me a mix tape back in eighth grade with songs he'd breakdance and pop to. On that tape was RUN-DMC's "It's Like That." The USA Network's *Night Flight* also kept "King of Rock" in rotation when they weren't showing reruns of *Reefer Madness* or footage from Reggae Sunsplash.

In May 1986, RUN-DMC released *Raising Hell*, the album featuring their "Walk This Way" collaboration. Carlton and I made a trip to Tower Records in Tacoma to pick it up. We took my mom's white Ford Tempo because it had a tape deck, but also because I didn't have a car of my own.

Album in hand, we drove all the way back to Port Orchard with *Raising Hell* blasting through the stock speakers of my mom's Tempo. By that time, "Walk This Way" was kind of played out, so we gravitated toward the other tracks—"You Be Illin'," "My Adidas" (which I always thought was a borderline novelty song and ground zero for product placement in rap for the next four decades), and "It's Tricky." The latter managed to do something most hip-hop songs never do: it had real staying power. "It's Tricky" still shows up in movies, TV shows, and sports arenas to this day.

The success of "Walk This Way" broke hip-hop's video barrier on MTV. From the summer of 1986 on, rap videos began creeping into regular rotation—and pop culture would never be the same.

Fast forward two years to August of 1988. We spent that summer in flux, caught in that awkward and anxious space between high school graduation and the rest of our lives. Eric and Carlton were counting down the days until they moved into their college dorms, and quite a few others from our extended friend group were doing the same.

What should come as a shock to absolutely no one: I wasn't exactly college material at that point. I'd failed so many classes my sophomore year that I had zero cushion when it came to having enough credits to graduate. In fact, me graduating *without* having to attend summer school wasn't even a real possibility.

As senior year wrapped up, I was carrying a big, fat "F" in algebra. I hadn't turned in a single homework assignment all trimester. With a week left in the school year, my algebra teacher pulled me aside and told me that if I scored a 90% or higher on the final, I'd be within screaming distance of a D-minus. He had weighted the grading system to give jamokes like me a fighting chance.

I had a week to cram three months' worth of algebra into my head. So I did what I'd done for most of that school year — I put off studying until the night before. I sat in my basement room with my algebra book and a six-pack of Jolt Cola, trying to absorb as much math as humanly possible in one caffeine-fueled night.

For everyone else, the last day of school was a formality. Most of my class spent the day in the commons signing yearbooks and taking Polaroids. Not this guy. I had algebra first thing that morning. I wandered into class like a dead man walking, fully aware that scoring 90% on the final was all but impossible.

My teacher handed me the test and escorted me to a small room adjacent to the classroom. I was allowed nothing but the test, two pencils, and a sheet of scratch paper. My mood was grim, but I was determined to give it everything I had. He set a timer for forty minutes and walked out, closing the door behind him. The metallic thunk of the lock sliding into place felt like foreshadowing—I wasn't going to graduate, and they'd probably just leave me in that room all summer.

I took a deep breath and got to work.

There's a scene in *A Beautiful Mind* where the John Nash character looks at a board filled with random numbers. We see his brain light up as he decodes the patterns, revealing the hidden logic behind it all.

That did *not* happen to me. I had to grind through every problem, never entirely sure if I was doing them right. I worked feverishly, on the edge of a breakdown, scribbling and erasing until my scratch paper looked like a ransom note written by a lunatic. Sweat rolled down my back, my head pounded, and I finished the final problem just as the timer buzzed.

My teacher unlatched the door and let me out. He took my test, and as I started toward the exit, he said, "Don't leave." Then he pointed to a chair by his desk.

"Let's see how you did."

He placed my test next to the answer key, pulled a red pen from his shirt pocket, and brandished it like an executioner raising an axe.

After several excruciating minutes—and what felt like a billion red marks bleeding across the page—he turned to me, expressionless. He capped the pen, slid it back into his pocket, and sighed.

I opened my mouth to ask if I'd passed, but he cut me off.

"Had you given any effort at all this trimester, you wouldn't have been in this position."

I failed. That's what he was telling me. I braced for the verdict.

"You got a 95 on the test. You can graduate with your class."

I just sat there, stunned. I thought all those red marks were wrong answers, but it turned out he'd been marking each one *right*.

As I got up to leave, I tried to thank him, but he waved me off.

"You're the most frustrating student I've ever had," he said. "You're lazy, distracted, and unmotivated—but you just proved that when you put in the work, this is easy for you. It's infuriating to watch. Apply yourself in life, and you'll move mountains."

I'd love to say that speech lit a fire under me—that I never coasted again, never procrastinated, never put myself in that position. But that would be a lie. I walked out of that classroom elated and relieved, and over the next few decades, I pretty much ignored every bit of advice he'd given me.

High school was officially over. What none of us realized was that we were stepping into the last summer we'd all spend together.

The rest of that summer blurred into a familiar rhythm: working, going to the lake, and playing basketball. I washed dishes at a local restaurant, Carlton installed windows, and Eric manned the counter at an electrical supply shop.

By mid-August, the friend group started to shrink. Some left for freshman orientation, others for boot camp. Finding enough people for pickup games became harder every week.

August 28 was the last day we had enough bodies for full-court games at Orchard Heights. It was hot and clear, the kind of late-summer day that feels endless. Everyone was there — Eric, Carlton, Mike, Arnold, Duane, Richard, and a few underclassmen. The games were tight, physical, and full of trash talk.

As five o'clock approached, I noticed Carlton checking his watch between plays. Then, at 4:50, he grabbed his bike and said, "I gotta go."

"Why? We just won — we're still up!"

He didn't smile, didn't even hesitate. "*Yo! MTV Raps* comes on in ten minutes."

And with that, he pedaled off down the gravel trail that led out of the school yard and toward his neighborhood.

You never know when something's happening for the last time. For me, that was it — the final day that whole crew was together, not counting the occasional reunion or, worse, a funeral.

I can still see Carlton disappearing into the trees, hear the doors of Arnold's Chevette slam shut, the back seat littered with tennis balls. Eric climbed into Mike's Ranchero and the two of them sped off.

For a moment, I stood alone on the empty court, the echo of the game still hanging in the air. Then I tossed my basketball into the passenger seat of my '73 Mercury Comet and drove home to watch MTV.

The last video that played during the debut episode of *Yo! MTV Raps* was "It Takes Two" by Rob Base & DJ E-Z Rock. It was a high-energy, infectious closer. The track is anchored by a sample from Lyn Collins' 1972 funk classic "Think (About It)" — the source of the iconic "Yeah! Whoo!" shout. Other samples include Go Public's "Check It Out" for the bassline, The Meters' "Cardova" for the drums, and James Brown's "Funky Drummer" for the snare. Together, they form a brilliant collage that Rob Base raps over with confident, cocky, playful swagger. The call and response — *"It takes two to make a thing go right / It takes two to make it outta sight!"* — made the song an instant, enduring dance-floor favorite.

"It Takes Two" was all anyone talked about the next day, which led to another trip with Carlton to Tower Records in Tacoma. Tower was the only record store that had a dedicated hip-hop section at the time, so we made the twenty-mile drive to buy new releases. Cassette in hand, we headed home in my Comet. My dad had bought me an Audiovox tape deck for my birthday that year, so we no longer had to rely on my mom's Tempo to listen to tapes while driving.

The album was a disappointment. Outside of "It Takes Two," the rest of the tracks were dull. The only other song that came close was "Joy and Pain," but even that one paled in comparison. It was our first taste of what would plague albums across all genres for years to come — a strong lead single surrounded by filler.

The next week, Eric left for the University of Puget Sound. A week after that, Carlton moved into his dorm at the University of Washington. By mid-September, only a handful of my friends were still in Port Orchard. Mike left for the Army, Arnold for the Navy. I stuck around washing dishes and making omelets at the restaurant where I worked until December, when I finally left for Air Force boot camp.

The weeks after Eric and Carlton left were odd and lonely. They had moved on, and I was left behind in a hometown that felt empty. I still had friends to hang out with, but it wasn't the same.

"It Takes Two" was the song of the summer of 1988, even though it wasn't released until August. It's the sound of basketballs rattling through chain nets at Orchard Heights, friendly trash talk that sometimes went too far, the rumble of Mike's Ranchero, and the echoes of tennis balls at the high school courts.

Rob Base provided the track that signified the beginning of the end of adolescence.

But my friend group fading into the haze of real life wasn't the only change in the air. Music was shifting too. It was evolving into something different—more authentic, less gloss; more raw, less glam.

The same could be said for me and my friends. We were changing too, and our evolution into young adulthood didn't come without growing pains. But through it all, we managed to never drift too far apart. The echoes of basketballs rattling through the chain nets at Orchard Heights always remind us which way is home.

SHE DRIVES ME CRAZY

I left for Air Force boot camp on December 12, 1988. My recruiter, Sgt. Brad Correll, drove me from home to the hotel where I'd spend the night before flying to Lackland AFB in San Antonio, Texas. Sgt. Correll and I had become friends during the months between my graduation and enlistment date. He'd sometimes take me—and occasionally Carlton—to the local naval base to play basketball with other new recruits and active-duty servicemen.

Fun fact: Sgt. Correll looked *exactly* like Rob Base.

The pickup basketball games were also Sgt. Correll's way of keeping an eye on my weight. I had to be under 195 pounds when I arrived at MEPS to sign the last of my enlistment papers. If I showed up overweight, my enlistment would be delayed—bad news for both of us. It would blow his recruitment quota and derail my plans.

Port Orchard had two gyms in the late '80s. One was a blood-and-sweat powerlifting joint full of boxers, bodybuilders, and guys who looked like they'd learned to lift in a prison rec yard. The other was a new-fangled "health club," wall-to-wall with Nautilus machines, mirrors, racquetball courts, saunas, and a strange new contraption called the StairMaster. The first gym smelled like BO, gym socks, and open-air PED use; the second like lavender cleanser and women's perfume.

I joined the latter.

My workout routine consisted mostly of testing my one-rep bench press max and then spending fifteen minutes on the StairMaster. Some days, if enough people were around, I'd play Wallyball—which was just volleyball inside a racquetball court.

A week before my MEPS appointment, Sgt. Correll had me step on the scale in his office. I tipped in at a whopping 218 pounds.

Panic ensued.

I had to lose twenty-three pounds in a week. Sgt. Correll lost it, insisting it was impossible. I reassured him I could do it and walked out of his office looking confident—but panicking inside.

For the next seven days, I lived on lettuce and water. My mom freaked out, convinced I was developing an eating disorder. To counter it, she made my favorite dishes every night—enchiladas, chicken mole, chile colorado, and piles of homemade tortillas. I had to pass on all of it, much to her dismay. Cooking was her way of coping with stress—even if, in this case, her cooking was partially to blame for it.

I've never been much of a runner, but at the health club I became a fixture on the treadmills, churning out miles in layered sweats and limping through shin splints. I ran in high-top British Knights—basketball shoes that prioritized looks over function, stability, or comfort. After each run, I'd head into the sauna to sweat out whatever water I had left in me. The sauna was always uncomfortable, and not just because of the heat or dehydration. It was always full of old guys who were *way* too comfortable chatting it up while completely naked. I went in fully clothed, sometimes throwing on an extra sweatshirt. Not these guys. They sat on towels without a care in the world, debating nonsense like they were on a talk show.

After a week of lettuce, water, and misery, I returned to Sgt. Correll's office for an unofficial weigh-in the day before my MEPS appointment. The mood was solemn. The good sergeant was skeptical that I'd lost the necessary weight. He gestured toward the scale. The moment of truth.

One foot. Second foot.

Sgt. Correll slid the large counterweight toward the two-hundred-pound hash. The beam teetered, clacking softly against the top of the balance indicator.

Shit. Still over two hundred.

He adjusted the smaller counterweight until the beam leveled out.

Two hundred and one pounds.

"You're still a fat body," said Sgt. Correll. "You're not going to make weight."

I was crushed. That meant delaying enlistment—and losing my guaranteed slot in the Administrative career field. If that happened, I'd likely be reassigned to some manual labor job.

In desperation, I asked, "Do you take your shoes off for the medical exam and weigh-in at MEPS?"

Sgt. Correll's eyes lit up. "Yes!"

I kicked off my heavy-ass British Knights, peeled off my bulky sweatshirt, and stepped back onto the scale. The beam rocketed upward, then slowly began to settle. Correll slid the small counterweight to zero. The beam didn't move. Then he shifted the large counterweight to the left.

At one-ninety-eight, the beam floated upward.

At one-ninety-five, it hung just shy of even.

He tapped it gently.

One hundred ninety-three pounds.

Sgt. Correll congratulated me, then told me I couldn't eat or drink anything until after my official weigh-in. I agreed.

The next morning at MEPS, I easily made weight—coming in at one hundred eighty-seven pounds—which made me suspect Sgt. Correll's scale might've been rigged.

The day after that, I left for boot camp.

Air Force boot camp isn't like basic training in the other branches. It's not nearly as physical as the Army or the Marines. We didn't run or do pushups and pullups until we puked. Physically speaking, even the Navy had it tougher. There's a reason the other branches call us the "Air Farce," and Air Force basic training "summer camp."

What they get wrong is that while Air Force basic isn't as physically demanding, it's *mentally* exhausting. And it all starts on day one.

On the way to training, every new enlistee is handed a little handbook explaining what to expect. It says, "You will meet your drill instructor at the Air Force Training Reception Center and then enjoy your first Air Force meal."

That sounded downright pleasant.

It was also the furthest thing from the truth.

When you arrive for basic at Lackland Air Force Base, you are indeed greeted by your training instructors. And by "greeted," I mean immediately verbally annihilated. Every expletive and insult known in the English language is hurled at you, your family, your extended family, and even your unborn children.

I was called names I didn't even know existed. At one point, I made the mistake of smiling when Sgt. Gandy, our head instructor, delivered a masterful string of profanity that rang out into the cool Texas night like a Shakespearean sonnet. It was beautifully profane, and I admired the way it rolled off his tongue.

He caught my smile out of the corner of his eye.

For the next ten minutes, I was doing pushups—or as Sgt. Gandy put it, "Beat your fucking face on the ground until *I* get tired, you useless sack of shit."

And that was the moment I officially met my Air Force drill instructor, Sgt. Gandy. His uniform was immaculately pressed, the creases sharp enough to cut glass. He was lean, mean, and looked almost identical to our squadron mascot—an angry bulldog.

After the formal meet-and-greet, we were ushered into the dining facility — or, as the other branches would call it, the chow hall. This was where I would "enjoy my first Air Force meal."

We shuffled in single file, trays in hand, eyes locked straight ahead on the back of the head in front of us. The training instructors circled the room like vultures, waiting to pounce on the slightest misstep.

The rules were simple: no sweets, no sugar, and you had to drink two eight-ounce glasses of water before taking a single bite. That first night it wasn't so bad, but every day after that was brutal — especially at breakfast. Our stomachs were empty and growling, and flooding them with cold water caused stomach cramps so sharp a few guys actually puked. But the rule existed for two reasons: one, to ensure we were at least partially hydrated, and two, because water takes up space and makes you feel full after only a couple bites of reconstituted, quantity-cooked scrambled eggs.

The food that night was... surprisingly decent, or so I was told. We were served a cheesy chili-mac casserole with a piece of cornbread roughly the size of a cinder block. It actually looked pretty good after a long day of travel.

The problem was that the casserole was served at the exact same temperature as molten lava.

When we sat down — at the first available table, no hesitation allowed — we were given exactly ninety seconds to eat. At the end of that ninety seconds, roughly 98% of the Airmen in Basic Military Training Squadron 3708, Flight 159, had second- and third-degree burns on the roofs of their mouths.

We couldn't taste anything for the next week.

To this day, I hate my food served hot.

The rest of boot camp was a blur of classroom lectures on

the history of manned flight, Air Force tradition, and military protocol. When we weren't in class, we were learning to perform the most mundane tasks imaginable—like folding every piece of clothing into perfect six-inch squares.

Sgt. Gandy told us it was his job to break us down, mentally and physically. His logic was sound in a twisted way: *if you can't fold a T-shirt into a perfect six-inch square, how can you be trusted to work on jet engines or load explosives onto fighter jets?*

(In my case, it probably meant "type without using too much correction tape.")

We may not have run or rucked like the other branches, but we also never slept. Air Force regulations required a minimum of eight hours of bed rest per night, which was adorable, considering how often we were yanked out of bed for "bed drills."

The process went like this: jump out of your bunk, get dressed, make your bed perfectly, run down several flights of stairs, form up outside, then sprint back upstairs and do it all in reverse. Over and over. For hours. After six or seven rounds, we were exhausted, sweaty messes. Sgt. Gandy loved having us do bed drills.

It was insane.

If Sgt. Gandy was the architect of our suffering, Sgt. Rodriguez was the freelance contractor who showed up just to make life worse. He had it out for me from day one, and I never fully understood why until one morning during drill.

My legal name is Jesús, very Hispanic, but I'd listed myself as Jesse on my Air Force forms because that's the name I'd always gone by. Sgt. Rodriguez took this as a personal betrayal. The fact that my last name is Taylor—a relic of my father's Anglo heritage—pushed him over the edge. He stormed up to me, got so close I could feel the spit hitting my eyelids, and screamed:

"Taylor?!? Jesús Taylor?!? That is a fucked-up name for a Mexican!"

There was no correct response to that. I just stood at attention, eyes locked forward, wondering if anyone else in the history of the United States Air Force had ever been verbally assaulted for their *name* being insufficiently ethnic.

So I had that going for me.

I also had the unfortunate luck of being in basic training for Christmas, New Year's Eve, and my nineteenth birthday. It was lonely and miserable, and there were days I wondered if I'd made the right decision. Then I remembered I had burned all my academic bridges. I either made it through or returned home to... what, exactly?

Quitting wasn't an option. Like Richard Gere in *An Officer and a Gentleman*, I had nowhere else to go.

Or something like that.

But over the next several weeks, I found myself adapting to this new reality. When reveille played at 4:30 AM, I was one of the first to leap out of my bunk, get dressed, and fall in for morning formation. Every day started the same way: we'd form up, receive the daily safety briefing—which was always identical ("stay away from the cats, bats, and rats, as they will all infect you with rabies!")—sing the Air Force song in a tone-deaf, half-awake caterwaul, then march into the dining facility to shovel down as many mouth-blistering calories as we could during the allotted ninety seconds we were given to eat.

Good times.

I did well at the physical drills and the classroom portions of training, and even earned a Small Arms Expert ribbon (the Air Force equivalent of "Marksman" in the other branches) for my proficiency with an M-16. I like to joke that it just meant most of my shots landed somewhere in the vicinity of the target, but my score actually qualified me as a marksman across all branches of service.

Christmas Day was like every other day in basic, except for one thing: during dinner, Sgt. Gandy lifted his moratorium on dessert. Several guys in my squadron took full advantage and loaded their trays with cookies, pie, and anything and everything sweet they could wedge onto the plastic rectangle. I abstained—not because I didn't want a chocolate chip cookie, but because I knew exactly what awaited those who indulged.

The next morning, every single airman who'd eaten his body weight in sugar the night before passed out and hit the deck—hard. Their systems couldn't handle the previous days sugar rush followed by the brutal crash eleven hours later. Medics raced around checking heads, ribs, noses—anything that might've made contact with the floor. And there was Sgt. Gandy at the front of the formation, wearing a knowing smirk.

That day was one of the few days we ran hard and often in basic training. Sgt. Gandy was hellbent on burning every last gram of Christmas sugar out of us.

Recreation time mostly meant sitting in the day room of the barracks and shining our boots. We'd use the standard applicator to smear on the shoe polish, then switch to cotton balls dipped in water to buff the leather until it gleamed. It was tedious, but it gave us a rare chance to relax and talk without the threat of Sgt. Gandy screaming in our faces.

The only other free time we got—aside from one day of base liberty in downtown San Antonio—was a two-hour break on New Year's Day at the Chaparral, the base recreation center. The Chaparral had a small dance floor, an arcade, a snack bar, and gave us a chance to mingle with the opposite sex.

I gravitated to the arcade, where I played John Elway's Quarterback until I ran out of quarters. From there, I wandered toward the dance floor, where several of my squadron mates were doing their best to dance in BDUs and combat boots with girls from our sister flight. It looked exactly as awkward as it sounds.

Just as I was about to get more quarters, the DJ announced, "Here's a new one from... the Fine Young Cannibals!" The dance floor emptied as people looked around, confused, asking, "Who the hell are the Fine Young Cannibals?" Luckily, I knew the answer. I'd picked up their debut album on my sixteenth birthday after seeing the video for their incredible version of "Suspicious Minds."

I stood at the edge of the floor as the opening chords of "She Drives Me Crazy" blasted from the speakers. The song is a falsetto-fueled, snare-driven, blue-eyed soul banger—1989 pop perfection that turns tormented obsession into dance-floor gold. Roland Gift's voice is weaponized, slicing through the verses in a razor falsetto before dropping into that reedy tenor for the chorus: *She drives me crazy... ooh ooh... like no one else... ooh ooh...* The snare is relentless, the bass pops, and Andy Cox's guitar scratches along like a blend of Prince and Andy Summers.

Before I knew it, I was on the dance floor doing this weird kind of swaying half-dance, completely transfixed. It was my first moment of musical bliss since arriving at Lackland, and for three minutes and thirty-eight seconds, I wasn't in a beige-and-gray Air Force rec center. I was somewhere else entirely.

That two hours of free time went by in a blink of an eye, but the song stayed with me.

Three days after turning nineteen, I graduated basic training and was sent to Keesler Air Force Base in Biloxi, Mississippi. On the way there, our bus stopped in New Orleans. It was Mardi Gras, and the city asked if they could use us—a bus full of fresh-out-of-boot-camp Airmen—as float guards in the parade that night.

Next thing you know, I was walking beside a float, holding a giant hurricane cup, and tossing beaded necklaces into the crowd. Throwing necklaces seemed to be the only official duty of being a Mardi Gras float guard. One of my fellow airmen got spectacularly drunk and was arrested for disorderly conduct—which is really hard to do during Mardi Gras. He managed to take drunken debauchery to a level that required police intervention.

It was a great night that I wish I remembered more of, but those hurricanes are no joke.

Tech school at Keesler was also a blur. I wasn't even there a week when I tore the ACL and medial meniscus in my right knee during an intramural basketball game. I tried hiding the injury for a few days, but one of the instructors spotted me limping across the courtyard on my way to the dorm. He walked over, asked what happened, then drove me straight to the base hospital. A stability test confirmed what I already feared: my knee was shredded.

This was devastating news—not just because of the injury, but because I'd already received my permanent duty station assignment: Lakenheath AFB in England. A dream posting. In my mind, I'd already mapped out a magical mystery tour through London and Liverpool, hitting all the places immortalized in "Penny Lane" and "Strawberry Fields." Those orders were immediately pulled once the severity of my injury was discovered and reported.

I slipped into a quiet, determined depression.

For the rest of my time at Keesler, I was either in class or in physical therapy. My right leg was locked in an immobilizer, and I had to use crutches to get around. Meals were a challenge—I had to rely on classmates to carry my tray for me. Worse, I couldn't really leave the base because of the injury.

When I got my first post–basic training paycheck, I hobbled over to the Base Exchange and bought three things: a dual-cassette Sony boombox, a pair of headphones, and the Fine Young Cannibals' *The Raw and the Cooked*, featuring "She Drives Me Crazy." My days became a loop of Roland Gift, classwork, and physical therapy. My career field had an accelerated graduation path—the harder I worked, the faster I could graduate and get new orders and, eventually, knee surgery.

Tech school was supposed to last three months. I passed my final exam after less than four weeks.

The day after graduation, I was called to the base personnel office and was handed my new orders...to New Jersey. Definitely a downgrade from Lakenheath. A young female airman stood next to me reading over her assignment with equal disappointment. She was headed to Edwards AFB in California. I tried to cheer her up.

"Hey," I said, "at least it's not New Jersey."

She frowned. "I'm from New Jersey."

A moment passed. Then she said, "Maybe we can switch?"

It turns out you *can* trade orders, as long as the staffing needs match and both people hold the same rank. By some miracle, everything lined up. The next day, my orders were officially switched from New Jersey to Edwards AFB.

Forty-eight hours later, I was on a plane back to Washington before reporting to Edwards, duffel bag in one hand and my Sony boombox in the other. I was home for two weeks—long enough to buy a Subaru Justy. It was powered by a three-cylinder engine that cranked out a whopping seventy-three horsepower and took about twenty minutes to reach sixty miles per hour. It also had no air conditioning.

I didn't know much about Edwards AFB, only that it was ninety miles east of Los Angeles. My dad looked it up in his Rand McNally atlas and showed me its exact location: smack dab in the middle of the Mojave Desert.

The lack of AC in my Subaru was going to be a problem.

After my brief stay at home, I headed south on I-5. The Justy was loaded with clothes, a few mementos, and millions of cassette tapes.

A few months later, in July, I underwent the first of three knee surgeries. The Air Force surgeon gave me thirty days of convalescence leave. I spent the first three days on base, miserable and bored, before making a decision that was equal parts impulsive and medically questionable: I was going home.

My right leg was in a massive brace, the sutures still tight and angry, but I climbed into the Justy anyway and quickly realized the manual transmission was going to be a problem. I had to operate the accelerator with my right foot while using my left foot for the brakes and clutch.

Before attempting the eleven-hundred-mile drive with an immobile leg, I practiced for fifteen minutes in the dormitory parking lot: starting, shifting, easing off the clutch without stalling, braking without locking the tires. It was awkward and jerky at first, and every time I lifted my right leg too much, the incision lit up with hot, needle-sharp pain.

But eventually the movements clicked enough that I felt—not confident, exactly, but capable—of making the drive. As long as I avoided heavy traffic or bad weather, I might survive.

I left early the next morning and drove through day and night, stopping only for gas and the occasional agonizing bathroom break. Meals were strictly drive-through. McDonald's had cheeseburgers for forty-nine cents. Those would do.

The drive was brutal. Every exit required a clumsy ballet of twisting, lowering myself out of the car, and hauling myself back in without bending my right leg. And the Justy's supposed top speed—ninety-five miles per hour—was complete propaganda. I had the gas pedal welded to the floor through central California, and that little three-cylinder go-cart never cracked eighty. And it only managed that while drafting behind an eighteen-wheeler.

But eventually, sometime after midnight, I crossed the Tacoma Narrows Bridge and rolled back into Port Orchard.

Home looked the same, but felt completely different.

I'd only been gone eight months, but it felt like eight years. It's not true that you can never go home again—of course you can. But when you do, you realize you've changed. The lens sharpens. The town doesn't look different so much as *smaller,* like someone nudged the camera back a few feet.

My friends were back from college for the summer, but it wasn't like it used to be. Personalities had sharpened. Priorities had shifted. We were still friends, but the edges didn't quite line up the way they had before.

Growing pains.

Being on crutches meant no basketball games. My incisions prevented me from going to the lake. And both Eric and Carlton had summer jobs and were gone until afternoon. I'd wait for them to get off work, and we'd hit the movies, wander the Kitsap Mall, or hang out at my parents' house playing Nintendo. It didn't feel like summer vacation; it felt disconnected, transitional—like we were all already headed somewhere else.

Pop music that summer was just as disjointed: Milli Vanilli, Paula Abdul, Bobby Brown, Janet Jackson, Madonna—bright, glossy hits that felt thin and weirdly artificial. Milli Vanilli turned out to be exactly that, but I'll still go to bat for "Blame It on the Rain." Great song, no matter whose voices were on the tape.

Luckily, 1989 was the year of the Fine Young Cannibals for me. *The Raw and the Cooked* became the soundtrack of that first year away from home—the album I leaned on when I felt disoriented or lonely. A somewhat shady Jamaican guy who worked at the Edwards hospital installed a tape deck in the Justy for me, and from that point on Roland Gift had co-pilot status. I played that tape to death.

I returned to Edwards and the blast-furnace heat of the Mojave in mid-August and got to work on my knee. Rehab was grueling, but I didn't let it stop me. As soon as the surgeon cleared me for activity, I got after it. I played a lot of basketball, rode my mountain bike through the desert, and even played keeper on the base soccer team. What I lacked in mobility and kicking strength I made up for with grit. After a tough stop on a shot on goal, a player from the opposing team told me I was the meanest keeper he'd ever played against. I took it as a compliment.

My Air Force career lasted four years, and I grew up a lot during that time. I had to learn to be self-sufficient and responsible, especially when it came to taking care of myself. There was no physical therapist on base—I had to rehab entirely on my own. And because my first surgery was in 1989 at a military hospital, it wasn't exactly cutting-edge ACL repair. A nasty zipper scar still runs up the inside of my right knee. It wasn't until 1997, when I tore the ACL and medial meniscus in my left knee, that I finally got a modern arthroscopic surgery.

Even though I never made it overseas, I still got to do things I never would have experienced otherwise. Edwards AFB had a small detachment of the UK's Royal Air Force for the U.S. test pilot program. I befriended a few RAF pilots, and they invited me to join their darts team—even though I'd never thrown a dart in my life. Once a week, I'd meet them at the Officers' Club to play and drink pints of Harp lager. It wasn't Lakenheath, but it was a small taste of what might have been.

I still have a slight limp in my right knee, and some days it aches with arthritis, but it hasn't stopped me. If anything, the discomfort is a reminder of what I've already pushed through—and that I'm still capable of pushing forward. It's the proof I carry with me, every day, that growth leaves a scar.

HEY JEALOUSY

In January of 1993, I landed a customer service job with Washington Mutual Bank. I was less than a month out of the Air Force and knew next to nothing about banking.

On my first day of training, we were told to transfer any customer calls about IRA accounts to a senior agent. I raised my hand and asked the trainer if that was because of the political situation in Ireland.

She blinked. "I'm sorry?"

I doubled down. "You know... the Irish Republican Army? Are these accounts being used to fund their struggle against British occupation or something?"

Her eyes went wide. Then, very calmly, she explained that IRA accounts were *Individual Retirement Accounts* — not banking instruments used by paramilitary organizations.

I might not have known anything about banking, but thanks to Bono, I had a rudimentary understanding of The Troubles.

My office was located in the heart of downtown Seattle's financial district. Key Bank, First Interstate, and Seattle First all had headquarters within earshot of the Washington Mutual Tower—WAMU Tower for short. The dress code was strict business attire, so I wore a tie every day. Business casual hadn't been invented yet, at least not for us.

I was living in a rental house in Port Orchard with Eric and my brother Chris. It was a decent place, except for one detail: every wall and shelf was decorated with portraits and figurines of clowns. Everywhere you turned, a clown stared back at you. The owners told us we weren't allowed to move or remove any of them. We didn't ask why. After a month, we all silently agreed the house was haunted and left it at that.

My mornings started at 5:00 AM. I'd get ready, drive to Bremerton, and catch the ferry to Seattle. The ride was fifty-five minutes long, and most mornings I slept with my head on a table in the boat's galley. After docking, I'd walk four blocks uphill to my building, where I spent my day trying to talk senior citizens out of their passbook savings accounts and into deposit accounts — a $2.75 commission each time. The rest of my shift was spent reassuring those same senior citizens that yes, the Social Security direct deposit *did* hit their account.

My base pay was $1,500 a month. Not every two weeks — *per month.* Even in 1993, that wasn't much. But it covered rent, my car, CDs, and the occasional night out. It wasn't glamorous, but it worked.

Most lunches I grabbed a bagel from Mel's Diner at the base of the building. That's where I formed a crush on the bagel girl. She was shy and didn't say much, but three times a week she'd hand me a toasted salt bagel with a smile, and that was enough to keep me coming back. Well, that and the fact that a toasted bagel with cream cheese in 1993 cost less than two dollars.

I'd eat while wandering around downtown before returning to take calls from customers convinced the bank had robbed them of three cents in interest the previous month.

My desk was tucked in the corner of the floor between my coworkers Scott and Todd. We shared a radio tuned to 107.7 The End — Seattle's alternative rock station. We kept the volume low, but not so low we couldn't hear the steady rotation of Nirvana, Red Hot Chili Peppers, Pearl Jam, and Smashing Pumpkins. The afternoon DJ was British and occasionally slipped in The Smiths, The Verve, Hot House Flowers, or Morrissey. I welcomed the break from all the so-called grunge.

On May 24, The End played “Hey Jealousy” by the Gin Blossoms for the first time. I had just returned from the breakroom with what I called the homeless man’s mocha, which was a packet of Swiss Miss hot cocoa swirled into plain black coffee. It tasted awful, but I had to make that $1,500.00 last a whole month. There was no way I could drop three bucks on a latte and expect to eat, at least not in the same day.

I sat at my desk, girding myself to return to the endless queue of angry seniors, when then the jangly pop rock of the Gin Blossoms hit my ears. The song felt and sounded different — not just sonically but, emotionally. There was an unpretentious self-awareness in the lyrics that set it apart from the well-rehearsed performative angst of the likes of Eddie Vedder.

That same day, we learned our office was being moved from downtown Seattle to Lynnwood. Goodbye high-rise in the financial district; hello strip malls stitched together by an endless maze of parking lots. The move meant I’d have to relocate too. There was no way to keep living in Port Orchard and survive the commute. It would destroy me mentally and financially.

I rented a small room in a house shared by other call center workers. Rent was affordable and the commute was decent, so I agreed sight unseen. What I found out my very first night was that this house was the location of one long party. People were always coming over or stopping by to drink, smoke weed, watch the Huskies/Seahawks/Sonics/Mariners play, or jam downstairs in the makeshift studio. The house was always loud, always raucous, and there was always some kind of drama. I’ve never been one for communal living as I enjoy really my solitude. A lot. So I had to make a choice; be the weird roommate who just stayed in his room, labeled all his food, and complained about everything, or learn to adapt and join in. I chose the latter. Before long, I was smoking enough weed to captain a reggae cruise and drinking like a pirate who’d raid it.

My new roommates introduced me to a seasonal beer called

Snow Cap that tipped the scales at 7% ABV. It's a rich, malt bomb of a beer that tastes terrible, but that didn't stop me from drinking my body weight in the stuff one night at the Wedgwood Ale House. On an empty stomach. I became psychotically drunk to the point my roommates had to drag me home, where I then spent the rest of the night barfing in the bathroom. I eventually passed out on the bathroom floor, facedown on a heating register. I awoke the next morning, a work morning mind you, with an imprint of the heating register stamped on the right side of my face. My right eye had partially swollen shut from the metal grate and warm air pushing into it all night.

Panicked, I scrambled to get it together so I wouldn't be late. I arrived at my office with my polo shirt on inside out and a pair of Marvin the Martian flannel boxers over my regular boxers. I literally forgot to put on proper pants. I shit you not, I showed up for work wearing two pairs of boxers.

How I didn't get fired on the spot remains one of life's greatest mysteries.

Those early WAMU months after the move to Lynnwood became a blur of hangovers, overdraft disputes, and the slow death of my liver and lung capacity. I suddenly had a new cast of characters in my life, too. Scott and Todd were still around, but worked different shifts. I became fast friends with two new hires, Jonathan and Ron.

I actually interviewed Ron while in the midst of a DEFCON 3 hangover. My head was pounding, I had a flop sweat going, and was seconds away from vacating my stomach into the nearest trash can during the interview. Making matters worse, Ron was a talker. His answers were elaborate, detailed, and endless. By the time we got near the end of the interview, I was barely hanging on.

Then I made a near fatal mistake. I asked, "Do you have any questions for us?"

Ron perked up. "Yes!" he said, before producing a yellow legal pad *filled* with questions—about the job, future career opportunities, and possibly the meaning of life itself. To this day, it remains the longest interview of my career. But he got the job, and we became good friends, so I guess we both survived.

Life then became a routine of chaos. I kept spare clothes in my car for the mornings I didn't make it home, taking what can only be described as a "restroom sink shower" before skulking to my desk, waves of nausea hitting me harder than the ones that sank the *Edmund Fitzgerald*.

We argued with customers, suffered through mind-numbing team-building sessions, and endured surreal "diversity" workshops—including one street poet who threatened to kill us with his righteous rhymes and a Holocaust Survivor who made us lie on the conference-room floor on top of each other to better understand trauma.

It was *The Office* before *The Office* existed.

Amidst all of that, I was still trying to figure out who I was supposed to be. By the time spring of 1994 rolled around, I was juggling work and playing in a bar band. My co-worker and bandmate Patrick and I spent most lunch breaks huddled in a corner booth of Alfy's Pizza, refining setlists and arguing over which cover songs deserved to stay. Did the drunken rummies at The Anchor Tavern in Everett really want to hear Icicle Works' "Whisper to a Scream"? Probably not. But we kept it in anyway because it was a hell of a lot of fun to play.

I was also dating a woman a couple of years older than me, someone with a proper corporate job at the bank—far removed from the barely contained mayhem that defined telephone customer service and sales. We made it about a year before she dumped me for a cardiologist or something. A guy with career plans and actual ambition. Meanwhile, I was still wondering where our next gig was and hoping we'd get at least two free drink tickets at the door.

It was my first adult breakup, and it hurt. But it also taught me something: nothing changes if nothing changes. Getting dumped is never easy, but it hits harder when someone finally says out loud what you already know — that your mopey bar-band persona had gone from mysterious and fun to exhausting and boring. She didn't have the energy to continue pretending that her goals weren't bigger than mine, and she'd run out of patience waiting for me to figure things out — and honestly, I don't know how *I* had the patience to put up with me either.

Christ, I unironically wore a Sub Pop shirt with the word *LOSER* printed in giant bold letters across the front. Sometimes I wish I could time travel so I can go back and smack myself in the head.

The Gin Blossoms' "Hey Jealousy" had been floating around the radio for close to a year at this point, but it really took hold for me around this time. The song — and the album it came from, *New Miserable Experience* — became a kind of companion as I stumbled my way through early adulthood. Doug Hopkins' songwriting mattered to me. His lyrics carried a self-awareness that resonated when you're in your early twenties and trying to navigate through life.

New Miserable Experience wasn't just an album I liked — it was a mirror. Doug Hopkins wrote about alcohol-fueled insecurity and self-sabotage, and I was becoming fluent in both.

It isn't a coming-of-age record; it's a confession disguised as jangly power pop. Seen as a whole, it's a stunning collection of songs where Doug Hopkins — and by extension the entire band — laid bare everything that haunted them: unfulfilled potential, the weight of expectations, and the resentment that grows when you realize you may never become the person you're supposed to be.

Every track lives in that impossible tug-of-war between who you are and who you're expected to become. The lyrics orbit that tension — wanting to grow up but being dragged backward by old habits, old pain, and the gravitational pull of familiar demons tugging at your ankles. Staying the same is always easier. You can't fail if you don't try to move forward.

At twenty-four, that was me in a nutshell. I wore self-doubt like a uniform. I joked about my insecurities before anyone else could. You can still see echoes of that self-deprecation in my writing today.

Back then, I felt a kinship with Doug Hopkins the songwriter — the guy who penned most of the album's best tracks. Now, I feel sympathy for Doug Hopkins the human being. His life wasn't just shaped by alcoholism, depression, and what was likely bipolar disorder — he was *shackled* by them. You can hear it in the way he wrote, how the songs crackle with hope one second and whipsaw to despair the next.

During the recording sessions for the album in 1992, those battles spilled into the open. His drinking increased and his behavior became more erratic. A&M Records pressured the band to fire him before the album was even finished, terrified he'd sink the whole project. Hopkins accepted a small settlement but lost all future royalties on songs that were unmistakably his. This decision haunted the band for years.

On December 5th, 1993 Hopkins killed himself with a .38 pistol in his Tempe apartment. A week earlier, he had smashed his framed gold record for "Hey Jealousy." He was thirty-two.

Unlike Kurt Cobain, Hopkins isn't treated as a cultural icon or the voice of a generation. But maybe he should be. For guys like me, trying to stumble into adulthood with a head full of doubt and a belly full of cheap beer, songs like "Mrs. Rita," "Lost Horizons," and "Hey Jealousy" hit closer to the bone than anything on *Nevermind*. Cobain articulated generational disillusionments with blunt force; Hopkins articulated something more intimate and fragile. Young adulthood is fraught with aching hopefulness, a belief that life could still shake out in your favor if you'd just get the fuck out of your own way.

The song "29" strips away the pretense of the bar-friendly brightness of the other tracks. It's written from the perspective of a man who realizes he has nothing left. Musically, it's one of the prettiest tracks on the album: shimmering guitars, Robin Wilson's warm vocal, that perfect jangle-pop sheen. The darkness of the lyrics, woven through the melody, are a brutal self-assessment of a life spent chasing highs that never lasted and revisiting relationships that ended in wreckage. He's staring down thirty and sees only the abyss. "29" is Doug Hopkins' raw and unflinching suicide note disguised as a song.

Unbeknownst to Doug, his writing also captured the emotional texture of the early '90s — that strange in-between moment when the present was slipping into the past, and the future felt unsteady underfoot. The cultural landscape was shifting fast. The internet was about to change everything. Music was evolving. The world felt both wide open and impossibly uncertain. Hopkins wrote straight into that tension.

"The past is gone, but something might be found to take its place" turned out to be a prophetic line.

As my twenty-fifth birthday approached, I could feel my own inertia closing in. My attitude, my drinking, and the general disarray of my life had burned every bridge I had in telephone banking. If I wanted any chance at a future, it wasn't going to be there. So I bet on myself, took what was essentially a demotion, and started over.

The self-destruction didn't stop — not yet, not for a few more years — but that new job was my first small step, or maybe a clumsy stumble, toward something better.

In "Hey Jealousy," Robin Wilson sings, *"If you don't expect too much from me, you might not be let down."* That line used to feel like a warning label I should've worn on a shirt. Now it feels like an artifact of somebody I used to be. These days, I expect a lot from myself.

New Miserable Experience will always be one of my favorite albums from that era — not out of nostalgia, but because of how precisely it mirrors the path I was on. It's a record about unraveling and trying again, about the shaky hope hiding beneath self-destruction. Back then, I related to the collapse. Now, I relate to the recovery.

It took me years to understand what that album had been trying to tell me:

You can fall apart — but you don't have to stay that way. You can choose the harder thing, the better thing, and keep going. That's the real confession hidden inside those jangly guitars.

And in 1995, for the first time, I was finally starting to listen.

Or was I...?

LIVE FOREVER

On April 5th, 1994, Kurt Cobain was found dead inside his home by electrician Gary Smith. Cobain had ingested a lethal dose of heroin and then shot himself in the head. At the time, his suicide was being treated like the death of John Lennon. David Fricke went so far as to say that Cobain's voice was so similar to Lennon's that if you ran them both through a spectrogram, they would be indentical. This was a phenomenally stupid take and was immediately recognized for what it was: a boomer's attempt to hijack a current pop culture event and tie it back to an icon of the 1960s.

Nirvana was a great band, there's no denying that. There have probably been a million or two words written about how Nirvana, with Cobain at the helm, completely redefined the pop music landscape. Which they did, but not in one fell swoop. And they also had help from Pearl Jam, Soundgarden, Alice in Chains, Smashing Pumpkins, Green Day, and even Stone Temple Pilots.

Now, had you asked me in March of 1994 which of the above-mentioned bands would still be around thirty-one years later, I would have said none. Yet, here we are in 2025 and every single one of those bands, minus Nirvana, are still out touring and churning out albums only the most die-hard fans buy.

Cobain's death, Dave Grohl's success with Foo Fighters, and Krist Novoselic doing whatever it is he's doing, served as roadblocks to any type of Nirvana reunion. Nirvana operated as a band behind the scenes, everyone contributed to Cobain's compositions. But in the end, Nirvana was Cobain, and Cobain was Nirvana. Going on tour with another lead singer would be seen as sacrilege. I'm kind of surprised Courtney Love never pushed for it.

Cobain's suicide affected me in an odd way. Yes, I was sad that he'd killed himself at twenty-seven, but what struck me more was the feeling that something had been exposed — as if a veil had been ripped away. At the time, it was treated like the death of an icon, and in a sense it was, but it also revealed a rot that had been there all along.

Cobain's death didn't just shock the city; it highlighted a truth that had been hiding in plain sight. It came on the heels of Andrew Wood's overdose, and only a few weeks before Hole's bassist, Kristen Pfaff was found dead of an OD as well. Several years later, Layne Staley would die the same way. Cobain's suicide was the most high-profile, but it wasn't an isolated tragedy. The scene had a problem — one everyone knew about, but no one wanted to say out loud.

That day, Seattle felt different. Not like a part of the city had died, but like something had finally been unmasked.

That night — April 5th, 1994 — I had a blind dinner date arranged by a friend and his wife. The girl I was being set up with was the wife's friend, so the four of us went to dinner together. My date was a nice enough girl, a little shy, and that's pretty much all I remember about her.

I arrived at the Italian restaurant where I was meeting them, said my hellos, and then I proceeded to get shitfaced drunk.

I was three or four vodka tonics into it before the salad and bread even hit the table, and threw back another three or four over the course of dinner. By the time the waitress asked if we wanted dessert, I was melting down faster than Chernobyl.

Cobain's death reverberated through Seattle, but it wasn't universal. My friend — the one who had helped set up the blind date — was Black, born and raised in Seattle's Central District, and he didn't feel the shockwave the same way I did. As I knocked back vodka tonics as if I had just absorbed the news of a family member dying, he kept asking what all the fuss was about.

Rock stars OD'd all the time. Why was this one being treated like a state funeral? Was it because Cobain was local? Because he was white? Because the alternative-rock world had been elevated into something bigger, broader, and more sacred than other genres and scenes? He wasn't being dismissive — he just didn't buy into the mythology Seattle had built around its music scene, and he didn't understand why we were eulogizing Cobain as if he were royalty.

His confusion only amplified my own unraveling. While the city mourned its patron saint of disaffection, I was melting down at an Italian restaurant, drinking like the world had tilted off its axis.

I excused myself and stumbled out to the parking lot. A chain-link fence separated the restaurant from the bar next door. I leaned across the top rail, the cold metal biting into my chest and under my arms—then wretched so hard I blacked out.

My date grew concerned after I'd been gone too long and came outside to look for me. She found me slumped over the fence like a derelict scarecrow left out to guard an empty field in the winter.

She managed to get me down off the fence, laid me across the backseat of my car, and drove me home. My friend—a former squadron mate from the Air Force—had seen this side of me before, back on my twenty-first birthday, so he knew I was a lost cause. Once I tipped too far, there was no rallying.

He and his wife led the way to my house, and together they helped me inside. My date even went so far as to peel off my puke-covered shirt and start a load of laundry. When I was finally in bed, and everyone was certain I wasn't going to pull a John Bonham, they left.

I never saw that girl again.

In the months that followed Cobain's suicide, countless think pieces tried to answer the same question: who would fill the void he left behind? Could that void even be filled, or had his death marked another day the music died?

The answer, at least on paper, seemed to be: "plenty" and "no". Quite a few bands were ready to step up. Weezer released their *Blue Album* in May. Stone Temple Pilots followed in June with *Purple*, the confident sequel to *Core*. In the months leading up to Cobain's death, Green Day had already dropped *Dookie* in January, and Soundgarden unleashed *Superunknown* in March. That fall brought new releases from Pearl Jam and The Smashing Pumpkins, both of which helped cement the next chapter of alternative rock.

On August 8th, the debut US single from Oasis, "Live Forever", slipped onto American alternative radio with no fanfare or hype campaign. It just appeared as a bright, defiant burst of color that cut through the grey. The opening alone, the unhurried thump-thump-da-thump-thump-thump of the drums, already sounded like something different. Then Liam Gallagher's voice slides in, nasal, fearless, and sneering, "Maybe I don't really wanna know / How your garden grows / 'Cause I just wanna fly...." It didn't feel like any of the mopey naval-gazing music we'd been wallowing in. It felt as if someone had cracked open a window in a musty, stuffy room. After months of grief, here was a song that defied despair.

For me, in that moment, the wreckage of Cobain's death was swept away.

Noel Gallagher has said the idea for "Live Forever" came to him in the days after Kurt Cobain's suicide. "I wrote it the week Kurt died. I didn't want to be him," he told *Melody Maker*. "We're not here to be like Nirvana. We're here to outlive them."

The Gallagher brothers were everything Nirvana wasn't—loud, brash, and unapologetically confident. Noel knew he had an album's worth of songs that could put them on the map, and in his younger brother he had the perfect front man: fearless, magnetic, and cocksure enough to make audiences believe every word he sang.

The first time I saw Oasis was at a small venue in Seattle, and to this day it remains one of the best live shows I've ever seen. There were no performative histrionics from Liam, no rock-and-roll posturing from Noel, Guigsy, or Bonehead, and drummer Tony McCarroll held everything down with a steady backbeat. The five of them walked on stage, tore through their set, and rocked that club's collective ass off for the better part of an hour.

They closed with a raucous cover of The Beatles' "I Am the Walrus," and it was glorious—loud, chaotic, and transcendent.

My ears rang for three days afterward, but I was all in on Oasis from that night forward.

I was surprised later to learn that "Live Forever" barely dented the US Top 100, and that *Definitely Maybe* only reached #58 on the Billboard 200 album chart. That song felt like it was everywhere in the summer of 1994—not just on alternative radio stations, but on mainstream pop stations too. Or maybe that's just how I remember it: ubiquitous, inescapable, and alive.

In retrospect, "Live Forever" was a rolling rumble of thunder crossing the Atlantic, a hint of what was to come.

By November 1995, the storm had arrived. Oasis unleashed "Wonderwall," their first U.S. Top Ten hit, and became exactly what they'd been predicting since 1994: the biggest band in the world.

Oasis was the last band I loved in that way you can only love a band when you're young. I'd hit up Bulldog Press in the U-District just to buy copies of *Melody Maker*, *New Musical Express*, and any other UK publication that featured them. They were rock stars, and they were ecstatic to be rock stars. They behaved like it too—loud, confident, and utterly unbothered by what anyone else thought.

They didn't take themselves too seriously or try to change the world. No haranguing the crowd about politics. No lectures on veganism or internal combustion engines. They just wanted to play music, drink, do coke, shag groupies, and write great songs.

I saw Oasis a second time when they rolled through Seattle again in January of 1995. After the show, I ended up at a bar called The George & Dragon — a British pub tucked away in a Seattle suburb. I'd been there once or twice before, but something clicked that night. Maybe it was the post-concert adrenaline, or the way the music inside the bar matched the music still ringing in my ears. Maybe it was that familiar sensation of being unmoored in my mid-twenties and needing a place that felt like mine.

The George & Dragon hadn't yet been infiltrated by hipster doofuses or scenesters; it was a proper pub — the kind of place you went to get pissed with your mates, not put on airs or act real cool. For that reason alone, the G&D became *my* pub. And if you looked at my bank statements from January 1995 through late 2001, you'd assume it was my second home.

For the next several years, I was there at least three nights a week, usually with my buddies Ron and Jonathan. All three of us would wander in after a long day of maneuvering through the insanity of working at the WAMU contact center. People drifted in and out of our orbit, but we were the core three. We talked about work, life, girlfriends (or lack thereof), and whatever fresh chaos we were navigating through at the time. We were young, half-broke, recklessly dumb, overconfident, and somehow convinced that everything in our lives was still wide open.

The décor didn't matter. The darts didn't matter. Even the beer didn't matter. It was the atmosphere — the feeling that you could walk in on any random Tuesday and know exactly who you'd see and what songs would be playing.

I was living out my own version of Chumbawamba's "Tubthumping"; *"he drinks a whiskey drink, he drinks a vodka drink, he drinks a lager drink, he drinks a cider drink/he sings the songs that remind him of the good times, he sings the songs that remind him of the better times."*

And the soundtrack was brilliant: Oasis, Blur, Pulp, Elastica, Black Grape, Ocean Colour Scene, The Charlatans. That bright, shimmering, guitar-driven Britpop that made everything feel bigger and more electric than it probably was. It filled the bar the way neon fills a city street after it rains — all glow and edge and possibility. I shed the dead skin of mopiness and insecurity and embraced self-confidence and alcohol-fueled swagger.

For a while, the G&D felt like the center of the world.

Maybe because it was.

The cast of characters we mingled with at the G&D were unforgettable: Jim the doorman, more interested in shooting pool than checking IDs; Pagey, the drunken building inspector who rode his bike everywhere after racking up too many DWIs; and Clyde the bartender, always ready with a refill and a pithy comment.

It was a happy, carefree time. I was finally making decent money —enough to have disposable income to blow on drinks, dinners, and splitting the cost of Sonics season tickets. I usually sold my bundle, keeping only the games when my beloved Lakers came to town.

Early in 1998, the day before my twenty-eighth birthday to be exact, the Lakers were in town to play the Sonics in an afternoon matinee between the top two teams in the Western Conference. It was a nationally televised game, and the area around KeyArena (now Climate Pledge Arena—Seattle still leads the world in pointless virtue signaling) buzzed with NBC Sports vans and local news crews setting up for pregame bits.

That night, Oasis played Mercer Arena on their *Be Here Now* tour, with Cornershop opening.

I had tickets to both.

Ron, Jonathan, and I started the morning with a liquid breakfast of Bloody Marys at the Mecca Café. By the time the game tipped off, I was already seeing double.

When we reached our seats, I was greeted by the Sonics fans who'd grown familiar with my antics over the past two seasons. I was always quick to berate the refs anytime a call went against the Lakers — which, in my mind, was every single one of them. There was a lot of playful back-and-forth with the locals, but it never crossed the line. I truly believed the Lakers never committed fouls, even when it was obvious they did.

The Lakers lost that afternoon, and I heard plenty about it from my Sonics-loving friends as I stumbled my way out of the arena shouting, "We'll see you in Inglewood!" before slipping on a wet sidewalk grate.

Since we'd been drinking since breakfast, someone suggested we should probably eat and sober up a bit before the Oasis show. So we went to another bar — the logic of the day remaining flawless. I couldn't tell you which place it was, only that a few more friends joined us. They weren't going to the concert; they just wanted in on my birthday shenanigans.

I ordered a burger at the bar, and when it arrived, someone commented that it looked good. I eyed them suspiciously. Convinced they were going to try and steal my burger, I grabbed it and hid between two pinball machines to eat in peace. At the time, that seemed like a reasonable thing to do.

After eating — and drinking even more so we would sober up — we went to *yet another* bar for the obligatory pre-func before seeing Oasis. Which, in hindsight, was insane; the entire day had already been one long pre-func with an NBA game as the intermission. Still, tradition was tradition. For the uninitiated, the pre-func was when you went to a bar to drink before going to the bar you had plans to drink at later. It wasn't unusual to say things like, "Let's meet at Bernard's to pre-func before rollin' to the Nitelite." Trust me, it made sense back then. Kind of.

The Oasis show was great—though not as magnificent as the

first time I saw them, or even the second. They were older now, and the cracks in the band were starting to show. The relationship between the Gallagher brothers had always been complicated, but after four years in the spotlight, it was clear this version of the band wasn't built to last.

But it wasn't just Oasis showing strain. Cracks were forming in my friendships with Ron and Jonathan too, hairline fractures at first, easy to ignore and paper over with drinks. Friendships built on late nights and drunken revelry don't collapse all at once; they erode slowly, imperceptibly, until the foundation you thought was solid shifts under your feet. We were still the core three, still laughing, still drinking, still pretending nothing was changing, but the truth was creeping in. We were growing up, and not always in the same direction or at the same pace.

That January night at Mercer Arena, I was shoulder to shoulder with friends and strangers, all of us swept up in the same electric wave of energy, singing along to every song. I would turn twenty-eight in a matter of hours, though I didn't feel it yet. Nights like that — full of noise and laughter and the illusion of permanence — have a way of tricking you. When five thousand people scream *"You and I are gonna live forever!"* it's impossible not to believe them. Impossible not to think your friends will stay close, your life will stay wide open, and none of it will ever change.

That night was the beginning of a long goodbye to that version of myself. It probably was for Jonathan and Ron too, though none of us would have known it then. Slow change had already started tugging at us with new jobs, new relationships, new responsibilities and all of the other quiet forces that loosen the knots of friendships pulled tight during late nights at the bar. It wasn't dramatic or sudden; it was more like watching the tide go out. Endings make space for beginnings, even if you don't realize you're standing on that threshold at the time.

People who once felt permanent eventually turn into names you scroll past in your contacts, relics carried over from one phone upgrade to the next. You still hear from them sometimes, almost always when the news is bad (someone from the old crew is gone, divorce, job loss). The only remaining thread between you is tragedy, but even those threads fray over time.

Mostly, though, they linger at the edges: a photo that sneaks into your feed, a reflex "Happy birthday!" you leave before scrolling on. Ghosts that flicker into existence for half a second, then dissolve back into the algorithm.

When I hear "Live Forever" now, those opening drum beats still feel like a door swinging open or the first breath of a morning that hasn't even happened yet. It will always be that defiant affirmation that says maybe, just maybe, there is something in us that is bigger than the years.

If I do get pulled back into the past, I feel like a phantom wandering through a landscape that died out a long time ago — familiar, but uninhabitable. The people, the noise, the bar lights...they're museum pieces now. I can look at them, acknowledge them, even appreciate them. But I don't live there anymore. I don't need to. The song remains the same, but the former life wrapped around it is nothing more than an exhibit, not a destination. The music kept its promise in the only way it ever really could: it outlived the version of me that needed it most, and it still makes the version of me that's here feel, for three and a half minutes, like everything is still beginning.

I also remember the soul-crushing hangover I had the next morning, the kind that makes you beg for sweet, merciful death. That part I could've done without.

HERE COMES A REGULAR

I would never go so far as to call myself an alcoholic. Even in the booziest stretch of my booze-hound days, I never drank alone, never woke up needing a drink, never got the DTs, and could go days or even weeks without touching the stuff. I was a social drinker who just happened to go out. A lot.

My drinking life was always tied to other people. Alcohol became personality fuel. I'm an introvert by nature—slow to warm up, slower to trust, and easily mistaken for standoffish, aloof, or outright unapproachable. I'm not a natural "people person." But alcohol made me one. A couple drinks in, and suddenly my wit sharpened, my dry humor caught fire, and I could hold court at any after-work happy hour.

Whatever I lacked in self-esteem, a double Maker's Mark neat with two Coronas on the side—my standard Friday-or-Saturday-night starter kit—more than plastered over the hole in my personality. After that, it was a steady diet of bourbon on the rocks, punctuated only by the occasional glass of water or emergency order of fries to keep me from sliding off the cliff from "gregariously drunk" into full blackout mode.

And I did my share of blacking out.

In 1998, I was working as a business analyst at Washington Mutual. We'd just launched a new version of our proprietary consumer lending platform, which of course meant celebration.

Someone booked an Argosy cruise, the entire consumer lending organization boarded, and we proceeded to drink the boat's bar dry. That night gave birth to the phrase "boat party drunk," a term created specifically to capture the level of catastrophic drunkenness we all achieved.

By the end, I was in no shape to drive, so I caught a ride home with coworkers. For reasons that remain a psychological mystery to me, I was embarrassed about where I lived—which was absurd for two reasons. One, I lived in a condo on Mercer Island, one of the most prestigious zip codes in Washington State, if not the entire West Coast. Two, these coworkers had already been to my condo before.

Still, alcohol convinced me I was some tragic version of Molly Ringwald in *Pretty in Pink*—too ashamed for Andrew McCarthy to see her sad house. So instead of being dropped at my front door like a normal person, I asked them to let me out about a mile away. Then I staggered home alone in the dark.

On a work night.

Calling in sick the next morning wasn't an option. Our boss was a stern, deeply religious Filipino woman who had warned us—very clearly—to "watch how much we drink" at the party. Naturally, no one listened, especially me. I was ordering double vodka tonics so fast that the bartender eventually poured them into pint glasses because he ran out of regular cocktail-sized ones.

My hangover felt like a Biblical plague. The headache was blinding, my mouth tasted like I'd spent the night licking sandpaper, and the nausea... good God, the nausea. It came in waves—tsunamis, really—while I lay on my back staring at the ceiling, the room spinning like a broken carnival ride.

Eventually, I found it somewhere within my rapidly decaying body to crawl—literally crawl—to the kitchen. There was a lone blue Gatorade in the fridge. I sipped it while taking a cold shower, praying that a combination of electrolytes and mild hypothermia would resurrect me.

They didn't. But I still had to get to work.

When I arrived, everyone looked shocked that I had survived the night, including my boss. Coworkers later told me she had been genuinely worried about me, which is rarely a good sign.

Thirty minutes into the day, I was in the men's room warning the poor bastard in the next stall, "It's about to get ugly in here." Then I threw up.

And when I throw up, it's a full-body, soul-ejecting experience. The capillaries around my eyes burst, my ribs feel like the support beams of a collapsing submarine, and my head threatens to detonate. Afterwards, I'm basically a spent casing.

The rest of the day I survived by chewing ice chips and nibbling stale animal crackers someone had stashed in a desk drawer.

It's not a moment I'm proud of. But at the time, it only reinforced my reputation as a "fun guy to hang out with."

The boat party is an extreme example of my shenanigans, but a version of that night played out over countless weekends for years. Eventually it got to the point where, if I walked into the Owl & Thistle after work, a double vodka tonic would already be waiting at the table before I sat down. At the Nitelite, the bartender didn't even speak—she just set out a double Maker's Mark and two Coronas like she was laying out communion.

My reputation as a partier was, at first, a badge of honor. I was outgoing, funny, magnetic—the guy who could glide into any social situation and stitch the whole room together. Then it became a crutch. Then the hangovers got worse. And somewhere along the way, my act—the rambunctious drunk lobbing zingers around the bar like a late-night talk show host—got old.

"Here Comes a Regular" is the closing track on 1985's *Tim*, The Replacements' major-label debut. The 'Mats, as they were affectionately called, had already put out four critically acclaimed indie albums before signing to Sire/Warner Bros. The year before, they released *Let It Be*, their masterpiece of bratty suburban punk. But "Here Comes a Regular" is one of their best songs. It's rumored that Frank Sinatra was interested in covering it.

Written by Paul Westerberg, the track is an examination of what happens when the bar is no longer a party—it's just where you go in hopes of outdrinking regret. It's loneliness set to music. The arrangement is sparse—just a guitar, a brief piano break, and Westerberg's cracked, pleading voice. "Here Comes a Regular" smells like a bar rag. It sounds like glasses clinking as they're loaded into the dishwasher at closing time. It looks like drunks shuffling toward the door and out into the night of their empty lives.

The melody, simple and haunting, carries the lyrics like watercolors on a brush, gently painting those images: the bellied-up rummies, the glass rings on the tables, the loudmouths in the back of the bar.

There's no redemption arc to the song; it ends with the narrator turning away from a "pay-you-back-last-call," coat turned up to face the cold of the outside world. We all know he will be back the next night, and the night after that, and the night after that.

It's vulnerability without hope, and that's what makes it so devastating.

What made it worse was my friends' expectations of me. I wasn't just part of the group—I was the designated fun one, the guy who would be the drunkest, the funniest, the brashest, the loudest. That became my role, and once people start expecting a performance, it's hard to step off the stage. Even on nights when I didn't feel like drinking much, or didn't feel particularly charming or clever, the show had to go on.

It was exhausting. And expensive.

As soon as the drinks hit the table, I'd start grabbing tabs. I was that guy too—the overly generous one, the guy who'd pick up the check because it seemed easier than dealing with the awkward dance of who owed what. Sure, every once in a while someone would split a twelve-egg omelet and hash browns with me at Beth's Café at three in the morning, but most of the time I was just lighting money on fire and calling it camaraderie.

I'm not sure how close I got to that place where "fun guy" turns into "don't be that guy." Luckily, I was able to move out of that space before it engulfed me. Fatherhood had a lot to do with it, but in the months and weeks leading up to my first daughter's birth, I was still out drinking with my friends. Not every weekend, but enough that my behavior was as concerning as it was alarming.

Then those hard-drinking nights—and whatever alter ego the ol' demon rum dragged out of me—were slowly cast out. And I don't miss it. At all.

The Replacements are a band I still listen to a lot. Their early work perfectly captures those small, awkward moments of young adulthood—the ones where you're unsure of yourself, unsure of your place in the world, unsure of anything except that you feel something and have no idea what to do with it. A song like "Customer" may sound like a blistering punk anthem, but the lyrics are about a guy with a crush on the girl working the checkout at a convenience store. He invents excuses to talk to her—"Where are the Twinkies? What's on sale?"—which is both silly and painfully accurate. That was always Paul Westerberg's gift: he could take the hyper-personal and make it universal. You didn't have to be from Minneapolis or know anything about punk rock to feel seen by what he wrote.

The Replacements never made it big—at least not as big as they should have, had they leaned fully into their talent. Instead, they mastered the art of self-sabotage like no band before or since. Showing up unprepared—or completely shitfaced—to important gigs was practically a signature move. The bigger the expectations, the bigger the implosion. But when the stakes were low? They could be transcendent. Magical. Unrepeatable.

And they knew it, too. The final track on *Hootenanny*, "Treatment Bound," practically winks at it: "the label wants a hit, and we don't give a shit."

Yet through all the chaos, all the blown opportunities and blackout shows, they touched people deeply. They touched me. When I discovered them in my late teens, they became the blueprint for how I wanted myself—and any scrappy little band I played in—to be: raucous, rowdy, belligerent, unhinged in all the best ways. But as I got older, the way their music landed changed. Songs like "Hospital," "Johnny's Gonna Die," and "Takin' a Ride" eventually took a back seat to "I Will Dare," "Favorite Thing," and "I'll Be You." The Replacements grew up in their own uneven, sideways way, and so did I. Their music moved with me, soundtrack to both my chaos and my coming to terms with who I was.

Of all their songs, though, the one that still the most personal is "Answering Machine." It's The Replacements at their most vulnerable—no swagger, no distortion, no drunken bravado—just Paul Westerberg alone with a guitar, trying and failing to bridge the gap between himself and someone he desperately wants to reach. The song is basically him pleading into a void, pouring out everything he can't say in person to a tape recorder on the other end of the line.

"How do you say 'I miss you' to an answering machine?"

That one line can still make me wince. It's so nakedly honest. Anyone who's ever sat there, phone in hand, dialing a number they shouldn't dial, hoping for a voice but getting a prerecorded message instead... you know exactly what that feels like. That mixture of humiliation, longing, fear, and hope. That tiny, pathetic moment where you're reduced to negotiating with a beep.

I've been there. More than once. Wanting connection, wanting someone to hear me, wanting—just for a second—not to be alone. And instead all I got was that cold electronic voice calmly informing me that no one was available to take my call. No emotion. No heartbeat. Just the emptiest sentence imaginable.

Westerberg somehow captured all of that—the futility, the ache, the loneliness of wanting someone who isn't there and may never be—better than anyone else of his era. Better than most people, period. It's the sound of reaching out and finding nothing. The sound of being young and uncertain and convinced that the universe should at least offer you a sign that you matter to somebody, somewhere.

"Answering Machine" is heartbreak distilled. It was then, and it still is now.

It's easy to see how the heartbroken voice pouring itself into "Answering Machine" eventually becomes the narrator of "Here Comes a Regular." One is reaching out in desperation; the other has stopped reaching entirely. That progression—the slow slide from wanting connection to numbing yourself against the lack of it—always felt uncomfortably close to home. With a few bad choices, a few more nights leaning too hard on the wrong crutches, I could have slipped into that life. I could have become that guy.

But I didn't. I was saved from that fate by timing, by luck, by fatherhood, by the people who cared about me even when I didn't care enough about myself. So now those songs are exactly what they should be: snapshots of a life I could have lived, but didn't. Sad postcards from a parallel universe.

That doesn't mean I love them any less. I still listen to The 'Mats all the time. Paul Westerberg was the underappreciated voice of my generation—it's just that almost no one realized it back then. His songs weren't just about youth or drinking or heartbreak; they were about insecurity, longing, self-sabotage, and all the quiet emotional weather patterns you don't have words for when you're young. He sang the things we felt but didn't know how to articulate.

SOMETHING MORE THAN FREE

There's an unspoken cutoff point where you age out of pop culture — a moment when you realize, with a mix of surprise and resignation, that you are no longer the intended audience for certain movies, TV shows, and especially music. I remember the exact instant it happened to me for the first time.

End Fest. 107.7's annual summer concert. Korn was playing the side stage, sandwiched between sets by Better Than Ezra and Gin Blossoms. I wandered over to see what the fuss was about. It took less than thirty seconds to understand—whatever this was, it wasn't meant for me.

I was all of twenty-six years old, standing in front of a side-stage at the Kitsap County Fairgrounds, when my musical adolescence finally gave up the ghost.

Oasis was the last band I loved in that superfan kind of way. After them, I went through different phases — Dwight Yoakam, Steve Earle, a second Led Zeppelin period in my early thirties (the first Zeppelin phase ran parallel to my heavy Rush stage in my twenties). I'd still do deep dives into back catalogues, reading up on old interviews, and absorbing the history. But there were no more posters on the walls, no concert shirts, no rushing out to buy every magazine with a familiar face on the cover.

Music was still important to me, and discovering new artists still mattered, but it wasn't the same. Something shifts as you get older. There's a dignity line you cross, somewhere around thirty-five, where being a superfan of anything looks...well, a little unbecoming.

And yet, at forty-five, I drifted toward the outskirts of superfan territory. I may not have been ready to buy property there, but I was definitely checking Zillow and asking about walkability.

In 2013, Jason Isbell released *Southeastern.* Fresh out of rehab, he wrote a record that was both brutally personal and universally recognizable. The album held everything at once—devastating honesty, hope, tenderness, humor, and a clarity that only comes from crawling back from the edge. Many consider the album as his defining work.

Two years later came *Something More Than Free,* the record that cemented him as one of America's great modern songwriters—mentioned in the same breath as Townes Van Zandt, John Prine, even Dylan.

Around that time, my life was collapsing in slow motion. I had moved out of the house where I'd lived with my daughters and their mother. I threw myself into work, into running, into anything that would keep me one step ahead of the emotional tsunami bearing down on me.

Isbell's albums—and his earlier work with the 400 Unit and the Drive-By Truckers—became the soundtrack to my survival. I listened to them constantly while grinding out miles, trying to keep my mind from slipping into places I didn't want to go.

It worked—but only for a while.

Every time I felt like I was clawing my way back to solid ground, something else would knock me flat. In mid-2016, it was a layoff. Suddenly I was unemployed, living alone in a small one-bedroom apartment, staring at the numbers and trying to figure out how the hell I was going to keep myself afloat.

It was terrifying. A layoff used to mean extra time with my daughters when there was a dual income. Now I was on my own.

My days became a blur of job applications—jobs I was qualified for, jobs I wasn't, and jobs I had no business clicking on. Unemployment and severance barely covered rent and the car payment, but I kept spending like I still had a six-figure job, because acting unemployed felt like admitting defeat.. It wasn't a winning strategy, but I clung to it.

In September of 2016, everything finally gave way. I was sitting at a cheap fold-out table in my apartment, staring at a negative balance in my checking account, with no idea when money would come in again.

I don't talk about my faith often. It's personal, and I'm not sure other people want to hear about it. But that night, I had one of the most honest conversations with God I've ever had. I told Him that, because of the seasoning on my life insurance policy, I was worth more dead than alive. And that I didn't see the point in going on.

Then I wrote my sister an email saying the same thing.

If you're ever trying to figure out whether you're in a crisis, here's a tip: if you're calculating the ROI of your own death, you probably are.

And after that, I took my kids to the pool. The pool was a place they were happy, and their lives had to go on, even as I was contemplating something I'd always believed to be unthinkable.

And after that, I took my kids to the pool. It was a warm late-summer afternoon—blue sky, sunlight bouncing off the water, my daughters laughing like nothing in the world could be wrong —while I sat there pretending I wasn't disappearing inside myself.

Later that evening, after dropping the girls off at their mother's house, my phone rang. The number was unfamiliar. The caller said he was from a company I'd applied to months earlier, but I had never heard from.

"Do you have a few minutes for a phone screen?"

I did.

When we hung up, he said I'd know soon whether I was moving on to the next round. A couple of interview rounds later and I landed the job, which was a huge relief. The only problem? It was almost two-hundred and fifty miles away and my start date was in less than a week. I was going to have to relocate - fast.

Moving day meant stripping my apartment down to almost nothing. Everything went into a storage unit except a single mattress on the floor. My lease ran through mid-November, which at least meant I'd have a place to sleep on the weekends when I came back to see the girls.

I reserved the day before the move for them. We spent it at Flaming Geyser State Park, grabbed lunch together, and tried to ignore the clock ticking down. Saying goodbye was brutal. Becoming a "weekend dad" was no longer a hypothetical — it was real, and it was immediate.

Late that afternoon, I loaded the car with clothes, a few personal items, and started the four-hour drive toward my new life. I tuned Sirius Radio to something like "Roadhouse," and when the Zac Brown Band's "Highway 20 Drive" came on, my eyes brimmed with tears. Turning onto Highway 18, I headed east with no idea what was waiting for me.

I arrived in Kennewick knowing exactly no one and with no place to live. For two weeks I bounced between Airbnb, killing the evenings at Gold's Gym and eating whatever I could grab at Safeway before going back to a rented room.

Luckily, one host was a very sweet older LDS couple. They let me stay for five days, only charging me for three. I ate dinner with them some evenings, and on my last night we had homemade Salisbury steak, a dish I honestly thought existed only in school cafeterias.

Airbnb aren't economically viable when you've gone over six months without a real paycheck. So again, I leaned on my faith. One afternoon I was sitting in the breakroom, staring at the shrinking balance in my checking account. Payday was still ten days away, and I did not know how I was going to stretch what was left. I took a deep breath and silently prayed, *"Things are looking pretty bleak, but I trust You."*

Just as I stood up to leave, another new hire sat down beside me. She was on the phone with her mom, saying she wished she could find someone to rent out her basement to.

That became the lifeline I needed — affordable rent, stability, an actual place to land.

After I moved into the basement apartment, I found the one thing that finally made Kennewick feel less like exile: a local CrossFit gym. It was the first place outside of work where people actually knew my name. They took me in fast — no questions, no conditions. It was genuine warmth and a sense of belonging that I needed.

My days were still simple and predictable, but for the first time since everything collapsed, I wasn't drifting through them alone. These people looked out for me. They gave shape to the evenings and something to look forward to besides the quiet of the basement.

But even in the middle of all that sweating, laughing, and suffering through burpees, the absence of my daughters never left me. There was a giant hole in my life where they used to be — coaching their soccer teams, going to their games, just being near them. Community helps. Friendship helps. Movement helps. But nothing fills the space your children occupy. Not even hundreds of deadlifts performed next to people who feel like family.

Somewhere in the middle of all that, Jason Isbell found his way back into my ear. The song that hit me the hardest was "Something More Than Free."

It's not a song about triumph; it's a song about endurance —waking up every day and doing the work, even when the work feels like the only thing holding your life together. Being hundreds of miles from my daughters felt like a slow death. I was cut off from the three people I loved most in the world, doing everything I could just to keep my head above water. Everyone around me knew how much I missed them; it hung over me like a permanent shadow.

But, I was grateful to have a job—grateful for anything that pulled me forward, even if it pulled me away from the only thing that truly mattered. When Isbell sings, *"I don't think on why I'm here or where it hurts / I'm just lucky to have the work,"* that was exactly where I lived. I tried not to dwell on the pain. I just clung to the gratitude. The work healed nothing, but it kept me moving.

I slipped into a relationship I knew was doomed from the start—an emotional painkiller that made the day-to-day easier. For the first time since the collapse, someone would look me in the eye and ask if I was actually okay. But it also kept me from pursuing what I wanted most: a job closer to my girls. When it ended, I was right back where I'd started—adrift.

My friends rallied around me as I sorted through the wreckage. I'm not sure what I would have done without them. Everything I owned was back in a storage unit, and I was couch-surfing again — only this time I wasn't entirely alone.

She also decided she no longer wanted to care for her dog. Colt, the world's sweetest chocolate lab, became my responsibility by default. We spent hours at the park, and I stood on the bank while he swam, anxiety chewing a hole in my stomach.. I dropped nearly twenty pounds without realizing it; eating felt impossible.

At night, Colt and I stayed wherever we could. He'd curl up beside me, rest his head on my chest, and fall asleep — his own quiet way of telling me to breathe. In the middle of all that uncertainty, he was the one steady thing I had.

Again, I had to trust that God was looking out for me. And He was. A job offer came in from Seattle — suddenly, the thing I'd been praying for was actually happening. They wanted me to start right away.

I spent that last week in Kennewick saying teary goodbyes to the friends who had carried me through a dark stretch of my life. They'd given me shelter, community, and more kindness than I ever expected. My boat had been taking on water for a long time, but they helped keep it afloat until I could make my way home.

Jason Isbell's music became the lighthouse in all of this — steady, unblinking, cutting through the fog even when I couldn't see ten feet in front of me. *Southeastern* and *Something More Than Free* didn't just resonate; they *named* what I was feeling long before I could articulate it.

In "24 Frames," he sings:
"You thought God was an architect, now you know/He's something like a pipe bomb ready to blow/And everything you built that's all for show goes up in flames."

That line rattled around in my head for months. It isn't true for me — not exactly. God wasn't the pipe bomb. I was. I was the one who detonated in the middle of my own life, scorching everything I cared about and calling it fate. It took me a long time to understand that.

But Isbell's songs helped me get there. They held up a mirror I needed to see, even when I wanted to look away. And it wasn't until I finally stopped trying to force my life into the shape I thought it should take — stopped clinging, stopped fighting, stopped white-knuckling my way through every disappointment — that things finally made sense again.

When I finally came home—almost two years later—nothing was the same. The girls had grown in all the ways kids do when you only see them on weekends: taller, more independent, with new priorities and inside jokes I wasn't part of. Reintegrating into their daily lives wasn't simple. I felt like a guest in a house I used to live in, trying to relearn the rhythms, the routines, the unspoken shorthand we'd once shared.

So I picked up my shovel and got to work. Not to "make up" for the time I missed—because you can't. Time is merciless. Once it's gone, it's gone. All you can do is show up now, in the present, and keep showing up.

So that's what I did.

Coming home didn't erase the years I'd spent away. If anything, those two years in Eastern Washington — my self-imposed exile in the desert, wandering around like Moses minus the staff and the tablets — made me understand what actually mattered.

Before I left, I tried to love my girls the way I thought fathers were supposed to: buying them things, surprising them with whatever they wanted or thought they wanted. I mistook presents for presence. Inside that apartment with a mattress on the floor and living in someone else's basement, all of that fell away. None of the stuff mattered. None of it survived the blast radius. Like Isbell sings, *"everything you built that's all for show goes up in flames."*

And it did. Every illusion I had about what made me a good dad — poof.

What remained were the memories I couldn't replace and the moments I couldn't get back: bedtime giggles, noisy breakfasts, car-ride conversations, the hum of ordinary life lived side by side. That was the real cost of my exile. Those little moments are priceless, and they're the currency I'd been spending too carelessly.

Two of my girls are young adults now, moved on into their own lives. Sometimes I look at them and wish I had never left, never taken that job hundreds of miles away. But I had to. That job was the bridge that eventually brought me home again.

"Something More Than Free" became the song that carried me across it. It's a reminder that sometimes the work — showing up, enduring, trying again — is the only thing that keeps your life from collapsing. That sometimes God isn't building an architecture for you to live in; sometimes He's clearing the rubble so you can start over.

I'm back now. Not trying to rewrite the past, but trying to be present for the days I still get. The little ones. The ordinary ones. The ones that matter.

And that's enough.

IN MY LIFE

There's a moment in life when you realize that your childhood isn't simply behind you — it's been quietly shaping everything you've become. For me, that realization didn't arrive in some grand epiphany in adulthood. It started much earlier.

When we arrived in Bummertown — I mean Bremerton — in mid-August of 1980, we stayed at the Bremerton Motel just off Highway 16 for the first few days. The motel sat in a town with the unfortunate name of Gorst. After that, we packed up the motel room and moved our small world — U-Haul and all — into a campsite at Illahee State Park, where we camped for a week.

The weather was perfect. It was warm, but nothing like the blast-furnace heat we'd left behind in El Paso. My brother and I spent our days exploring the trails and walking the rocky beach, turning over stones to watch sand crabs scatter. The air smelled of salt water, seaweed, and the thick, tarry scent of creosote from the wooden pier pilings.

At night, my dad built a campfire, and we ate burgers or hot dogs beneath a sky thick with stars. I missed my friends — both the ones I'd left in El Paso and those back in Montclair — but the flicker of the fire, the steady lapping of waves on the beach, and the novelty of sleeping in a tent softened the ache.

Each morning felt like an adventure. Having spent most of my short life in either Southern California or the desert of El Paso, the thick woods surrounding us were new to me. There was a lot to do and see — until one night, when I woke to something stomping through the trees near our campsite.

Bigfoot. I was sure of it. Absolutely sure.

From that night on, I was more cautious about venturing too deep into the woods. What started beneath the canopy of trees in Illahee State Park became an irrational, bone-deep fear of Bigfoot.

But I digress.

Later in life, I learned the truth about our circumstances: the move from Texas to Washington was a huge financial burden. My parents barely broke even when they sold the house in El Paso, and we had arrived in Bremerton out of money and running on fumes. That's why we moved out of the motel and into the park. For that week, we were, for all intents and purposes, homeless.

My parents eventually found a rental house — affordable, but off the beaten path. Instead of a neighborhood filled with families and other kids, we were surrounded by silence. There wasn't another house within a mile.

To the left of our driveway, about a quarter mile down the road, was a small self-storage facility. To the right, beyond a thin strand of trees, sat a half-vacant strip mall. And behind the house stretched the woods — acres and acres of them. Woods I was certain were also inhabited by a Bigfoot.

By September, we were enrolled in school for the start of fifth grade — my fourth school in a single year.

My brother thrived on being the new kid. He was good-looking, confident, and charming — the kind of kid who walked into a new classroom and instantly drew attention, especially from the girls. Perfect teeth, perfect hair, a cleft chin, and an easy smile that made teachers and classmates alike warm to him instantly.

My sister was still too young to realize what was happening, although she too would experience some of the instability that my brother and I did. A new pre-school was just a new adventure for her at this stage.

For me? Different story.

By ten, I needed glasses. Thick ones — the kind that could probably stop a bullet. My hair was a wiry thicket of cowlicks anchored to a wicked widow's peak. No matter how often I washed it, it still managed to look oily and unkempt, to the point where I started to believe it was behaving with willful disobedience.

Physically, things got weird fast. I'd been a skinny kid for years, but somewhere around eleven, my legs thickened, my backside expanded into what can only be described as a bubble butt, but my upper body stayed rail-thin. Clothes stopped fitting properly. Shopping became an exercise in humiliation, as I was steered toward the dreaded "Husky Boys" section at Sears or JCPenney.

Husky pants weren't designed to look good — they were designed to survive. Heavy fabric. Reinforced seams. Two color options: blue or brown. That was it. It was a sad, muted world we husky boys inhabited — scratchy, stiff, and profoundly uncool.

I showed up for my first day of fifth grade at Viewridge Elementary dressed in those unfortunate pants, an ill-fitting polo, and a pair of discount Pro-Wings sneakers my mom had picked up at Payless. Unlike my arrival at Glen Cove, there was no formal introduction or poetry reading to greet me. I was just a goofy-looking kid no one remembered from the year before.

About a month into the school year, just as I was settling into a semblance of routine, several of us fifth graders were called to the office. The principal greeted us and explained that Viewridge was overcrowded, and we — by luck or misfortune — had been randomly selected to attend school several blocks away at Armin Jahr Elementary. Unbelievable. This would make my fifth school in eighteen months.

Making matters worse, the weather shifted dramatically from when we arrived that August. Late summer had been glorious — warm and bright. Early fall was crisp and pleasant. But by mid-October, the rain had settled in for good. The days turned into an endless parade of gray dampness.

Halloween and Thanksgiving came and went, and we prepared for our first Washington Christmas. The days were short, and the sun seemed to set the moment I got home from school.

Our rental house used heating oil, which was expensive, so to save money we relied on the fireplace as much as possible. It was my job to keep the wood box by the back door stocked. That meant walking out to the detached garage — the one pressed up against the Bigfoot-inhabited woods behind our house — and loading a wheelbarrow with firewood.

I'd fill the wheelbarrow with wood, careful not to stack it too high after a few tip-over incidents, and carefully maneuver it out of the garage.

Then came the sprint.

I'd haul ass back to the house, pushing the wheelbarrow with all my might, absolutely certain Bigfoot was chasing me down. Every snap of a branch, every rustle of leaves convinced me he was right behind me. I'd reach the back door, unload the wheelbarrow, and barricade myself inside.

Good times. Repeat every night until spring.

On the evening of December 8, 1980, I sat watching Monday Night Football with my dad — the New England Patriots versus the Miami Dolphins. The game was tied, and the Patriots were lining up to kick the game-winning field goal at the end of regulation. Before the attempt, Howard Cosell's voice broke in:

"An unspeakable tragedy...John Lennon, outside of his apartment building...shot twice in the back, rushed to Roosevelt Hospital, dead on arrival."

The kick was blocked. The Dolphins went on to win 16–13 in overtime.

My dad, never one to show emotion, simply said, "Huh. John Lennon is dead," and went about his business. My mom told me about hearing The Beatles' "I Want to Hold Your Hand" for the first time at a dance in Ciudad Juárez, Mexico, when she was a teenager. That's when it clicked. John Lennon was in The Beatles. And he had been murdered.

Over the next several days, the airwaves were flooded with Beatles and Lennon songs. Just like when Elvis died, the television filled with retrospectives and documentaries about Lennon's life, music, and legacy. Everyone had something to say about his genius, his activism, his contradictions.

That moment began my deep dive into The Beatles — and especially John Lennon.

Lennon quickly became my favorite of all the Beatles. His wit in interviews was sharp and mischievous, but there was always something more underneath. The way he squared up to the microphone, head tilted back, legs bent slightly, made it seem like he knew something the rest of us didn't. Even his guitar playing looked different — worn high on his chest, almost awkwardly, his rhythm attack sending the chords at you from sharp angles. It wasn't just music. His guitar playing had a presence.

Even at their most basic, The Beatles sounded different. "Love Me Do" might seem simple, but its use of a G-seventh chord added an R&B element that pop music rarely had at the time. And while it was the frenetic opening chords of "I Want to Hold Your Hand" that first grabbed me, it was the subtle dips into minor chords that kept me listening.

My dad still had his reel-to-reel system, one of the few surviving relics from his bachelor days. He would sometimes listen to *Abbey Road* while working in the basement, the layered harmonies of "Because" drifting up through the floorboards. I dug through his catalog looking for Beatles albums. Having learned a lesson from my Elvis obsession, my parents invested in a pair of headphones for me.

After school I'd sit in front of the stereo, headphones clamped over my ears, and lose myself in the songs. Their catalog was rich and sprawling, touching nearly every genre. "A Day in the Life" swirled with orchestral chaos, "Tomorrow Never Knows" looped itself into a single droning chord, and "Norwegian Wood" wove the sitar into a pop song for the first time. There was always something new for me to discover.

By then I'd learned to record off the radio onto reel-to-reel. My dad bought me a stack of blank tapes from Radio Shack so I could capture the Beatles songs he didn't already have from the marathon Beatles blocks local stations were running in the wake of Lennon's death. I would disappear, deep into my own head, imagining a version of life that wasn't my own — one with strawberry fields, cellophane skies, and yellow submarines.

For Christmas that year, my dad got me a portable 8-track player along with The Beatles' Red and Blue compilation tapes. They were used, picked up at the local Goodwill, but I didn't care. For the first time, I had easy access to The Beatles' greatest hits. The 8-track player became my constant companion. I carried it from room to room and even outside to the garage when I had to split and stack firewood — Bigfoot be damned. He could jam out to "Revolution" along with me as I carried out my chores.

One track quickly became my favorite — an introspective song reflecting on past places and friends. "In My Life," written by John Lennon, marked a leap forward in the band's musical maturity. Though never released as a single, it remains one of The Beatles' most celebrated songs, universally praised for its lyrics and musicality.

I didn't know what to call the ache it stirred in me, the way that melody pressed on something old and unformed inside my chest. All I knew was that the song felt true, even for a kid who'd barely lived anything yet. Maybe because, by then, I already understood how it felt to leave people behind. To start over. To be shaped by places I'd never asked to live.

"There are places I remember, all my life, though some have changed..."

I'd sit in our living room, headphones on, thinking back to all the places I'd already been. The small house and apartments in Detroit. The sad trailer and welfare hotel in El Paso. Our house on Flora Street in Montclair. The memories of "people and things that went before" would come flooding back.

Riding bikes with Sean, Larry, and Raymond. Football with Francisco and Freddy. The day we ate pizza and rode go-karts with David and Javier. The smell of lukewarm Chef Boyardee ravioli heated over an unreliable hot plate. The sound that tub of butter made when my mother threw it against the wall, overwhelmed by sadness and frustration. My mother struggling to hold it all together, desperately broke after the divorce. The way my father could light up a room with his smile. Shifting the gears in my dad's VW bug.

The song remains one of my favorites, and as I've grown older, it's taken on new significance. As a child, I didn't understand what Lennon meant when he sang:

"And these memories lose their meaning, when I think of love as something new..."

The song followed me as my life expanded and contracted through marriage, fatherhood, heartbreak, catastrophic mistakes, reinventions, and that long, disorienting stretch of living away from my daughters. I didn't understand Lennon's line about memories "losing their meaning" until I met my wife — until we built a life and love became something lived again rather than imagined.

"Though I know I'll never lose affection, for people and things that went before..."

Each person who drifted into and out of my life, the friends, teachers, girlfriends, coaches, coworkers — all left something behind. A lesson. A scar. A kindness I didn't appreciate until years later. Even the moments I tried hard to forget ended up becoming part of the foundation I stand on now. Every new beginning was built on the wreckage of the last ending.

"I know I'll often stop and think about them..."

Not a day goes by that a memory doesn't surface — a song, a scent, an image. In those moments, I stop and think about the people attached to them. Sometimes the memories are good; sometimes they're not. Either way, I've learned to appreciate them all. Because without them, I would not be where I am today. The tears, laughter, heartbreak, and happiness were all signposts on the journey that led me here. None of this would be possible if it weren't for the people and things that came before.

For my daughters, I hope that when they hear "In My Life," they think not just of me but of the people who made me: their grandfathers, Eddy and Stan; their uncle Chris; their grandmother Nora; the little boy in the welfare hotel in El Paso; the awkward kid running wheelbarrows of firewood away from imaginary Sasquatches; the teenager clutching an 8-track player; the young man still trying to make sense of the world.

For my wife, my hope is that the fractured pieces that formed the person she met and married are less jagged now.

I hope they think of the good times too — accordion lessons taken out of spite, bike rides with friends, football cards traded under streetlights, Star Wars unfurling across a giant movie screen like a universe that suddenly seemed full of possibility.

But mostly, I want them to know this:

Every move, every song, every memory — sweet or painful — was part of the long road that led me to them.

And in my life, I loved them more.

AND IN THE END...

There are dozens of other songs I could have written about. Maybe hundreds.

Some I skipped on purpose, some slipped through the cracks, and some I just wasn't ready to revisit. Maybe one day I'll collect the leftovers into a companion volume — *My Life, the B-Sides* — or, if I really want to be over-the-top pretentious, *The Besides of Life*.

But this book was never meant to be comprehensive or a jukebox with every song option illuminated.

What I've laid out here are the songs that formed the emotional architecture of my life — the ones tied to the moments, big and small, that still resonate. These songs still carry that weight. They are the ones that knock on a door I thought I'd long since closed and remind me of who I was, who I became, and who I'm still trying to be.

These songs have followed me across states, across decades, across the whole uneven arc of becoming a person. They've been lifelines, mirrors, map markers, warnings, and comfort. And when I hear them now, at fifty-something, they no longer send me crashing back in time so much as they tap me gently on the shoulder and say, *You're alright. You made it.*

I wrote this book for my daughters.

Not to impress them, or lecture them, or turn them into carbon copies of me, but in the hope that they might gain a clearer sense of who their dad was before he became "Dad." I want them to know the kid who moved too many times, the teenager who lived inside headphones, the young man who stumbled more than he strutted, and the adult who tried to figure things out as he went — often poorly, occasionally beautifully.

It was written for my wife, too — the woman who met me when I was fifty years old and already formed. She didn't get to see the prequel: the awkward chapters, the messier acts, the scenes where I still didn't know my lines. But she got the person those years shaped, and these songs shaped me as much as anything else ever did.

My daughters and my wife can't live the memories I lived or feel the things I felt. No one can. But maybe, when they hear a song from this book — whether it's Elvis or The Replacements or Larry Norman or whoever else shows up — they'll recognize something. A tone. A feeling. A flicker of understanding. Maybe they'll hear a younger version of me singing under the track, a voice they never met but still somehow know.

Music doesn't preserve who we were, it reveals who we've become.

And if these songs have taught me anything, it's that I'm going to be okay.

I hope, in some small way, they tell my family the same.

There's one more thing I want to leave you with.

This book wasn't only written for my daughters and my wife.

It was written for you, too — whoever you are, wherever you're reading this, whatever songs have stitched themselves into the seams of your life.

I hope, in some small way, these chapters nudge you toward your own soundtrack.

I'm not suggesting you write a book — God knows I didn't exactly plan to write one either — but maybe pay attention to the songs that have followed you through the years. The ones that carried you, startled you, embarrassed you, saved you, broke you open, or held you together.

We all have those songs.
The ones playing faintly in the background of our memories.
The ones we didn't realize were shaping us until much later.

Talk about them.

Bring them up at dinner. Mention them on a long drive. Tell your kids why that one cheesy '80s track still hits you in the heart. Let your friends know why a song they've never heard before can bring you to the brink of laughter or tears. Don't let those stories stay locked inside your head.

I say this because I waited too long with some people.

My friends Doug and Mike are both gone now, and I never got to tell them how much they meant to me — in different ways, at different stages of my life. My father has been gone twenty years. And my dad…the man who raised me…he's in the end stages of dementia and Alzheimer's. Neither of them will read this book. Neither will ever hear the stories behind the music that reminds me of them.

So tell yours while you can.

The next time that old song comes on — T'Pau's "Heart and Soul," or New Kids on the Block's "Hangin' Tough," or whatever track transports you back to some version of yourself you haven't visited in years — don't just stare off with that faraway look in your eyes.

Tell someone why it matters.
Tell them what you felt, what you feared, what you hoped for.
Tell them who you were then, and who you became.

Music is memory, but it's also connection.
It's a bridge — sometimes fragile, sometimes sturdy — between who we were and who we love.

So start your list.
Start your conversations.
Start your soundtrack.

And don't wait.

www.ingramcontent.com/pod-product-compliance
Lightning Source LLC
LaVergne TN
LVHW010649110826
845149LV00014B/2996

* 9 7 9 8 9 9 4 2 2 7 4 0 4 *